"There's Baxter," someone said. He is one
name like Thor. I was afraid. Him with h
smoke wafting up like a white thundersto
and black checked, and his eyes piercir
voice deep as the old woods. And he has a heid of bee
royalty like d.a. levy and tangled with politicians to give the Niagara River
back to people. This is a lifetime. This is the book. "Everything is connected."
This prose is a life's work of writing the pattern of living. Reflective composition, digression is unique and compelling if the creative mind is mature and
honestly vowed and woven. Sure it is with Baxter's. This is Baxter's design
in form. It has been long in the making, as a life is, as is his life. I just kept
reading. So it will just keep you reading as you just keep your living on the go.
    – Michael Basinski, poet, author of *All My Eggs Are Broken*

An amazing combination of in-depth descriptions of the Niagara area, deal-
ing not only with Baxter's own personal experiences, historical and familial
history, so that he really brings the place alive for you....but....then he throws
in all kinds of totally in-depth meditations on other authors and their works.
And not just ordinary, everyday authors, but the kings of the Avant-Garde
like Tristan Tzara, Lawrence Ferlinghetti, d.a. levy, D.H. Lawrence and the
mimeo revolution. So you have a combination of real-place and real-time and
brilliant, wildly original thoughts about the most original authors that have
been surrounding us for the last century. The key here is brilliance, forceful,
totally captivating.
    – Hugh Fox, author of *Who Me?*

GODDAMN. Goddamn. That was like going back to a time in youth i would
love to have had but never came close to having and having it even though
i didn't. you know – i just don't read fiction, although this is not fiction, nor
is it what i think an essay is; i just don't anymore.... i have given up reading
anything other than information about something i have to know about for
one purpose or another but this was a real pleasure, reading this memory that
had to be written down so it could be somewhere and not disappear when you
die, if you ever get around to that – it needs to be published. Herman Melville
would be jealous. What a graceful job of work. My compliments sincerely.
Thank you for sharing that. It was a privilege to read. o.k., o.k., i will just
shut up now.
    – James Copia, resident of Niagara Falls, NY.

Niagara Digressions

E. R. Baxter III

Starcherone Books   Buffalo, NY

ISBN 978-0-9837405-2-0
© E. R. Baxter III, 2012
General editor: Ted Pelton
Book editor: Rebecca Maslen
Cover design: Julian Montague
Proofreaders: Emmett Haq and Jason Pontillo
Special thanks to Ed Taylor

Cover photo by Harry T. Brashear

Library of Congress Cataloging-in-Publication Data

Baxter, E. R.
  Niagara digressions / E. R. Baxter III ; [introduction by] Eric Gansworth.
    p. cm.
  ISBN 978-0-9837405-2-0 (pbk.)   .
  1. Baxter, E. R. 2. Authors, American--20th century--Biography. I. Title.
PS3552.A8554Z46 2012
813'.54--dc23
[B]
                                2011044245

Starcherone Books thanks Medaille College for general support. We also thank
supporters of this book's publication through Kickstarter.com, and are particularly
thankful for a generous gift from Brian Lampkin.

State of the Arts

This book is made possible
with public funds from the
New York State Council on
the Arts, a state agency.

NYSCA

In Loving Memory of
Loraine Lefrancois Baxter

Introductory Digression

Okay, first things first. Yes, I know E.R. Baxter III. I am even a "character," appearing briefly in the first chapter. A fair number of people have *suggested* I'm a character, as in "what a character," or "who's *this* character?" so I guess now it's true. I'm a member of the Onondaga Nation, having been raised at the Tuscarora Nation and my Indian name is definitely not Straight Arrow. This assertion will come to make sense once you go forward in this book.

These days, I'm a professional writer and a professor at Canisius College, in Buffalo, New York, but I met E.R. Baxter III, at Niagara County Community College, where he was teaching, and where I'd gained admittance only because the college had an open-admission, "no SAT Exam required" policy. It was a long time ago, and we've known each other ever since. It's possible I know him better than most people still around. There are many ghosts in this book, and a lot of them knew him longer, better, more than I do, but they are not in the position to be writing this introduction.

To those who are prone to looking askance at two writers being "connected" to one another, I ask, why *would* a stranger be invited to write an introduction, anyway? So for the record, at the writing of this introduction, we've known each other for 27 years. We met when I was a student in his Creative Writing class, the year I began college.

As that fall 1984 semester started, almost every other student I knew advised me to drop the class. I hadn't yet taken the advised prerequisite course, Writing II and Introduction to Literature. I'd gotten a grade of C in Writing I, from a professor who'd had very odd ideas about writing, and who, as a side note, was a firm believer in reincarnation. I believe she claimed to have been the "Handmaiden of Isis" in one of her former lives. No reincarnates ever seem to have had ordinary former lives. Is it that the farmers and house-cleaners don't get to go on to enjoy more than one of their possible lives because they squandered the first? As she has subsequently passed on, I have to wonder who, or what she is now.

My friends said Baxter didn't suffer fools (I did *not* miss their implications about me in this statement) but I dismissed their advice. In part, I saw this class as perhaps my only chance to formally experience what I really wanted to do. I was enrolled in a heavy-requirement medical technology program, and had no idea if my scarce "free elective" time slots and the Creative Writing class would ever align again, and I'd been lucky enough to get a seat in advanced registration. The class often filled so quickly that many students never got in. I wasn't giving up my winning lottery ticket.

The first day of the semester arrived, and I had still never seen the man. Somehow, his hard-ass reputation had conjured up a cliché college professor image in my unadventurous imagination. I pictured the usual tweed-jacketed slight graying man with short, wavy hair and tiny wire-framed glasses. As a bunch of us stood near the hallway ashtray, smoking last cigarettes before class (yes, it was that long ago), I kept waiting, thinking "where is this guy, anyway," sizing up the rest of the class.

There was a broad demographic, which was often true at this community college. It was a place for people like me, who'd been told in high school that college wasn't for us, for people who'd flunked out of four-year residential colleges, trying to get their grades back up, and for people who'd missed the opportunity of college at earlier ages and who were generally eager to get their educations. I tended already to like these people the best, because they brought with them their interesting pasts and usually had a strong commitment to making class an engaging experience.

Among the general college-age population that made up half the class, one young woman talked with wild animation, as if on stage, delivering monologues. Her designer clothes were so coordinated, I imagined her hair had perhaps been cut by Vidal Sassoon, himself. A couple of women in their mid-to-late twenties seemed earnest and quiet, probably the people I would gravitate to.

An ex-military guy in his thirties with a neatly trimmed beard, jeans and sneakers, had an easy way about him, chatting with everyone as if we'd all known each other for years. At a later date in class discussion, he asked Baxter a question, inadvertently starting, "Mr. Bastard." Everyone cracked up and, being the easy-going guy he was, the ex-military man accepted that we weren't going to let it go for the rest of the semester, mostly because it simply wasn't true. Whatever chemistry in a group that comes along maybe once or twice in a lifetime – you know you've had it – well that chemistry sat with this group. For those fifteen weeks in 1984, everyone in that room seemed to be fond of everyone else, not a bastard in sight.

Among several other non-traditional students there was a bald man in polyester dress pants, suspenders, tooled cowboy boots, and a dinner-platter sized belt-buckle. Throughout the semester, he steadfastly insisted that every poem, every short story, every personal essay we read, was secretly, symbolically, about the atom bomb. Within this past year, I read his obituary in the newspaper. His initials were N.M., also the initials of the state where the first U.S. nuclear tests were done. N.M. had a long life, and I've wondered what preoccupied him once the Cold War ended.

Also in that group milling about was a grandmotherly type in a thick wool sweater despite it being the Wednesday after Labor Day, and thus still about 75 degrees outside. Near her was another older guy with a bushy beard and really weathered hands, wearing a plaid shirt, an overshirt on top of that, and shiny black dress boots. I couldn't help but speculate about their backstories, which is, I suppose, a fiction writer's habit. Some, I'd gotten right, but as the ten minute period between class times ended, the bushy-bearded guy said, "Okay, it's time. Put 'em out and let's get in there."

That day and in the fifteen weeks to follow, I was to learn about a world of writing beyond the "Stephen King and Pink Floyd" frame of reference I'd entered with. I'd never heard of Kenneth Patchen, or James Dickey, or William Stafford, or even Allen Ginsberg. This is an embarrassment to me now, considering I'd actually met Allen Ginsberg years before, when he, Bob Dylan, Joan Baez and the rest of the Rolling Thunder Revue gave a free performance on the reservation that was my home. But I never felt embarrassed in this class-room, E-211, where I became a writer of more subtlety and sub-stance. I felt challenged, and sometimes lost. I also knew that doors were being opened in my head that I hadn't even known existed. This might seem more like a tribute to a beloved teacher and while that label's true, it's only partially true. I was, from the first, also interested in Baxter's creative work. Anyone who was as im-passioned and meticulous as he was about writing, and as well read, would surely have written work which I would find engaging and enriching. He'd published some essays, short stories and poems in what were known then as "the littles," journals dedicated to the sty-listically adventurous movement in American letters that flourished after the Beats broke the mold in the 1950s.

The college library had copies of poetry chapbooks Baxter had published but, irritatingly, they were in a "rare books collection," because of the limited print run nature of chapbooks. As a student, I was not allowed to touch these books. To this day, I have to wonder who *does* get to read them. What good is a "rare books collection," if no one has access to them? In frustration, I asked Baxter himself if I could read some of his work, and he lent me personal copies of publications. This one act changed the nature of our relationship. There were probably myriad small ways it changed in the first few years we knew each other, but it was in the thoughtful exchange, as writers, where we really found our friendship.

The night I finished writing my first novel manuscript, I called him up and asked him if he would read it. I was 23, and hadn't been a formal student of his for at least a couple years, but he immediate-ly said yes. I think of my life now, as a creative writing instructor, myself, trying to balance the complicated time demands of a "teach-ing writer" career, and in all honesty, have to wonder if I would be as generous a teaching writer. Many novels written by 23 year olds, frankly, are just not good. They're not good technically and their level of depth tends to reflect the limited perspective on life experi-ences that a 23 year old in America is likely to have. There are excep-tions, surely, but mine fell squarely into the "just not good" category.

In the same period, Baxter was completing a novel, and we swapped manuscripts. The convergence didn't happen so close that we read at the same time, but it was within the same year. We went, in three years, from being teacher and student, to friends, to writers who read each other's work. This is not to say that the earlier phases dropped off as new ones developed. This is a cumulative identity. We've been friends and early readers for each other since then, and even after all this time, I'm still learning. His is the voice I hear in my head when I know I've written a bad sentence.

The "early reader" is a tricky position to ask someone to be in and an even trickier circumstance to be the person asked. There are responsibilities, mostly in striking the balance of the honest appraisal with an understanding of the first-draft's fragility. Usually, we have each waited until we had something substantial, a completed manuscript of some sort, before contacting the other about it. But we've each had occasion to send off pieces that felt complete even if we knew they were parts of something else – a few thematically linked poems, a story that would become a chapter of a larger work.

Niagara Digressions, many years and manuscript swaps later, was a work I started reading that way. By this time, our friendship had survived my transfer to another college, graduate school, our time as colleagues and office mates when I was later hired by NCCC, even Baxter's retirement and my eventual move to another institution, Canisius College. As I grew into my new academic environment, every now and then, pages would show up in my mailbox.

These works seemed complete, personal essays, short bursts of memoir – what has come to be known as "creative non-fiction" these days, since the word "essay" has such bad cultural baggage for people who'd been forced to write essays throughout their college careers. "Thought of the Week" and "The Pencil" were two pieces that I distinctly remember reading.

A few months later, I saw a couple of the more stylistically adventurous passages and thought: what on earth is he writing? But this is not really a question you ask a writer in the middle of manuscript, when it is at its most fragile, when it's most easily derailed.

There was a long period of silence between us about this book and then, eventually, the completed manuscript showed up. I had my answer. There was no way to fully grasp the book's structure until I had read it all the way through, with its title, which serves as the key, the way any good title does.

The term "novel" first came into use as a description for extended prose works. While currently, "novel" has a very specific meaning – a meaning often challenged by bold small literary presses like Ted Pelton's Starcherone – it was initially chosen because each new work was composed in a form with which its readers were unfamiliar. Novels were "novel."

I don't have a citation for this assertion. You'll have to take my word for it. I learned this idea in a different college classroom. That professor, like so many of the voices in this book, has joined the world of memory and shadow. What you have in front of you, by this definition, is indeed a novel. It might also be considered a non-naturalistic memoir, or idiosyncratic treatise on the effects of environment on shaping one's personality. It is probably all of these things, and more. Or perhaps not. Allow me to, well, digress.

* * *

Most contemporary memoirs use novelistic devices. In the past, memoirs were written by people who were already public figures because of previous accomplishments. Now, with the rise of the "trauma narrative" model, it seems like the only requirement of a memoir is a terrible early life and a willingness to discuss it. I suppose that *is* the attraction. Really, who doesn't think they had a traumatic childhood? I have friends who read these accounts, telling me, a novelist, "it's like reading a novel, but better." And when I ask how it's better, they pause, look at me as if I am a child with an insight deficit. "Because it's true!" I don't tend to argue, but I suspect that the truthfulness in many of these books is usually closer to Stephen Colbert's "truthiness."

* * *

This book, in its more unorthodox style, is closer to truth than most of those memoirs with which you might already be familiar. It's an aesthetic representation of the way we really see our lives, if we are at all careful listeners and viewers, witnessing the way we perceive the world. If readers can be sensitive enough to absorb its complexities, they can also absorb its riches, and discover, as this book suggests, that they "can spread-eagle themselves on the ground and feel the earth's slow revolving and, simultaneously, here in Western New York, its rebounding, too, from its compression of thousands of years under ice."

When you finish, you'll come to understand the layers and permutations of interconnectedness in any person's life, recognizing some of your own paths along the way. As with any sophisticated work of art, this book strikes the balance between the individual and the universal. These renderings are, naturally, Baxter's own memories, thoughts, narrative decisions. At any moment, though, you are also witnessing that moment and aligning it with everything else you have ever witnessed or experienced, comparing the moment, filing it. These associations, in accumulation, are the sequences that make up a life.

So, a million years ago, Baxter used to tell me about a Lone Ranger silver bullet ring he had as a boy, and I happened to find one at a comic shop I visited regularly. The owner was – as dealers in collectibles tend to be – a vulture, so he totally gouged me because he knew I'd been looking "too hard" at it. I bought it anyway, so I could give it to Baxter. He talked about the one he'd had with such love and intensity, I felt, when I saw it in the shop case, that I was somehow meant to find that one. My Indian name is also not Tonto, but I passed the Lone Ranger ring onto its rightful owner.

I have no idea if Baxter still has it, but as I was writing this introduction, I thought about it, so did some quick research. Its motif was actually a marriage of the Lone Ranger's silver bullet and, you'll never guess… the atom bomb! I wonder if N.M. is laughing down from the heavens at me, proven right about the omnipresent specter of the atom bomb after all. The ring was a premium in a cereal box, Kix, to be specific, a puffed wheat product. This information, as well as some other passages here, will make more sense the further you get into this book.

An introduction is usually supposed to tell you something about the book, but I don't want to be a "spoiler" and I've already mentioned more than I had planned to, so I better stop here. As you turn the next page and begin this song to the marriage of biography and history, for the first or the fiftieth time, I have one last suggestion: remember when a novel was novel, and embrace the joy in discovering something new. In short, enjoy the ride.

Eric Gansworth,
Onondaga Nation,
Lowery Writer-in-Residence,
Canisius College

He's stretched out in bed, up in the small bedroom under the slanted ceiling. The night is windy, and it's raining, the power is out, and only the glowing end of a cigarette is visible in the room. Heavy rain is pounding on the roof, maybe on that corrugated tin roof of his childhood. It's going to be an all-nighter. And then a voice comes out of the dark. Tell me a story, it says.

1.

I have owned the shoulder blade of a deer for over fifty years. It has been painted gold. My father was of English descent, my mother Irish. I always wanted to be an American Indian. I once collected Straight Arrow cards from Shredded Wheat boxes. They were simple pieces of gray cardboard that separated the unwrapped biscuits, 4" x 7 ¼", with information about Indian skills and crafts printed on them. These were called "Injun-uities."

I am home alone as I write this. It is late February, snowing, the wind gusting, 22° F. The sound of Janis Joplin is cranked up, "Bobby McGee" vibrating the windowpanes. Outside at the bird feeder, four chickadees and one nuthatch are getting Janis with their sunflower seeds. The wire from which the feeder is suspended goes up through the hole of an old LP record. This unstable shield of silent tunes, 10,000 Maniacs, prevents squirrels from raiding.

On page 87 of the paperback *How to Know the American Mammals*, Ivan T. Sanderson writes, "You can go quietly insane trying to figure out the difference between hares and rabbits." This has never troubled me. I accept that Peter Rabbit was a rabbit and do not consider the possibility that he was a hare. Likewise, it was a hare the tortoise beat in that footrace, not a rabbit. There are multitudes of other ways to go quietly insane. Someday I will make a list. Snow will be blowing and drifting across the vast emptiness of the Great Plains tonight. A nuthatch is not a mammal. Do I digress? Of course – how else to tell the sad, glimmering truth about anything?

* * *

I have shot rabbits and eaten them, pursing my lips to spit lead pellets onto the plate with the distinctive clink that is impossible to mistake for any other sound once you have heard it. Out of season, and more than once, I have also seen a motionless rabbit in a thicket, sitting there thinking it is undetected, and kept on walking. To stop walking might spur the rabbit into unnecessary flight. "I've been spotted!" it thinks. How many thousands of years of predator and prey interaction went into the creation of this behavior? Human hunters try to use this knowledge. Hunting without dogs, the instruction is: Do not walk in a straight line, but meander. Walk, stop. Walk, stop. Walk, stop. Even then some rabbits overcome their anxiety and sit there anyway, until the last second, until the fallen leaves crunch right next to them. Some of these get away, too. It is the element of surprise.

These instructions, incidentally, meander, walk, stop, walk, stop, are also what parents should be telling their children about how to go through life. This advice should not be pushed too far.

Target detection is a skill taught to combat forces, such as the US Army Infantry. The trick is not to look at anything, but to look at everything, to stay alert for irregularity, pattern disruption, movement no matter how slight, sound, odor. Target detection is a euphemism for seeing where the enemy is before you kill him. But the enemy has been taught target detection, too, and the art of concealment as you were. So it doesn't matter how good you are, unless you can achieve 100% all the time, and nobody can. About the time you start to congratulate yourself on how good you are, the enemy rises at your feet and loads you up with lead. Surprise. You've been detected.

There you were thinking of some girl you knew, or of your buddy back home, and how he's with the girl, or how the brush and vines in front of you looked like good rabbit cover, or how the smell of the swampy ground reminded you of old sneakers – and then you were dead. Those thoughts were as good as any others you could have been having. What would you rather had been your last thought? How wonderful it was to be part of the great force making the world safe for Democracy?

If you are wounded and unconscious, the next awareness you have as you begin to awaken is the cold air of a field hospital, the probe and tug of something inside you, the band playing "Mustang Sally." You want to open your eyes to see who's singing. You're sure it's Meatloaf, but your eyes won't open. Then it's other words, "when your sweetheart writes a letter," and you're fading and coming back to "let your hair down and cry." Your mind is on random select, all those old tunes from your father's radio one after the other and you want to write yourself a letter, to give yourself a big bouquet of roses, a hug, but your arms won't move. A quiet voice says "There it is," and there's a sound and you know it's a bullet dropping into a stainless steel bowl.

You've seen it in the movies lots of times, so your eyes didn't have to open to see the bowl, bloody forceps opening above it, bullet falling. "Close him up. He's good to go," a voice says and you are off dreaming, sprawled out on your back in a sunlit meadow, white clouds chasing one after the other across the sky.

* * *

Many people in the world do not think it unusual to sleep outside, "out-of-doors" we call it, directly on the ground. Some of these people do not have doors to be out of, naturally. There may be a blanket or two or thin reed mats involved, a stone for a headrest, or nothing at all, a simple selection of a place and curling up or stretching out in it. This is what we call being close to the earth. Thus stretched out, arms spread, those who live in the northern regions and who are especially attentive can feel the earth rebounding from its compression during the last ice age and sense its slow, monumental turning. I have never felt this, though I would like to. Once, however, I stopped my car, in some western state of North America, Oregon, perhaps, climbed over a guardrail and down a slope to put my hand, palm down, in the still extant rut left by wagon trains that traveled west. There was a vast aching absence in there, vanished people, vanished buffalo, vanished prairie. Years later I saw a photograph of buffalo skulls piled up high enough to fill a K-Mart parking lot. After they'd been slaughtered to the point of extinction for their tongues and hides, the bone-pickers combed the great prairies for the bones to grind into meal for fertilizer.

Some buffalo are raised commercially now. I have never eaten a buffalo burger. Sanderson says buffalo "steaks are little inferior to prime beef," but I still don't want to eat any.

*   *   *

Buffalo, New York, is the home of deep-fried chicken wings. With a variety of sauces, mild to red-hot, these are consumed in huge quantities, bleu cheese in a side container, preferably while drinking beer. They are often called Buffalo Wings. They can be obtained in other cities now, and even the frozen food sections of supermarkets carry them, pallid imitations that they may be. Wherever they are consumed, many of us in Western New York believe they originated here, in the Anchor Bar of Buffalo, New York. But when I hear the phrase "Buffalo Wings" I think of the souls of millions of buffalo, ascending on ghost wings that grew to carry them into the ether. And then I think of the Ghost Dance.

*   *   *

The hottest of the hot sauces is called "Slap My Ass and Call Me Sally!" Where the name originated is difficult to say, but the rumor is that during the testing stages, tasters, when it hit the back of their throats, spontaneously screamed out that request – and after the third such utterance, the name stuck.

* * *

Toward the end of the 20th Century, the city of Buffalo obtained one hundred and fifty-four fiberglass replicas of buffalos to help with a fund raising idea. Many were nearly actual size. Some of these had been primed battleship gray. This was to prevent their being easily seen, to safeguard them against enemy attack from the air. These were decorated, painted, and so on, by various artists based on their personal inspirations, positioned in various locations around the city for a time, and then auctioned off, the proceeds going to charitable causes. Some turned out to be impressive, glittering creatures, covered with mosaics of colored glass bits and costume jewels. None were painted with blood. None were gilded. These ideas were either inconceivable or rejected as being too biodegradable or too banal, respectively. Banality, like vulgarity, apparently has its limits.

All this was accomplished in the full glare of the media, newspapers, television, radio. The whole effort was called "Herd About Buffalo." Or was it "Heard about Buffalo?" Of course, we've heard about it. That's where chicken wings were invented. Before that chickens had to walk.

Eric Gansworth, an Onondaga, replicated the three-foot image of Indian Head nickels on the sides of his buffalo. This coin is also known as the Buffalo Nickel for its reverse side. I don't recall seeing his buffalo on TV or in a newspaper photo. It eventually went to Rex, Georgia, where it had found a home at a flagship chicken-wing restaurant named Mo-Joe's. The owners were previously residents of Buffalo. There is some potential there, on a rainy night, because the customers do not have Buffalo, New York as part of their consciousness, for the whispering thought of buffalo wings as I think of them to float through their minds.

Although I haven't eaten buffalo meat, I'm not squeamish

about what other flesh I've chewed and swallowed. Excluding fish, I've eaten frog legs, squirrel, both red and gray, opossum, rabbit, raccoon, bear, deer, moose, elk, duck, goose, woodcock, pheasant, turkey, ruffled grouse, and pigeon. Call the latter rock dove if you like, but they were the same birds that hang around city parks, though that isn't where I got them. I haven't eaten five and twenty blackbirds baked into a pie, nor, unlike a past president of France, any songbirds, either. I think of the old saying "You are what you eat." What am I? Inside me is some spirit of all those animals I've consumed, even though I'll never be able to sing.

Over a century ago when millions of buffalos grazed the Great Plains, migrating for hundreds of miles in herds, they were accompanied by a variety of blackbird which came to be known as the "buffalo bird." They found the living easy in the good old summertimes, feeding on the swarms of insects stirred up by moving hooves, even perching on the beasts themselves to capture flies and other morsels. But their nomadic lives made it impossible to build nests and raise young. They were never in one place long enough.

It is difficult to imagine how their adaptive behavior evolved, but over hundreds or even thousands of years, these birds had learned to lay eggs in the nests of other birds, where their hatchlings would be raised, long after the herd had moved on, accompanied by the biological parents.

This species survival strategy wasn't so great for the adoptive parents, whose own young were often ejected from the nest by larger, earlier hatching buffalo birds. Defensive behavior evolved. Some birds learned to recognize a different egg in the nest and toss it out. Others abandoned the nest altogether and started anew, or built a new nest on top of the first effort and produced additional eggs. If the herd had moved on by then, their nest was safe. But enough buffalo bird chicks were successfully hatched and raised to continue the species.

Then, in a relatively short span of years, the great buffalo herds had all but vanished. Did the buffalo bird vanish along with them? Interspecies relationships in nature are often so strongly symbiotic that when one species goes extinct, the other goes, too. In this case, as the buffalo herds diminished, cattle raised by ranchers were on the rise and the birds shifted their allegiance to the cattle drives. Loyalties often take a backseat to survival.

Now that the huge cattle drives are also part of the past, these birds migrate all on their own, but still keep company with the smaller northern cattle herds across the country during the summer. Even a few head of cattle on a family farm will have the birds following along, very visible in a short pasture, inches from the hooves at times, alert for whatever meal might reveal itself. The buffalo bird still lays eggs in the nests of others. Old habits are hard to break. They are known as cowbirds, now, and you can look them up in any field guide.

* * *

I still want to tell about eating Shredded Wheat, and eating pigeons and frog legs, and my father singing, and a few other forgotten things and times that will come back to me eventually. Everything is connected.

* * *

Eat lead, cowboy. Don't mind if I do. I live on the Niagara Frontier and I've eaten worse.

* * *

In broad daylight one late summer, I fell asleep on the ground near the brushy edge of a pasture where I'd been rebuilding the fence to hold cattle. The grass was short, having been grazed, the ground warm from the sun, the air still. When I woke up, I knew exactly where I was, curled on my side in the sunlight at the pasture edge. After a time, without having moved, I opened my eyes.

A cottontail rabbit was sitting about three feet away from my face in a sparse growth of brush. The lower part of the growth was leafless and spindly, pale sunlight dappling through the upper foliage. I was so close, its whiskers were visible. It must have come near after I was asleep, and had no idea I was anything other than part of the landscape – just a big motionless clump. It might have been dozing itself, napping, for all I know. About three-quarters grown, it had been born that spring. Abruptly, it stood up on all fours, if a rabbit can be said to stand, a posture not often seen or depicted in drawings. Then, back feet remaining in place, it moved its front feet forward as far as it could, extending its body to full length – and stretched its back, a slow, luxuriant downward arching of spine that rippled its smooth fur and ended with its head tilted backward, front legs stiff, a pose it held for a few seconds before its back legs took a little hop forward and the moment was over. I could almost imagine the sigh. How good that felt. After a few minutes more it took two unhurried hops and disappeared from view.

I got up myself and went back to work. This completely ordinary moment and others similar to it, are repeated thousands of times each minute throughout the animal kingdom. The Nature Channel provides a surplus of them. But this experience was important to me – at another time, I wouldn't have seen it at all, but that same rabbit in the fall or winter out running in front of the hounds and I'd have shot, field dressed, and later, eaten it. Right up along both sides of that same backbone that stretched are two of the finest pieces of meat on a rabbit, and they come cleanly away from the bone after roasting just as slick as if they were designed to do so. On a healthy rabbit, well prepared to last the winter on slim rations, there are two irregular flakes of pale yellow fat at the top edge of the shoulder blades, about the size of flattened dandelion blossoms. These are usually discarded. I have never saved the shoulder blade of a rabbit.

* * *

The way a cottontail rabbit eats a dandelion: It nips off the bitter stem near the ground so that when it raises its head there's a long stem extending from its mouth with the blossom bobbing at the end. The rabbit nibbles rapidly, without using its paws, and the stem grows shorter until, just for a moment, the yellow blossom is poised right at the end of its nose, a tiny sunburst. Then poof – it disappears into the mouth in one quick motion and the rabbit chews busily. It saves the best for last. Bitter, bitter, bitter, sweet.

* * *

It used to be that children playing would hold a dandelion bloom under another's chin and say "Let's see if you like butter," or ask "Do you like butter?" If the sunlight reflected yellow to the skin – and it always did – the answer was yes. Who didn't like butter in those days? This little ritual probably goes back to the pioneers or even further back.

* * *

Young girls also used to compress the center of a red rose petal between their lips, which would then fold back, creating the look of a lush red mouth. They'd posture for a moment, tilting their faces up for friends, before they couldn't stand it anymore and broke down giggling. That probably still happens across the country, but not as often. Roses aren't as much cultivated in home gardens these days, and some girls, by the time they are eleven, are wearing makeup and saving their allowance for collagen injections. They want to grow up fast and be adults, but there's no cow to milk and no butter to churn.

* * *

Location: In the countryside, a few miles south of Lake Ontario, lights of passenger planes, landing or leaving, moving across night skies to and from airports in Toronto, Canada, and Buffalo, New York. The road here has city water and cable TV. An opossum is run over in the dark by a fuel-injected Nissan. Two fields away coyotes argue near a woodlot, nearer, then far again, interrupting one another, throwing their shrill voices. We live in an old farmhouse. Now it has electric lights, indoor plumbing, and central heat, but it was built before the buffalo herds were slaughtered to remnants. There are fewer working farms in the area than there were a generation ago. Old barns shrug off their outer boards, open their roofs to the elements, lean a little, preparing for the final collapse. New houses advance from the cities. Some of their inhabitants complain about the smell of manure. This is all background.

On the high windswept creek bank behind the house there is a piece of stone that doesn't belong. It is almost at my feet. I'm standing in the thin band of woods along the creek, where at intervals a few aged pear trees have grown tall and scraggly, surviving from years when even marginal land was put to use. The flattened, palm-sized stone is chert.

I recognize it from pictures in books, or from handling a piece in a classroom or at a mineral show I've long forgotten attending. Its surface is dense, nearly shiny, very different from the granite and fieldstone native to the area. That's what caught my attention.

About four seconds passed between the time I saw it and picked it up. It fit comfortably in my palm, fingers curled over one edge, the other extending just beyond the heel of my hand. Another human hand had shaped this. Flakes had been pried from both sides, resulting in the edges being tapered. Thickened at the center of one side, it sloped toward the outer edges, and this ridge matched the fold of my palm when I positioned my hand as if it were ready to scrape something, a hide, the tough outer skin of a plant root. It was a dark slate gray, except for a two-inch stripe of tan through the center, almost a decoration.

I started back toward the house, looking in all directions through the woods as if to make sure I hadn't been seen. Had I been detected? Was I stealing it? Would its owner return for it, having been gone on a journey only temporarily for several hundred years? Had I been the next one to hold it since it had been lost or left behind on that early creek bank?

And then I turned and went back to where I'd picked it up, replaced it exactly into the slightly molded impression in the earth, flute to reverse flute, ridge to valley, next to a small patch of moss, not far from a tree root protruding above the stony soil.

That was years ago. The undergrowth in the woods is not heavy and I've been going there to check on it every so often, every year or so. I haven't picked it up again. Its owner has not yet returned.

What else was I to do? Take it home and place it on the window ledge next to the gold-painted shoulder blade of the deer?

* * *

Any questions so far? Let's summarize. You can go quietly insane trying to figure out the difference between lips and rose petals, between the sun and a dandelion, between a Rainy Night in Georgia and the Trail of Tears, between a lone hitchhiker and yourself. Construct a sentence, if you are able, using these words: field, hare, hunter. What have I left out?

2.

Years ago I registered for a course in American Literature at the State University of New York at Buffalo. We were to meet once a week for three hours. The day the course was scheduled to begin, I drove about twenty-five miles to the campus, found parking, walked to the Hall that was listed, took the elevator to the second floor, and located the classroom. The Professor never showed up. After thirty or forty-five minutes we all left.

He appeared the following week, made an obscure reference to his previous absence, and said we'd understand when we got to know him better. When the semester ended, however, the reason he'd blown off that first class still hadn't become clear.

We'd started out by having read *The Autobiography of Benjamin Franklin* in preparation for his lecture. "Why," he began, "do we consider this to be an example of American literature?" He paced back and forth in front of the classroom, holding a paperback edition of the *Autobiography* aloft in one hand. "Well," he said, after a long pause, during which he'd feigned listening and then disappointment that no answer was forthcoming, "we might say because it was written by an American."

He paused again to give us time to consider this.

Well, he had me hooked right there.

I don't remember another thing he said that day or during the rest of the semester. I was too busy imagining and reimagining how, on that first day, I should have casually risen from my seat, walked to the front of the room and put him to the floor with a roundhouse right. It would have been noisy for a little bit while he yelped and scrabbled around on all fours, his dropped copy of the *Autobiography* forgotten, lurching into his desk, as he tried to get up and I pummeled him back down amidst a modest spattering of blood, and then, for good measure, kicked him a couple of times while he was down. "Shoot him again. He's still breathing," as my father used to say, though he'd never owned a gun in his life.

Other students would have pulled me away by then – there always seems to be a couple of those – or maybe not. Perhaps there'd have been scattered cheering. The Professor, I've forgotten his name, would have been hurt, frightened, even terrified, certainly baffled by the attack. "Unprovoked assault on UB English Professor," *The Buffalo News* would have reported the next day. I'm sure, however, that over time, as he got to know me better, he'd have understood.

* * *

If there's one maxim that no longer reveals the essential American character if it ever did, it's "a penny saved is a two-pence dear," which is more easily recognized in its contemporary translation: "a penny saved is a penny earned." The real thing is probably something closer to what my father used to say, that expression of violence slightly contaminated with mercy.

* * *

I once saw a young man with a handful of pennies, maybe fifteen or so. He was standing in a hallway, head down, pushing the coins around in his palm with a finger. He flipped a few of them over, studied them for a moment, then tossed them all toward a wastebasket. Most of them clattered inside. "Wrong dates," he said, looking at me, then walked away.

* * *

So there's this man: he's frugal and generous, he's self-educated, he reads, he writes, he invents things, he's brilliant. He helped to create the place we all wake up in and walk around in every day. He's a citizen of the world. They loved him in France, even more than Jerry Lewis. It's not fair, but many of us recognize him right away as a cartoon. He wears odd little spectacles, perhaps bifocals, which he invented. He told a story about flying a kite into thundering skies and coaxing lightning to strike a key tied to the string. This is the key to rural electrification, to a steamer trunk, a strongbox, the key to unlock those secrets everyone's always talking about, the key to capitalism, the key to heaven.

* * *

Well, I've got a story for you. That kite string floated out there for over a century and came down on Nicola Tesla, whose bronze statue now sits on Goat Island, Niagara Falls, NY, radiating alternating current, scorning the shrinking wilderness. Niagara Frontier electricity chased darkness away. People celebrated this by parading through the streets with torches ablaze. Manufacturers of kerosene lamps went out of business overnight. Darkness hid in the Niagara Gorge where it had been for thousands of years. Johnny Weissmuller's long, wavering cry was frequently heard echoing down there in the forests on moonless nights, over and over. John Burroughs spent some of his declining years there, exploring, fishing for sturgeon, keeping secret journals, growing that prototypical ZZ Top beard, and creeping out at dusk for supper at a boarding house in the city. You like that story? I've got a million of them.

* * *

Burroughs inherited that key. You may think I'm still referring to Edgar Rice Burroughs, *Tarzan of the Apes*, *Tarzan and the City of Gold*, *Tarzan and the Lost Empire*, and all the rest. All those saved up pennies rolled into a city of gold. All those made-up Tarzan stories rising into a real city, Tarzana, California, population 27,337.

The neighborhoods of our dreams may be lost empires. Of

course, I am referring to Edgar, but also to John Burroughs, the great naturalist, whose writing documented and celebrated the forests and trout streams and experiences of the natural world in ways that inspired the crowds of nature writers who came after him. He didn't romanticize nature too much. He was more a transitional figure than transcendental, who revered the creatures of the wilderness and also casually killed them. He admired Thoreau. He carried a pistol in his pocket. John Burroughs is one of ours, isn't he? He had the key to the woods. Most of us don't know where the door is anymore. Do you think John has high name recognition these days? Take a poll. Ask the first ten people you meet tomorrow.

So we have Edgar, John, and also William S. Burroughs, who wrote *Junkie* and *Naked Lunch*, probably the most widely known of his books. He loved pistols, guns in general. There was a lonely puritan mystic wandering around inside him. William S. had a whole key chain full of keys – keys to the underworld, the overworld, to ancient and future worlds, skeleton keys, etc. People are still looking for some of the locks they fit. He also had an encyclopedic knowledge about keys, who had them, who didn't, and what they opened.

A character in his novel *The Place of Dead Roads* said, "Stay out of churches, son. And don't ever let a priest near you when you're dying. All they got a key to is the shit house." Does any of this add up?

*   *   *

When I first discovered *The Place of Dead Roads* I was certain it was about the Niagara Frontier. This was, after all, the land of Love Canal, and a place where road work turns up radioactive slag. In one location it was too hot for the local landfill to accept. The material, it was determined, had probably "fallen off trucks" years earlier and the level of radioactivity that could be accepted at the landfill was revised upward. And it was William S. who described six young boys wearing jock straps colored like rainbows, like souvenir postcards of Niagara Falls. Even the rainbows that once played in the mists of the falling water were finding new places to live.

* * *

It's gone now, of course, as gone as the first library at Alexandria, as those tall Buddhist statues in Afghanistan, the towers of the World Trade Center. Vic Figler called it Castle Rock. Emmie Lou Dias Tucker called it Chimney Rock. I knew it as Indian Lookout. My father often said you've got to make your own fun. Unlike Robert Zimmerman, I've remembered. Once, on some televised award show, Zimmerman stood there behind the podium, holding his award, and said, "Well, as my old man always used to say..." and the audience fell silent, because this was going to be good, this was going to be a life's lesson, a piece of advice, father to son, passed on to them. This was going to be comprehensible, something to live by, no vandals stole the handles stuff. And they stayed silent, waiting, waiting – and, finally, he said, "Oh, my old man. He used to say so many things."

* * *

The library at Alexandria has risen from the ashes and is once again collecting books.

* * *

So I'm six, I think, and my father is going up and down the lawn pushing an old steel drum roller filled with water. I'm helping. He's singing. The lawn is 60' x 120'. Our house is on the edge of the city, on a cinder road paved with slag from the coke furnaces of nearby industries, sometimes still smoking when the trucks spread it out. The half-dozen children who live across the road from us, sometimes accompanied by their mother, got out in the newly spread cinders with little boxes, bent over, sifting through to find the pieces of unburned coke for their winter stove. Some of these pieces are as large as a nickel, large as a dime. There are railroad yards to the south, smokestacks and factories to the west, northeast and north, close enough so that we'd hear the noon whistles blow, the overhead cranes screech in the factories, and freight cars slamming into one another as they put a train together.

The lawn is full of dandelions and plantain, and a variety of other grasses and plants that came in from the surrounding fields. My father doesn't care about any of this. It is his lawn and he cuts it and, in the spring and early summer, rolls it. I'm walking in front of him, arms raised over my head so my hands can reach next to his on the wooden handles of the roller, which squeaks once each revolution as we go. The sun is blazing down on us. He is smiling, singing, as if there's nothing he'd rather be doing: "Old Man River, he don't do nothing... he just keeps rolling the lawn." This is called making your own fun.

I'm picturing an old man named Mr. River. He's skinny with a long narrow white beard that reaches almost to his belt. His main pleasure in life is rolling the lawn. Somebody wrote a song about him and my father was singing it. This made perfect sense to me. I don't know how old I was when I heard the right words. Oh, my old man. He used to sing so many songs.

*   *   *

Speaking of being at home on the range, back in the saddle again, back where a friend was a friend, back when it was US Government policy to exterminate the buffalo to deny Indians a major food source, railroads sold tickets to people who wanted to ride passenger trains across the Great Plains, shooting buffalo from the windows as they went. What could be better than that? This was American Ingenuity and target detection, and something to do. People are always looking for something to do. The railroads made money, it was patriotic, it involved travel, and people got to kill something, or at least to wound it and let it die later. They were making their own fun.

Theodore R. Davis sketched this activity and the sketch was reproduced in *Harper's Weekly*, 14 December 1867. The title of the sketch is "Shooting Buffalo from the Trains of the Kansas Pacific

Railroad." The sky in the sketch is aswirl with almost solid dark cloud, like oil on water. In the lower left corner is a buffalo skull. Of the six buffalo in the foreground, five run desperately to rejoin the herd, a path which keeps them parallel to the direction of the train, and the sixth faces in the opposite direction toward the left edge of the sketch, toward the skull. Perhaps it has been mortally wounded. Its tail is held lower than those of the other five who believe they are fleeing toward safety.

The sketch is accompanied by the following:

"Our engraving represents a sport that is peculiarly American. At this season of the year the herds of buffalo are moving southward, to reach the canyons which contain the grass they exist upon during the winter. Nearly every railroad train which leaves or arrives at Fort Hays on the Kansas Pacific Railroad is 'slowed' to a rate of speed about equal to that of the herd; the passengers get out firearms which are provided for the defense of the train against the Indians, and open from the windows and platforms of the cars a fire that resembles a brisk skirmish. Frequently a young bull will turn bay for a moment. His exhibition of courage is generally his death-warrant, for the whole fire of the train is turned upon him, either killing him or some member of the herd in his immediate vicinity.

"When the 'hunt' is over the buffaloes which have been killed are secured, and the choice parts placed in the baggage-car, which is at once crowded by passengers, each of whom feels convinced and is ready to assert that his was the shot that brought down the game. Ladies who are passengers on the trains frequently enjoy the sport, and invariably claim all the game as the result of their prowess with the rifle. This solution of the case is, of course, accepted by all the gentlemen, and a more excited party of Dianas it would be impossible to imagine."

* * *

And it is almost impossible to imagine a more excited party of Dianas engaging in this most interesting and peculiarly American sport, isn't it? The *Harper's Weekly* writer had the decency to put quotation marks around the word "hunt," but not around "sport."

* * *

Nowadays there are "game ranches" where exotic animals from around the world, zoo "surplus," can be shot by those who are so inclined, if they are willing to pay.

* * *

What I remember about Indian Lookout is this: it was a natural upcropping of stone tower rising out of the Niagara Gorge, shaped by water, wind, erosion, freezing, thawing, and all those forces working in concert over hundreds or even thousands of years. About sixty feet around at the base, it rose some thirty-five or forty feet, tapering gradually to a flat top about three feet in diameter. Many pictures have been taken of such formations in the southwestern deserts of this country. It was located near the top of the gorge, its top extending nearly to the rim, a perfect lookout. But it was very unstable, comprised of crumbling layers of shale, slabs of limestone, and fractured dolostone.

At exactly what point along the Niagara Gorge Indian Lookout existed is difficult to say now, but I can say this much. It was perhaps within two hundred feet of where the Devil's Hole Massacre took place in 1763. It was a short distance from where Lewiston Road and Hyde Park Boulevard now intersect, near Niagara University, established in 1856. Hyde Park Boulevard used to be known as Sugar Street.

Both road and boulevard have now been widened from two to four lanes, the gorge rim has been leveled to accept an additional four lanes of concrete called the Robert Moses Parkway, and an access road to the water's edge Power Plant has been blasted through the gorge wall. But everything was intact the bright morning my father climbed to the top of Indian Lookout, hauling and boosting me along with him.

He was wearing dress shoes, or what used to be called dress shoes, leather, with leather soles. About halfway up he was sweating and swearing, footholds giving way, shoes slipping, chunks of stone coming off in his hands. I was perhaps two years older than I was that summer I helped him roll the lawn. Today, he'd be arrested for child endangerment. Back then it was the greatest adventure I'd ever had. In some ways, it still is.

When he got to the top, there wasn't room for both of us to be up there together. He pushed me up first. After a moment I stopped trembling enough to stand, crouching, then all the way up. I could see the lower gorge and river flowing, all the way to Lake Ontario it seemed and, as I think of it now, the feeling that if I'd stood on tiptoes, all the way to North Bay, or even the North Pole. I was on top of Indian Lookout. Then I clung below the edge as my father clambered up and stood there for a time, looking.

I wonder now what he was thinking about up there, but there is no way of knowing. It would be interesting if he were thinking about the British wagon train being heaved over the gorge at Devil's Hole by the Senecas. That would fit right in. But I doubt very much that he was.

Had he been drinking that morning? It's possible, I suppose. How else to explain taking such a risk? But he had smelled like he always did, that mixture of Burma Shave, pipe tobacco and cigarette smoke, empty beer glasses, and hot milk poured over Shredded Wheat biscuits, the finest breakfast in the world.

*   *   *

Some time later I had questions about Indian Lookout. Was it the lookout where an Indian watched for the wagon train that would be attacked and rolled over the gorge rim? Or was it the place where a settler or soldier would be on the lookout for Indians?

*   *   *

I watch television. A person would have to eat four hundred and twelve Shredded Wheat biscuits to equal the nutrition in one bowl of Eternalife Flakes. Big deal. What would I do with all that nutrition, anyway? So Shredded Wheat might be something like stone soup, but that's part of its charm. Those who have never heard of stone soup need to ask their great grandmothers, who may have eaten it as children.

The versatile Shredded Wheat biscuit is made from wheat, the staff of life grain, with whatever nutrients it has obtained from the soil, no steroids, color, flavor, or trisodium phosphate added. Or at least that's the way it used to be. And I'm not taking the advice in the song, "forget about your used to be." I'm going to work on forgetting songs that dispense such advice. When I want advice, I'll talk to a bartender, like any other good American.

*   *   *

In 1762, a small creek was fulfilling its destiny by flowing down cliffs and shale slopes into the river of Niagara Gorge about a mile downstream from the whirlpool. This creek didn't have a name, but it flowed along just the same, doing what creeks do, sparkling in the sunlight, attracting dragonflies, being home to crayfish and frogs and minnows and hellgrammites and other creatures. Deer drank from it, as did birds, foxes, raccoons, the occasional wolf, and other animals in the surrounding forests. It is possible that the woods bison, the buffalo of the Niagara Frontier, also once drank from it.

The creek probably intended, by design, to keep on doing what it was doing forever, with changes so gradual that it wouldn't even notice. Like most creeks, it had no idea about what was going to happen.

If it had possessed a different sort of consciousness, it might have guessed, though. Two years earlier, western Indians, fighting alongside the French, had killed eleven British soldiers nearby. This news should have traveled along the forest floor, and the creek had an ear to that. A Britisher wrote in a letter that the Indians had "cut off their heads and arms and fix'd them upon poles. I suppose *in terrorem* to us."

This was almost a hundred years before the slaughter of buffalo began.

This was 242 years before Daniel Pearl had his head cut off by his captors. That they didn't also cut off his arms and "fix" all three body parts on a pole shows the advance of civilization.

So the little no-name creek kept flowing, oblivious to everything that wasn't its business, until the bright morning of 14 September, 1763, when Seneca Indians ambushed a wagon train, killing all but two of those accompanying it, and ran the twenty-five wagons over the gorge rim, into that declivity at Devil's Hole. This was a stone's throw from where I climbed Indian Lookout with my father 184 years later. On that autumn morning, close to eighty died, wagon train drovers and military escorts. Many had tried to escape into the woods, and ended up splashing into the creek where they were shot, axed, stabbed, and scalped. Or maybe they were killed and thrown into the creek afterward. Would-be rescuers who heard the gunfire found the water running red and named the creek Bloody Run.

So, this is how, on the fourteenth day of September, in the year of our Lord Seventeen Hundred and Sixty-three, the anonymous little creek got its name.

* * *

During September, monarch butterflies are observed in their great southwestern migration across North America. There were undoubtedly monarchs fluttering and gliding along the gorge rim the morning of the Devil's Hole Massacre. But where they were going no one knew. That they were embarking on an incredible flight over the continent to a destination in Mexico would not be known until 1976, over thirty years after the German Blitzkrieg had inflicted heavy bombing and fire damage to many cities in Britain, killing 14,000.

*   *   *

Let us count the ways: 1) one to three biscuits in a bowl, sweetened, or not, to taste (white or brown sugar, honey, etc.) add milk. 2) pour hot water from teakettle or tap over biscuits, drain, sweeten, or not, add milk. 3) sweeten to taste, pour hot milk directly over biscuits. 4) crumble biscuits into bowl, add fresh fruit, sliced bananas, peaches, strawberries, etc., add milk or light cream.

*   *   *

Once, on the way down Indian Hill, my mother told my father to pull the car over while she got out and gathered handfuls of pods from milkweed growing on the side of the road. These were about four inches long, tapering from a blunt rounded end to a point, with soft, bumpy, green skins. My sister and I called these pods "fish." Each time we rode down the hill, my father announced "We're going down Indian Hill, now. Look out for Indians." I'd get my face up next to the car window, staring into the wooded hillside, but I never saw any.

*   *   *

There used to be a lot of wheat grown on the Niagara Frontier. The township named Wheatfield testifies to this, though in recent years scores of "subdivisions" threaten to make the name a relic of history. Each year some of the just-harvested wheat was sold to the Shredded Wheat factory in Niagara Falls. This was back when combines weren't the efficient kernel-saving machines they are today. They'd miss some in the fields, leave some still attached to the straw as it flew out the back, leak some as they worked, spill some in transfer to the field trucks. Then the trucks would trail kernels along the roads and the railroad cars would lose some in transport. The fields and roads and railway tracks were scattered with wheat kernels during harvest time.

After wheat, acres of feed corn dried off and the combines and corn pickers went to work on that. Kernels of corn and those shattered into fragments by the machines overlaid the landscapes, strewn nuggets. In some parts of the world people with small baskets would have been kneeling at the roadsides as if praying, picking up kernels, one by one.

Here it was an annual bonus for field mice and birds, especially pheasants and pigeons. Pheasants strode up and down the railbeds like furtive chickens, and pigeons whirled to the ground in large flocks. During wheat harvest and corn picking time and for weeks afterward, they were grain fed.

* * *

The wheat grown on the Frontier was nothing compared to the tonnage that came from the Great Plains when the sodbusters moved in during the years following the buffalo slaughter. "Sod busters" was a negative term, though today it's used for mild, archaic humor, the hatred and scorn it once embodied all but evaporated. Cattlemen, ranchers, and cowboys used it. Farmers threatened their unrestrained use of the open range. Initially, calling someone a "cowboy" was also intended as an insult. This was a term used by the real men – the frontiersmen, buffalo hunters, trappers, scouts, and Indian fighters, those solitary figures out into the wilderness and across the plains ahead of the settlers. Cowboys were boys who tended cows. It took Tom Mix and Gene Autry and John Wayne to make the country forget that.

* * *

Try to imagine that happening to the word "scab." Workers struggled and sacrificed much, including their lives, to establish unions in America. Struggle makes for long memory. You think the words "sodbuster" and "cowboy" got scrawled in outhouses and scratched on stagecoaches years ago? Although it's a common belief the Devil's Hole Massacre was actually an extreme labor dispute, there were, of course, mitigating circumstances and complications. Happy trails to you.

* * *

Many of the frontiersmen were at the very least anti-social loners if not outright sociopaths. Daniel Boone, his television gentrification aside, felt threatened by a neighbor settling in close enough so that the smoke from his chimney was visible. Boone said that was a signal it was time for him to move. This could have been a thin spiral of smoke rising from another mountainside, across the valley. My Uncle Bill would have been a frontiersman if he'd been born a hundred years earlier. Known as Kid McCoy in his boxing days, both he and Uncle Earl, nicknamed "Pee Wee," would have been fine frontiersmen.

I have a friend whose nickname is "Cowboy." He wears western hats, has a Stetson for dress, tooled cowboy boots, pearl-buttoned, embroidered cowboy shirts. The bug-shield mounted across the hood of his pickup has "Cowboy" lettered across it. He's never owned a cow in his life. Or a bull or a steer, either. He did own and ride horses for a number of years, but now the horses at his rural home belong to his daughters. He was very happy when all that was finished and he didn't have to bale hay every year. He's read all of Louis L'Amour, listens exclusively to Country, what used to be called Hillbilly until marketing changed that. I keep mentioning Zane Grey to him, *Roping Lions in the Grand Canyon*. Now the mountain lions are eating pets and killing joggers. Suburbia sprawls and the wilderness either dies quietly, becomes a nuisance, or snarls back. Sanderson says mountain lions are also known as puma and cougar or, more accurately, that puma are sometimes known as mountain lions or cougar. You get the idea. In March of 2011, the U.S. Fish and Wildlife Service concluded that the eastern cougar was extinct. Many people in Maine do not believe them.

* * *

For a time when Cowboy and I were kids, his father ran a two-pump gas station at Hyde Park Boulevard and Nevada Avenue. This was about a mile and a half south of Indian Lookout. In the front of the station lot was a large, red, circular sign, painted on sheet metal, suspended from angle-iron legs. About four feet in diameter, it proclaimed in white letters: "IF YOU DON'T STOP SMILE AS YOU GO BY."

That's my old neighborhood. I still go by, but do not often smile. The neighborhood is shrinking, smaller and smaller. Soon the streets and avenues will be too narrow to walk on, the houses too tiny for people to live in, smaller than doll houses, and then even smaller yet, and the giants who lived there when I was small myself will have all vanished.

3.

The house we live in is over a century and a half old. Over the last thirty-eight years the fieldstone smokehouse a hundred or so feet to the west has trembled invisibly as if subjected to a long, slow motion earthquake, its stone walls tumbling unnoticed into piles, and the outhouse, too, has gone through its own untended collapse. The years have streamed by, our plans for salvaging these relics unrealized. One of the oak support beams exposed in the cellar of the house is just short of twenty-five feet long, about eight by ten inches, hand-hewn, the adze marks still visible, of course, as descriptions of such timbers invariably mention. Of course. What would erase them?

How old was the tree from which such a beam was hewn in, say, 1854 or 1855? (The house was complete and inhabited in 1856.) If the tree had been 160 years old, which may not be totally unreasonable, then it sprouted from an acorn in the 1600s. Even if you think an 80 year old tree is more likely, it's still an old piece of wood.

Some day I may write about this house, but not here, not now. It's the barn I'm working toward, the first barn, the original one, the disappeared one, though not much is known about it. Given the importance of barns to survival in the Frontier's early years, in some ways they took precedence over the house. And the first house on these acres in the eighteen hundreds was not the one mentioned in previous paragraphs, but a log cabin, twenty by twenty-two feet, actually a two-story, that stood just to the rear, north of the present house. It was constructed in 1835.

To this location the family had used oxen to drag their few possessions through "the howling wilderness" of the swampy woods atop a sledge of logs. They may have had an adze packed away in there somewhere. About that time wolf scalps on the Niagara Frontier were worth ten dollars each, whelps five dollars, double the price of earlier years when fox and wildcat scalps were worth fifty cents each. As numbers of farmers and stock increased, the "wolf question" was to drive the price to ninety dollars for the scalps of adult wolves. Do you think there's a connection between these facts and the "scalpers" of today? Maybe not, but I'd like to think so.

Just a few miles away from that first log cabin was Quades Corners, a small village near which other homesteaders had begun to farm. Deer were so plentiful that one farmer fenced his small cornfield to protect it and dug stakes into the ground just inside the fence, sharpened ends slanted upward. One morning he found three deer impaled on them. Across the Great Plains the slaughter of buffalo herds was beginning. No wonder the wilderness was howling.

*   *   *

Years of my life have been spent in walking unconsciousness. Those who know me might suggest that this is a persistent condition and I can offer no evidence to refute them. Instead, I offer this. As a young man I spent an inordinate amount of time in the woods and fields of the Niagara Frontier, in the Southern Tier of New York State, and in other natural environments, hunting, training dogs, which we called "running the dogs," and simply wandering around, hiking, you could say, through the deep woods, Niagara Gorge, the second growth of abandoned farmland, through overgrown industrial sites, marginal ground, certainly, spring, summer, autumn and winter, in drizzle, driving rain, high winds, full hot sunshine, some great crisp days of frost and sun, in snowfall, and in blizzards.

I put in enough time out there to earn a college degree, maybe two of them. And what did I learn? You think it's something that can be passed on? That thorns and brambles can hurt you, that stepping into too deep water or on ice too thin can get you a soaker, that it can be real quiet out there, a good place to think, if only you had something to think about. Of the multitudinous plants, including trees, that I've looked at, sometimes closely and repeatedly, most of them remain unknown to me. They go on growing and blossoming, anyway, year after year, without me knowing their names. Thankfully, there are others who don't share my ignorance and, therefore, when plants become rare, threatened, or endangered, they can take the appropriate action. These are people who do not refer to wetlands as "drainage problems."

My walking unconsciousness has not been total. I can identify wild carrot, a couple of varieties of milkweed, chicory, dock, burdock, goldenrod, late-blooming purple aster, and maybe a half dozen others. I wouldn't know blue-eyed grass, though, if it winked at me, which it must have done as I slogged the fields. I can tell the difference between a raccoon and an opossum track in the mud of a drying creek. Deer tracks are easy: cloven, smaller than what the devil would leave, and the only creature it could be, because the buffalo are gone and their tracks would be much larger, anyway. A cottontail rabbit can routinely leap nine feet in a single bound. At a certain speed the rabbit's back footprints in the snow are ahead of its front paws, revealing the direction in which it's running. When a rabbit hops about slowly, this is reversed. Sometimes back off the road among the old farm fields going into succession, overgrown with thickets, occasionally near a small grassy clearing into which the sunlight filters, there suddenly appears a ragged stand of lilacs, usually the light purple variety. Sometimes the scent of the blossoms hits your nostrils before you see them. What are they doing there? You poke around a little and find the crumbling ruins of an old fieldstone foundation on which a farmhouse once stood, long since fallen or burned. Once, in such a cellar depression I dug around and unearthed an old ceramic pepper shaker, its metal top disintegrating. The pepper was as pungent as ever. I tucked it back into the rich mold of rotted boards. That's how you can find the locations of these old dwellings. Look for lilacs.

In an inch or two of fluffy snow the tracks of a squirrel and a rabbit are nearly indistinguishable. When the tracks lead to a tree and then disappear, it's a squirrel. On a winter day some insects move slowly to the sunny side of trees. Woodpeckers know this. The woods doesn't care about you.

Once during a light winter rain I crawled under an overhanging ledge high on the Niagara escarpment, into a layer of dry leaves that had blown in the previous autumn. Far below me the sepia countryside spread out, blurred and empty. After a little while a single crow floated into view, way down, tiny, wings beating slowly as if it had nowhere to go, but was going anyway, just for the hell of it. Then its caw sounded clearly, though far away, magnified by the silence. Then after about half a minute it cawed again, and then again, and again, repeated at about the same interval until it passed from sight. It had been getting smaller the whole while so it may have gone beyond my hearing about the same time. What did this mean? Everything. Beyond what I've written here, what can I tell you about its meaning? Nothing.

* * *

"Caw" is an onomatopoetic word.

* * *

Crows vocalize in a variety of situations. Scientists have undoubtedly studied this and can tell you how the sounds differ and what they indicate. The quality and frequency of their voices when they're harassing an owl they've discovered in the daytime, for example, is different from when they're calling others to a food source, or when the flock gathers at a roosting site at dusk, or when responding to an injured member of the flock. Why was the crow I described cawing the way it did? The scientists could probably tell you. But I believe it was cawing because it could, to break the silence, to declare its existence, to hear the sound of its own voice echoing across the countryside and to the distant escarpment. It was singing in the rain, unaware that it had an audience.

*   *   *

When I got out of the army, which I prefer to say rather than when I was "discharged," one of the first things I remember observing as a civilian, finally away from army bases and back on the streets again, was a sign, "Nails," over a small storefront at a shopping mall. I was cruising past in a car, on my way to nowhere, as I recall. This was the early sixties, when such shops first began appearing here. I knew there were many different kinds of nails, common nails, finishing, brads, spikes, aluminum, roofing nails, galvanized, and so on, but I never thought there were so many that a special store would be required. A regular hardware store couldn't handle them all anymore? I don't remember when the dawn came up on that one.

*   *   *

Somewhere on this property, which started out as a one hundred acre tract in 1835 and went down to ten before rebounding to fifty, there's a ghost of that two-story, 20'x22', first cabin. It's an empty space in air once taken up and made solid by this building, its second floor reached by a "substantial ladder." Birds fly through that space now, and butterflies, and leaves drop into it at year's end, and snow falls into it unrestricted.

When we moved in here and old-timers waved a hand vaguely at an area behind the garage and said, "And that's where the old house stood," and "the prune pickers used to stay in it," it never registered that the building they referred to was the original cabin. Why it didn't is now astounding to me, because it's so obvious the house we live in is genuinely old, and to have someone ignore that and mention the "old" house couldn't have been more of a clue. But the thought that the first 1835 dwelling could have been still standing within the living memory of someone speaking to me was obviously inconceivable. Then, too, they called it the old "house," which also threw me off. Perhaps, in later years, it had clapboard nailed over its outside walls and people stopped thinking about it as a cabin. Two locust trees flanked its front corners when the building was young and occupying its space in the world.

*   *   *

Even more astounding is that the building was torn down only twelve years before we moved into the "big" house.

*   *   *

Why now, after all these years, am I roused briefly to this awareness, to this detailed knowledge? Finally, I have carefully read a family history, written by Ruth Truesdale Townsend, in which there are numerous references to this homestead. A single ancient locust tree, battered and broken, half hollow, stands in the vicinity of where she noted that pair of trees grew. It's between eighty and a hundred feet tall, twelve feet in circumference at chest level, its trunk embraced by an American elm that towers alongside and lives, though disease has claimed other elms not thirty feet away. The elm itself is about five feet in circumference and may be helping to support the locust in high winds. The old locust trunk, almost fused with the elm, seems to have confused the Dutch elm beetles. Each year at the end of May into June, the old tree continues to blossom, sweet perfume filling the air, and to produce seeds, which are probably responsible for many of the younger trees in the nearby woods and on the creek bank.

Now, at long last the ungainly growth of lilacs in back of the garage makes sense. Stupid place to plant lilacs, I'd thought over the years, a swift, passing thought instantly shoved out of mind by others. But it wasn't stupid at all, of course, in 1838. They were growing next to the cabin then.

Over recent decades I've passed this thicket of lilacs on daily trips to the barn to do chores, during haying season, and so on, easily more than twice a day. I've walked by them over 30,000 times.

It never occurred to me to look for lilacs in my own backyard. Their forebearers were growing during Abraham Lincoln's lifetime, during the Gettysburg Address, when lilacs last by the dooryard bloomed.

* * *

It was built in 1900, so it's always easy to tell its age. This is the barn on the property now:

"Even the word 'barn' is solid and warm... the barn itself rests heavily on its fieldstone foundation, the beams and boards in place as they have been for over a century. The supporting beams are saw-mill-produced hemlock, eight by ten inches, some of them spanning over thirty feet. They might have been seedlings in the seventeen hundreds. Where these big timbers intersect they are mortised and pinned with oak pegs an inch in diameter. Vertical beams hold up the sill of the lower roof edge, braced on both sides with diagonal five by fives. The lower roof seems to almost float on these three-fingered candelabra. The rafters soar to the roof peak.

"Up in the winter loft when it is stacked full with hay bales, the dimness is broken only by the weak light that comes feebly between shrunken boards, through a nail hole, a knot hole. If it is snowing, the sounds from outside are muffled. It's as quiet as a cathedral inside. A mouse, perhaps, rustles in some far corner. Protected from the weather, a cow sighs in an open stall down below.

"The outer skin of the barn, tongue and groove siding applied vertically, keeps the cold wind from the animals. The barn had been painted red, darker than ox blood, so long ago that it may even have been the year it was built, and not repainted since. It's faded now, the blush of a half-remembered embarrassment that refuses to be forgotten altogether. A reddish chalk bleeds onto the palm or the shoulder when someone brushes against it.

"Inside, on the ground floor, there is almost a maze: rooms large and small, huge bays, dusty equipment, corridors, doors, a stairway, hay chutes, ladders. This is why city children like to explore barns.

What's in there, they wonder. Where does that lead to?"

This barn was built to replace the one that burned down in 1899. Little is known about that first one, its size, shape, or the materials used to build it, unless information exists in diaries or old letters, etc., that R.T. Townsend did not report. What she wrote was this: "Next year a blow hit the family – it was summer, and the barn burned."

That is a minor masterpiece of brevity and understatement. I should take a lesson.

*   *   *

It was one of those summers I ran barefoot the whole time. I was nine or ten, and you should know I had a healthy respect for fire even before my father asked me to step on that cigarette butt.

It was night. A fire of old boards was burning in a semi-circle of boulders in our backyard. My father and a half dozen or so of his friends were drinking beer. Their wives were there, too, and a bunch of kids running around into the dark and back into the light of the fire. Earlier, we'd all had corn-on-the-cob and hot dogs and we'd rolled potatoes in mud and baked them in the hot coals.

My father was taking a last drag on a cigarette when I ran up in front of the fire. He tossed the butt to the ground, which was mostly bare dirt from all the foot traffic, with a few blades of bedraggled grass. It made a couple of sparks when it hit.

"Step on that for me, will you, Joe?" he said.

So I did. I didn't hesitate. I stepped on it good. I yelled good and got right off it, too.

"Jesus," my father said, "I didn't think you'd do it!" Even in the firelight I could see in his face how sorry he was. "Come here," he said. He brushed off the sole of my foot and looked at it. "You okay?" He gave me a hug.

"It's okay," I said. "It hardly hurts."

"You'll be okay," he said.

And I was. Ten minutes later it didn't hurt at all and the next day there was no blister, no mark. The soles of my feet must have toughened up that summer.

Like most parents, he'd given his child credit for being smarter than he actually was. I never took up fire walking. You're supposed to honor and obey your parents, right? But you're also supposed to think for yourself. So what had happened there was a test. Did I pass or fail?

I have remembered the details of this minor event for many years. The best learning takes place in an atmosphere of love and a little bit of pain. We may have stumbled upon a new educational theory and practice here: "The Barefoot Boy," poem by John Greenleaf Whittier, 1855. Okay, step on those cigarette butts! No child left behind.

*   *   *

About 175 years after that early farmer sharpened wooden stakes to impale deer that leapt into his little fenced-in plot of corn, and just 30 miles away, a pointed wrought-iron fence surrounding a cemetery in a place called Williamsville was also impaling deer. Perhaps the deer were attracted to the quiet green space there, which was disappearing elsewhere. What, in the first place, were the pointed iron shafts designed to keep out, or in? Ghosts slip through unharmed. What the fence encloses, as expressed by the corny euphemism, is a marble orchard. After a half dozen or so deer were gruesomely impaled and had to be dispatched, concerned citizens began to make arrangements, at some expense, to render the points harmless.

*   *   *

That first barn was torn out of the woods, the trunks of trees, branch-lopped, dragged together, shaped by the adze, the ringing blows of steel on wood, the fresh cut sappy smell, levered into place, pegged, rising with sweat and fatigue, and most likely blood, for this kind of work can seldom be accomplished without it. For a number of years nearly equal to a person's retirement age it stood there. Barns don't usually look forward to retirement, but this one might have been feeling the passing years by then and decided to go down in flames. Or maybe you have your own ideas: struck by lightning, a coal-oil lantern fallen over, spontaneous combustion of hay stored too green.

The first is an act of God. The use of a lightning rod, then, is an attempt to thwart God's will. You think God couldn't override a lightning rod if He wanted to? Not much you can do after the fact, anyway, so you say a little prayer and vow to pray harder and get to work building another barn. The first barn? Oh, that one burned, a reminder that it will be the fire next time.

The second two are carelessness, but once the fire gets a good start there's no calling it off. You stand back, sick at heart, and watch it go, flames and sparks roaring into the sky, smoke swirling in huge, choking veils, timbers crashing into infernos so bright that it's painful to stare into them, pupils narrowed to pinpoints. You've got to look away. Your mind is incapable of forming the thought of pumping a clenched fist into the air and screaming, "Burn, baby, burn!"

You also look away because it was your decision to balance that lantern where you did, where if the calf bumped during your minute or two absence, it might go over. You'd taken the chance. Or those four wagon loads you hay-forked in off the wagon to beat the rain, that you thought might be a little too green, but you shrugged, stubborn, and said it would be all right. Then somehow five days slid by without enough hours in them and it was steaming hot in the barn and though the odor of silage wafted to your nose once, you still didn't climb up and dig into the mow. Tomorrow, you thought. And now flames shoot into the night sky, glowing, and for miles around people see it and wonder. They'll know soon enough.

A big fire like that takes days, even weeks, to finally burn out. The slightest breeze sifts ashes as light as feathers, kindles flames licking along the charred remains of a beam. The sour smell of smoldering lingers for a long while. And you're out there stirring the ashes, the embers, raking around, trying to get it all to burn completely, be gone, already planning the new barn in your mind.

It's that kind of resilience and doggedness and willingness to sweat and bleed again required to move forward, that and the taciturn description of what happened, the lips scarcely open as the words come out, "the barn burned," almost as if it had done so on its own, no fault of yours. And the new barn rises, full of promise, on the dead ground where the old barn had stood, and begins to gather its own cloak of years and its own stories,

4.

I have seen foxes... mating. "Mating" was not my first choice of words. The word that should have been there would have created alliteration, and would have been more fun to read.

But I'm trying very hard to keep the vulgar and obscene out of here. You haven't read anything vulgar or obscene yet have you? Actually, I think you have, but you're so used to other kinds of vulgarity and obscenity that you're reluctant to recognize new possibilities.

* * *

I'd ended up spying, though I hadn't planned on it. A huge, swung-open barn door blocked my view of the pasture from where I worked inside. Then, through a hole in the door about the size of my fist, a motion in the pasture attracted my attention. A red fox was trotting fluidly alongside the fallen, hollow trunk of an ancient Greening apple tree – and a few feet behind it, another. Who wouldn't have watched?

The fox behind sped up and the one ahead did, too. When the pursuer had nearly closed the distance, the other turned and raced in the opposite direction. The other reversed quickly and followed. After a minute or two, while this chase continued, it seemed the fox being pursued was female, a vixen, a name that took on new meaning. She leapt into the air several times and he shot past under her. She streaked through the hollow trunk and went the opposite direction on top of it, went part way through and emerged from the hole where a huge branch had broken off. Over the log, back over, into the hole, out one of the ends. All this time now, he was only a few feet or even closer behind her. Their motion was swift, but not frantic, the graceful choreography of their movement followed by the plumes of their tails, trailing like afterthoughts.

Several times during this chase, in what seemed agreement, the female allowed herself to be caught, and they had joined in what appeared to be brief couplings. Then in mid-chase once again, they stopped, ears perked forward, staring across the pasture toward the woods, where I had heard nothing. Light rain continued. It was a very quiet day. When they began to nose around in the grass for field mice, I cleared my throat discreetly and they disappeared as quickly and completely as if they'd been imagined.

* * *

I have seen people doing it, too. That's nothing special, nothing at all like foxes. Lots of people have seen that, including people with mirrors. But I have seen people doing it in a Henry J.

By the time I had become a teen, we had moved further into the city, where houses were close together along paved streets. One soft summer night after midnight I sat on the front porch, behind the vine-covered latticework, the rest of the family asleep. I was smoking a little corncob pipe filled with tobacco I'd stolen from my father's Prince Albert can. Wind chimes, those made from strips of glass, tinkled from across the street and down the block. I was probably just pretending to smoke, puffing away enough to keep the pipe going, inhaling just a wisp every now and then. Then the man who lived next door pulled into the driveway between the houses in his Henry J. and he had a woman with him.

The engine and lights went off, but they didn't get out of the car. There was enough illumination from the dim streetlight that it showed them kissing. After a few minutes they went out of sight below the top edge of the seat. This was magic trick enough. The Henry J. was a very small car. You can check this out. Those who owned them, loved them, but they seemed to have been modeled after the car in the circus out of which seventeen clowns emerge –

and it's thought to be hilarious because everyone knows that even two clowns would be crowded in it. Okay, it's not that funny, but people who go to circuses don't seem to know this.

The car seemed to adjust itself a little, shift on its springs, and one of the woman's bare legs rose up above the seat, and draped itself gracefully over its top edge. Then the car started to buck and heave, sideways, up, down, back and forth, springs squeaking gently. All this time, the leg was swinging, bending at the knee, foot nearly touching the headliner, not at all in rhythm to the car's awkward jouncing. Suddenly, everything was still. The wind chimes continued their clinking.

Two heads appeared in the front seat again, the passenger side door opened, and the woman got out. She came around the car toward my lawn, barefoot, wearing a long, full dress. She had hair down to her shoulders and kept moving, across my sidewalk, onto my lawn, in front of my porch, not six feet away, turned her back, gathered her dress up in her arms around her waist and squatted, peeing into the lawn, her round, white buttocks reflecting light from the streetlight, the moon, and every star in the sky. Finished, she stood, letting her dress fall, and pranced swiftly over the dewy grass back to the car.

I don't remember what happened after that. The car might have driven away. I might have crept off the porch, gone around the house and in the back door. I'm sure my little pipe had gone out. I did not tell my friends the next day. They might not have believed me and, besides, what was there to tell? It was something that happened, a street sweeper humming down the avenue next to the curb, louder, then fading, a black and white cat walking all by itself, stopping to sit under the streetlight, looking, pouncing at a moth, moving on.

* * *

Without the milkweed, the Monarch butterfly would disappear. This is the plant on which the female butterfly deposits her eggs and the only plant that can feed the growing caterpillar before it goes into the pupa to emerge as a butterfly. This is the plant from which my mother picked the seed pods on Indian Hill. This is one of the plants whose habitat disappears as a result of indiscriminate herbicide use and urban sprawl, under parking lots and driveways, lawns, carports, shopping malls, and so on. Those who love the Monarch are concerned. They see the Monarch on the World Wildlife Fund's Top Ten Critically Endangered Species list, along with the polar bear, the tiger, and the Mountain Gorilla. There are eighty-four varieties of milkweed, only one of which is federally listed as threatened. Of course, there were once billions of passenger pigeons in America. Alexander Wilson estimated the numbers of one flock to be over two billion in 1813. The flock was about a mile wide and 240 miles long. Three years later Audubon estimated the numbers of another flock at over a billion. Now there are none. In 1908, there were seven left, all in zoos. The last one, a female, died in 1914 in the Cincinnati Zoo, where she'd been the sole survivor since 1910. Those last four years had to be lonely ones. If passenger pigeons could have hung on for another century, cloning might have been a possibility.

Taxidermy, "the art of stuffing and mounting the skins of animals in lifelike form," has preserved this last passenger pigeon for the curious public who may view it at the Smithsonian in Washington. The bird was not mounted flying, however, and the remainder of the flock, all one billion or more of them, minus this one, are missing.

People ate a lot of them. They ate them by the millions. They ate them as squabs and as adults, fresh, dried, smoked, pickled, and salted. They shoveled them by the wagonload to feed hogs, then ate the hogs. If some member of your family was in America in the eighteen hundreds, it is highly probable that they consumed passenger pigeon meat in some form. This helped to give them the energy to engender you, or the people who did.

Research question: What was the name of the taxidermist who preserved the carcass of the last passenger pigeon?

It's true that a passenger pigeon is not a milkweed. There's no legitimate scientific way to compare them, to suggest the plant might go the way of the bird. But still. There are plants no longer with us, that have disappeared, and others whose existence has been strangled down to little fenced-in side yards of the earth, botanical zoos. Some of us go there to visit them. Buffalo grass is one of these. Milkweed is a friend of mine from childhood, the Common Milkweed, so called because it is common, which is why we became friends in the first place.

Milkweed gets its name from the sap which is white. The stems break easily. Sap oozes from the broken end, bitter, mildly poisonous, I read somewhere. The caterpillar that feeds on the sap-filled leaves not only tolerates the bad taste, but incorporates it into its body. The adult butterfly retains this quality. This is why most birds do not eat them. The one that gets a bite taken out of it has only the consolation that the bird has learned it is a snack to avoid. Other monarchs flutter about their business unharmed.

Inside the mature pods, the outer skin of which can be easily opened along a natural seam with a thumbnail, are the seeds, tightly packed, each with a parachute of silken floss. The seeds are flattened ovals about an eighth inch across, a rich brown, arranged neatly in overlapping rows like the scales of a fish.

In late summer the mature milkweed begins to dry, the pods shrinking, becoming brittle, and cracking open at the seam. The storehouse of seeds is exposed to the air and sun. On a windy day, gusts begin to tease the floss, fluff it up, tug at it, and the top layer of seeds drifts up, singly and in pairs or bunches, each with its spread parachute of silken fibers, floating off to new ground somewhere.

Typically, very few out of the hundreds set aloft will alight on the fertile earth where germination will result in a new milkweed the following year. Roads, parking lots, lawns, and rooftops aside, the milkweed seedling does not compete well in an environment supporting other vegetation. I once gathered at least a thousand milkweed seeds, a pod or two from each plant, and scattered them along fence rows where they'd be protected from mowing, about half into the grass already growing there, and half onto scuffed earth, a somewhat prepared surface. Four plants grew in the spring.

Later, I read that the preferred method of milkweed propagation is to start seeds in flats as other plants would be germinated, and to place the young seedlings in the desired locations. It turns out that after millions of years, nature has some of the processes pretty well worked out. If we want to intervene, even to mitigate, there's a lot of effort involved. How arrogant to think otherwise, even for a few seconds.

*   *   *

She was an older woman, older than me, anyway, who was exceptionally fond of squirming around on my lap while singing "I'm Sitting on Top of the World." She'd moved in with her sister and brother-in-law, who lived in the next-door upstairs apartment, to spend the summer. They worked during the day, and there she was, from Ohio, all day long with nothing to do. She claimed she was twenty-one, but I think she was younger, eighteen, nineteen, or twenty at the most. She had some sort of soft accent. I never saw her wear anything other than a nightgown all that summer. It might add to the picture if I told you that it was a sheer nightgown, but it wasn't. It was cotton, long enough to reach mid-shin, button front, halfway down. But she usually wore nothing at all underneath it.

I'd come slamming out of my side door on my way to somewhere and she'd lean out of the upper window all loose and falling out of that nightgown and call down in her slightly husky voice, "Are you coming up," followed by my name. I have never heard anyone draw a one-syllable name out that far. At the time I didn't realize this scene would be re-enacted in hundreds of Benny Hill skits and had probably been in hundreds before him, so I didn't appreciate that it was amusing. I was too busy going up the back stairs two at a time, to her apartment.

She, her name was Faye, had attempted to shape her eyebrows with a safety razor, which had slipped once or twice, and so she impulsively shaved them both all the way off. This gave her a look of perpetual surprise which seemed to complement her favorite activity. I once took a friend up with me. Faye seemed willing enough, and sat tentatively on his lap. He was embarrassed even at that and he never returned. He was a good kid, my friend, and I hope his life turned out all right.

As far as Faye goes, I have wondered over the years from time to time whatever happened to her. At summer's end did she go back to Ohio? Personally, I think she went to St. Catherines, Ontario, Canada, to pursue her goal of becoming a singer. This would be an almost perfect ending to this story, to have Faye settling in a place named after St. Catherine of Alexandria, virgin and martyr, singing her heart out, singing like a whiskey-throated nightingale while her eyebrows miraculously grew long enough to braid.

Unfortunately, I recently learned that the name St. Catherines, Ontario, has nothing to do with St. Catherine of Alexandria, or any of the six St. Catherines, for that matter. But that aside, people who do a great deal of thinking about these things assure me that in another fifty years lap dancing will be an Olympic event, and that in its very first year will attract tenfold more spectators than curling. There's no telling how popular the Synchronized Lap Dancing event will be. To think I may have been there in the very beginning is very humbling, indeed. And to think my father told me "Don't go up there. Stay away from her." That just goes to show that at certain stages of your meandering and stopping life, the advice of your father may not be the best advice after all.

* * *

The corner store was the mall of yesteryear, when the thundering hoof beats of the great horse Silver came out of radios across the land. This is where the pinball machine was, and bread, beer, milk, pop, ice cream, some delicatessen, penny candy, kites, kite string, greeting cards, buttons, thread, needles, pins, balsa wood airplanes, bandages, comic books, popsicles, Creamsicles, Mexican jumping beans, and other items too various and numerous to list here. A long painted sign over the front of the corner store usually stated what could be found inside, "Groceries, Beer, Candy, Sundries."

In the mid to late forties, one of the items that appeared briefly in the corner store of our neighborhood was probably a sundry. It was a fabric-covered box about the size of a Straight Arrow card, about an inch thick. In the center of the box was a red button. Words on the box said something like "Trapped Inside! Press button to hear shout of pain!" Of course, we knew there was some creature in the box, or even, although this was harder to believe, a little person. The boy who'd bought the box had pressed it first before we arrived and he said we could try it, but only one at a time, around the side of the corner store. We waited, full of excitement for our turns, all the more anxious when we heard yelps of pain from around the corner. When it was my turn I couldn't wait to press the button. And I did hear a shout. The button had a tiny hole in its center, from which a fine steel needle emerged when pressed. Spring-loaded, the button popped up, concealing the needle again.

After we'd all had our turn, we ran down the street with the box looking for children who hadn't yet seen it. What fun! What a joke on us! We all wanted to hear the yell of pain. We were eager to hurt that thing in the box, but hadn't stopped to think we might be the ones doing the yelling. We were introduced very early to the concept of hurting outside of the box. You can understand why this particular sundry didn't achieve the status of being constantly in stock.

* * *

During those years around WWII, the silken fibers of milkweed floss were used in life preservers because of their natural buoyancy. I've tried to imagine how such large quantities were collected. Did armies of children, women, old men and others roam the fields of America with sacks? Where were the collection depots? Was milkweed grown commercially? What happened to all the seeds? Were they tossed out in great moldering heaps in back of the factory? Did populations of monarchs drop off? Is there anyone still alive whose life was saved by a milkweed–down preserver? Does the person know what made him float in those cold waters waiting to close over him? How about all those green pods we picked to throw at one another in childhood wars and the pods my mother picked on Indian Hill? Were there fewer monarchs drifting on the breezes of the Niagara Frontier during those years? A person could go quietly insane thinking about these things, especially when so many other important questions demand priority. Like what's for supper?

My mother was thin, dark skinned, and loved big hoop earrings. Her hair was black and she had certain features unlike her other family members. She was always happy. She could make a faint whispering noise deep in her throat like a dog barking far away, the loneliest of sounds, a lost dog, or one chained with no one home, hungry, barking at something it couldn't see in the dark woods or across the fields. She had to put her lips up to your ear so you could hear it. The family joke was she'd been left by Gypsies, switched at birth with the real infant daughter and sister who'd been born to them. No one considered that a Gypsy mother wouldn't want to trade her baby any more than anyone else in the world. My mother died before I was old enough to ask her any serious questions about this.

The Indian Hill milkweed pods gave up their floss to my mother, who had plans for a glass serving tray with handles at each end. She removed whatever stained picture had been under the glass, perhaps one of those depictions of dogs sitting around a table playing poker, and replaced it with a compressed layer of silken milkweed floss, including seeds. She positioned a row of autumn red oak leaves around the outer edges.

This was during the last years and those just after the War, when friends got together in the evenings to entertain themselves by playing cards. I remember the word "canasta." The card table got pulled out, legs unfolded, and the collapsible chairs, metal, also unfolded, crowded around the table. The chairs had been painted Chinese Red, a popular color then. My mother served coffee or drinks using that tray. There was a lot of visiting and gossip and laughter during those card games. The chairs are scattered in the barn here, now, unfolded for many years, their dull and marred Chinese red under layers of dust, chaff, and cobwebs. Just for the hell of it, I am going to clean them up one of these days, bring one into the house and sit on it, while having a cup of tea. If I do, I will probably dream when I go to bed later. I will be in the old neighborhood in the dead of night. A dog will be barking so far away that its voice is scarcely audible, and under the streetlights, milkweed parachutes will be slowly floating, drifting as thickly as snow.

5.

So whatever happened to Bloody Run? Imagine that its headwaters had bubbled up from a magical spring somewhere deep in the ice-age fractured stone of the continent, from a hidden, slow moving river as broad as the Niagara. But that's probably not so. Chances are it was a typical stream with only two claims to fame: its final destination, its descent into the Niagara Gorge, and its christening by the large number of bodies that bled into it.

Creeks and streams that are not born from springs put themselves together from snow melt and rain, drop after drop gathering into trickles, into rivulets, joining forces until enough water accumulates to go somewhere. This is a miracle that happens continually before our eyes, this replenishing of the earth's moisture, necessary for life, until the ground is saturated, the water table rising, the swelling of brooks and streams that feed rivers and lakes that often flow to the sea.

With Bloody Run it would be difficult, if not impossible, to reimagine the 1763 landscape that sustained it, the swales and little swamps, the wetlands, the natural declivities in the woods, gravel beds and minor glacial moraines that may have guided its passage. We can speculate that lumbering and farming practices may have altered its character even before 1800. By 1856 the first buildings of Niagara University were completed very near the gorge edge terminus of Bloody Run, and during the next fifty years, industry began to establish itself in the area that fed the stream. Since low spots, swales and wetlands are not considered productive land by most commercial enterprises, some filling of these areas probably took place with whatever materials were available. Frequently, these materials were the wastes of production, cheap, and readily available. Over the next fifty years, the growth of industry in the area was enormous, especially in the processing of chemicals, other toxins, and radioactive metals. A fifteen-acre landfill about sixty feet high, now stands a short distance from a truncated remnant of the creek, which resembles a drainage ditch, choked with cattails. Where's the rest of it? Like any other self-respecting creek, it had gone underground.

It didn't do this of its own accord, but if it had been able to, it probably would have done so out of shame. By 1975 it was carrying a full range of contaminants from the Hyde Park Landfill, where 80,200 tons of chemical wastes squatted in the drainage basin of Bloody Run. Almost seventy steel-encased wells were planned, spidering out from the poisoned area, into neighborhoods, onto University property, on the landfill itself, where the migrating chemicals could be detected and, in some cases, intercepted for treatment.

The once sparkling, life-sustaining creek now flowed with acid chlorides, benzal chloride, brine sludge, BTC, BTF derivatives, CaF2, C56, chlorination products, chlorbenzenes, chlortoluences, DDM, dechlorane, LOS/MCT and inorganic phosphates, miscellaneous chlorination products, organic phosphates, TCP, and thiodan. It would never live again.

A DEC Update says "many of these chemical wastes are hazardous." Does this mean some aren't? Which ones would you add to your stone soup?

Ten years later the New York State Department of Environmental Conservation was referring to the "Bloody Run Risk Assessment Document" and defining for the public such terms as RRT (Requisite Remedial Technology) and NAPL, chemicals heavier than water, which do not mix with it and migrate through it into fissures in the bedrock.

In 1998, the DEC Inactive Hazardous Waste Disposal Report provides the following information:

"Surveys completed to date reveal that contaminants have migrated considerable distances in the overburden and bedrock aquifers."

"Contaminated bedrock groundwater flows into the Niagara River resulting in potential bioaccumulation of Hyde Park chemicals in the fish of the Niagara River and Lake Ontario system."

"A NYS Department of Health Fish Advisory is in effect for the lower Niagara River and Lake Ontario."

"Bloody Run Excavation was completed in early 1993."

So Bloody Run doesn't exist. Only the name remains. The short, straight ditches we see as the remnants of Bloody Run are not that at all. They are channels for the leachate, mixed with rainwater and snow melt, that comes from the landfill. Bloody Run is described in a DEC newsletter as "draining the area which includes the landfill, [running north]...." The landfill has become the point of origin, the magical spring we once imagined. Bloody Run was "excavated," gathered up with bulldozers and backhoes, front-loaded into trucks, dumped, and buried in the landfill. In some perverted sense it continues to flow from in there, through a conduit that runs under factory property, appearing in the daylight briefly, then sliding into "underground storm drains" that lead to the Niagara Gorge, where it seeps down a large area of the rock face into the river. It is an open sore on the gorge side, infected, weeping, unable to heal. The landfill is now listed as remediated.

*   *   *

In Richard Brautigan's *Trout Fishing in America* there's a piece about a used trout stream for sale at the Cleveland Wrecking Yard. It's stacked up in a warehouse in varying lengths, going for $6.50 per foot. That sounds about right for a stream between five and eleven feet wide. Trees, flowers, grass, ferns, deer, and birds are extra, insects free with a minimum ten foot purchase. It's too bad Bloody Run couldn't have been moved to one of the industrial warehouses on Buffalo Avenue before it was poisoned. A creek like that, with its historical significance and all, probably would have brought at least $18.00 a foot, maybe more. The little bit of dust that would have gathered on the sections in the warehouse while the owner waited for the price to go up would have flushed right out once it was installed. On the Niagara Frontier, though, it would have been discovered years later that in the three years after the first authentic half mile had sold out, that 2,434 additional miles of "Bloody Run" had been sold, all of it counterfeit.

* * *

Just south of the landfill, another factory had worked with uranium, thorium, zirconium, and radium. On that property, the Environmental Protection Agency reports radiation levels fifty times higher than expected background readings. No reports indicate that testing of Bloody Run effluents for radioactivity or radioactive elements was ever conducted.

So there you have it: ice age, chert, Seneca, Bloody Run, buffalo, Indian Lookout, gold-painted shoulder blade, silver-white metallic element, Lone Ranger ring with its secret compartment, glowing watch-face, Manhattan Project, God of Thunder, Hiroshima, Nagasaki, fallout. Got it?

* * *

When my father was in the hospital dying of cancer, he didn't know it until the very last. He was making plans for what he was going to do in the spring just a short time before he died. His doctors didn't believe in telling patients they were terminal, because it was counterproductive to patient care, or because they found it a convenient philosophy to embrace, because it permitted them to avoid an uncomfortable task. They told everyone else, though, all his adult relatives. The major surgery and radiation treatments my father endured kept him alive for the six months they predicted he'd live when the cancer had been first detected. This was good because "you never know when they'll find a cure." This was in 1954.

* * *

For thousands of unremarkable years a little stream tumbles into the gorge at Niagara. It didn't have a name and neither did Niagara. Then it got a name and a short time after that, for the span of twenty-two years between 1953 and 1975 there was a period known as the "Hazardous Waste Disposal Period." During that time rock and roll got invented. This time, though short, may have been more important than the Bronze Age. Don't name things unless you have to. Adam made a mistake naming all those animals. He should have said, "No, I don't think so. They're too marvelous to be named. You name them if you think they need names. I don't want to be the first one to go quietly insane trying to tell the difference between a rabbit and a hare."

* * *

When my father was in the hospital dying of cancer, he sometimes saw old men watching him from the wood grain veneer of the hollow core doors. The nurses and doctor said he was hallucinating from the heavy pain medication. They could have said his brain was being poisoned from the toxins his liver could no longer process. I think he saw old men watching him. Our druid ancestors refuse to be dismissed. The spirits of trees rise to the surface of those thin slices of wood. Are you absolutely positive that we know all there is to know about these life forms? Is Julia Butterfly Hill a lunatic? Toss another log on the fire. Let's talk about these things.

I also wonder now, if years before, when he had so quietly stared off into the distance from the top of Indian Lookout that he had seen something out there in the gorge forest, or at the horizon, staring back.

* * *

Sitting on the window ledge, across the room from the gold shoulder blade of the deer, are bronze-plated reproductions of a sculpture by Remington. The End of the Trail. They're bookends. Which books do you think should stand between them?

*   *   *

When my father was in the hospital dying of cancer his father stopped in for a visit. There we were, all in the same room, all bearing the same name, the elder, a Jr. and a III. I got out of the chair that I'd pulled up near the bed so that my grandfather could sit down. He wore an overcoat and a suit and tie, had come in after work, on his way home.

The conversation was halting, awkward, oddly formal, with long silences between topics. Maybe a little of it was that English reserve, the stiff upper lip business, but probably something else, too. My father, I think, had earned his father's disapproval. My father had his own way of doing things, buying a house on the wrong side of the tracks, marrying that shanty Irish girl, Florence McCoy. My grandfather went over how my father felt that day, the weather, best wishes sent by someone they knew in common, how things were at the office.

My father laid there, radiating pain, so thin under the sheet he was scarcely there at all, his lips cracked, skin yellow, making his dry mouth talk. The visit lasted about twenty minutes. I've spent many hours waiting for things since then, but no hours longer than that twenty minutes. Finally, my grandfather got to his feet, buttoning his overcoat, said, well, that he'd better get going, and went out the door.

It was the end of the day, getting dark in the room. No one had turned on the light. After a few moments my father said, quietly, "The old man will never know how glad I was to see the back of his head."

*   *   *

There's a curious tug and push going on along the Oregon Trail. Reports say it's vanishing, with modern road builders paving over long sections of it. This should not surprise us at all. At the same time, there are miles of the trail so deep, with the earth so compacted by those early wagon wheels, that it's said nothing grows there to this day. And some new highways have carried people away from the old pioneer towns – while much of the Oregon Trail, as a newspaper article describes, is "unkempt and abandoned." This we should be concerned about. Those portions of the 2,170-mile trail that are still identifiable should at least be kempt, don't you agree? At the very least, someone should be mowing the grass.

The Oregon Trail Interpretive Center offers tourists the experience of "standing" in the old wagon ruts. That wouldn't be enough for me. I want to drive my four-wheel drive RV in them. "That's not allowed, sir," the Interpretive Guide would probably say, hesitantly. "Oh, come on," I'd reply, in my most convincing tone, "What's it going to hurt?" And then deliver that line from Bukoski's poem "The Sex Fiend," full of cunning and promise, "I'll give you a dollar!" He thinks for a moment. "How about twenty?"

It's surprising no one's thought of that added attraction for the motoring public. It won't be long before a fully outfitted Conestoga wagon is available, pulled by oxen, on which tourists can book ten-mile journeys riding and walking behind that wagon as it rolls down the actual trail, wheels in the ruts. At some point, for the interested wealthy patron, an Interpretive Center employee dressed up like Straight Arrow will rise from the grass and shoot a feathered shaft into a non-lethal body area, say right in the ass. This will cost $12,000. There are complications to consider.

Perhaps transporting lengths of the trail into warehouses is now worth considering. How much would it be worth per foot?

We poke fun, of course. The Oregon Trail Interpretive Center and the End of the Oregon Trail Interpretive Center undoubtedly do a fine job of arresting time and providing a little of the experience of a bygone era. The vast emptiness I experienced years ago, however, with my hand in the wagon wheel rut, is vaster still, not lessened by museums, not filled by people who want to stand there in history, both feet in the ruts.

*   *   *

If you are one of those people who believe that when one door closes another always opens, you probably grew up in a funhouse. Or you know about that early apartment of mine where all the kitchen cabinets had been hung askew. In the actual world, where old men stare out from the grain of hollow core doors, sometimes doors shut and that's it. The sound of the deadbolt sliding home sends a short Morse code.

For a few weeks I worked in a door manufacturing company in California. These were hollow core, exclusively. Each morning the shift foreman, who'd arrived early, turned the heat on under the glue rollers and ripsawed up the frames and ribs of the doors we'd need to fill the day's orders.

The job of the assemblers was to arrange the wooden frameworks and ribs on a large table, staple them together with the pneumatic gun, then run sheets of veneer through the glue rollers, sandwich the frames between them and slide doors into a hot press, where the pressure and heat dried the glue, sealing the veneer to the frames. By nine in the morning it was sweltering, the doors smoking as they slid from the press, where we retrieved and stacked them, fingers burning. The assemblers were all Mexican-American, except for me, that displaced Irish English American. How had I ended up there? I wanted to be in the Niagara Gorge, cool river breezes blowing my hair back. For an hour or so each day, the boss's son, home from college for the summer, came in and made some fun for himself by stapling the assemblers' back pockets to their wallets. This made everyone sweat more. We all worked at top speed, trying to get the orders filled so we wouldn't get fired. Lots of doors opening and closing there.

Evenings I'd sit at my kitchen table drinking beer and drawing maps on old yellowed paper that I'd found in the back of a closet when I moved into the apartment. I'd make a bunch of squiggly lines and label it "ridge," and a curving banner labeled "river" or "river gorge," and "cliff top," or "three hills," all different. The only thing the same on each map was an "X," and every one of these was marked "Gold here." The pencil I used had soft lead and I didn't press down too hard, which made everything look as if it had been drawn many years ago. At work the next day, I'd slip these maps, folded into a square, into each hollow door as the veneer skin was glued on. In most of the California neighborhoods where these doors were sold, they were routinely opened up as if they were fortune cookies. Within five or ten years most of these doors would have been splintered open by a fist, a foot, a head, or a law enforcement battering ram. Hope needs some help once in a while. It was giving out little stories for people to tell. Hey, look at this! You'll never guess where I found it!

*   *   *

When my father was in the hospital dying of cancer a young man named Lloyd S. Harpham visited regularly on the long night shift and gave him back rubs with lotion to keep his skin from drying out and to help ease the pain. Lloyd had become part of our family for an extended period when I'd been very young. He was the son of my mother's friend. Family circumstances made it impossible for him to stay with her. After having served in the US Navy from 1944-1947 he worked at the hospital as an orderly. My father had always thought the world of Lloyd and often told the story at our house of how Lloyd survived tough times without complaining, of how, first married, he lived in a place so cold that the dishrag used to freeze on the kitchen sink overnight. I didn't find out about those backrubs for over thirty years, until a family member, not Lloyd, told me. Not too long ago, I got a note from him, telling me he'd received a Conspicuous Service Star for "service with a decorated military unit," and a Medal for Merit, for "service in peacetime or [service] in direct support of combat operations," both from New York State. Lloyd said in his note that it was "nice to be recognized after all these years." He signed it, "Your older brother." Some gifts pull broken pieces of years together. It took a while, but New York State got it right beyond what it knows.

6.

The Ticonderoga has always been my pencil of choice. It might have become my favorite simply because it was the first pencil I ever picked up. But even the name "Ticonderoga" is cloaked in powerful mist: Fort Ticonderoga, French and Indian Wars, gunfire, bloody battles, Benedict Arnold, death, and General Amherst, with his own unhappy history on the Niagara Frontier. A brand-new, freshly sharpened Ticonderoga No. 2 is full of potential, thousands of words ready to pour out of that slim vein of graphite centered in a cylinder of wood. It's a six-sided wand, with yellow paint as bright as new dandelion blossoms. There's a small bit of metal and rubber at one end. These are all natural elements that will be destroyed and discarded in the process of creation. It's a necessary sacrifice.

The preceding paragraph is a romantic rhapsody to a writing artifact poised to drop into the landfill of history. If I'd been born a few hundred years ago I'd be singing the praises of the quill pen, a few thousand years back, the stylus, how its sharp edges indented the moist clay, how easily it cleaned up with just a little water from the bowl, how writing in earth was the only way to do it. We come from clay and return to it. What better way to record our stories?

The graphite in a pencil, though, is derived from carbon, one of the elemental building blocks of life. The pencil drew a line to one of my first jobs, at International Graphite, which manufactured graphite electrodes for use in electric arc furnaces. One of those big electrodes, six feet long and nearly three feet in diameter, would have made a hell of a pencil. Stories, poems, plays, songs, novels, the whole history of the world could have come out of one of those babies.

You sharpen up one end, get yourself some paper and sit down at your kitchen table, hoist that thing up on your shoulder and start to write. If it gets a little heavy, knock back a double shot of Southern Comfort. That'll put some lead in your pencil, son. Write faster. Use it up. The more you write, the lighter it gets.

There was a time when getting a pencil box was part of a ritual for American grade-schoolers going back to school after summer vacation. These were made from light cardboard, with paper-hinged lids, and inside compartments, and were widely available in department and corner stores. They were designed to contain not only pencils, neatly aligned in their long compartment, but also a pink eraser and, in the more elaborate boxes, a plastic protractor, perhaps a wooden ruler, and a steel compass. All those little grade-schoolers were trudging off to school with their pencil boxes, ready to measure up the world, to protract it, to draw circle after overlapping circle until everything was connected, all the intersections beautifully visible and under control. I don't remember a teacher ever asking us to take out our compasses, though. And a good thing, too, since the compass was a vicious contraption, a remnant of some two-legged medieval torture instrument, with a stubby leg of a generic pencil clamped in on one side and a sharp steel needle for the other. Adjustable, the legs could be pushed so close together that points of graphite and steel nearly touched, ready to pirouette, or pulled so far apart that they pointed in opposite directions, the needle long enough to put out an eye, puncture a jugular, even reach a heart through some bony little chest. They'd be setting off the metal detectors today, wouldn't they?

The pencil ruled supreme. Does everyone have a pencil? All right. Take out your pencils, now. Raise your hand if you need to sharpen your pencil.

At one end of the pencil is its graphite point, used for writing, of course. At the other end is the delete button, used to eliminate mistakes. We knew it as the eraser, a soft rubber nubbin about a quarter of an inch long. This was very short compared to the length of the pencil, so it suggested something about the number of mistakes you were expected, or allowed, to make. We worked through long mornings and afternoons, heads bowed over our desks as we wrote with our pencils, copying from the blackboard, copying words from the workbook, or copying over, clumsy letters and words trailing one after the other along the lines of the cheap paper, page after page. On a hot day sweaty hands caused the smell of wood pulp to rise from the coarse paper, and the days passed filled with the sounds of erasers rubbing and breaths blowing the eraser shreds away, fingers sweeping across the paper, and the occasional grinding of the pencil sharpener at the front of the room. When an eraser was worn almost entirely away, the sharp edge of the thin metal band that held it to the pencil caught the surface of the paper and tore a ragged hole in it. Then there'd be a soft groan or sigh. Now the page had to be started over. This was work to turn in. A watchful teacher overseeing these classrooms could have taken notes and predicted the childrens' futures.

There were those children with their workbooks always open to the Palmer Method depiction of the perfectly formed letters of the alphabet, those who wrote slowly and with much labor, sometimes with the tips of their tongues protruding as an aid to dexterity, those who often snapped their pencil points from pressing too hard, those who erased entire words and lines with great, hard back and forth strokes, those who erased only the offending marks with short light motions, those who swept dramatically at erasure leavings, catching the page edge and wrinkling it with the palm, and those who brushed gently with the fingertips and blew softly until paper and desk were clean. There were children who gazed blankly out of the window for long spells, those who stifled yawns, those who were distracted by the loud double-click of the clock as it advanced each minute, there was the girl who delicately picked her nose with a baby finger and wiped what she'd extracted under her desk, the boy who watched from across the room with a faint smile, those who chewed their pencils leaving the dents of their teeth in the soft wood, some with the eraser end inserted into their mouths, others who wedged the pencil across their mouths like pirate's daggers and bit down.

Year after year the teacher watches these children come and go and thinks, "The future Harriet Beecher Stowe could be sitting at one of these desks. Or the future Jack London. Or probably not, but still."

The children had already been launched into the trajectories of their lives from families and neighborhoods, carrying their flimsy pencil boxes from which they had begun to write and doodle and draw their paths to somewhere, their unfocused dreams rising into the hopeful and beautiful daylight. The teacher disliked thinking these paths were fixed, though one day she gave in to the temptation and began to speculate about which of them would go on to careers in business, which ones would be aggressive, which shy, sullen, or radiating happiness as adults. She thought about which children would be occupational drudges, which hunters, which golfers, which bowlers, who among them would be adults susceptible to quick anger, who would be tender and thoughtful lovers, who would have an inventive sense of humor, be a loyal friend, which of them would be good and loving parents, which harsh and impatient, which among them would color inside the lines for the rest of their lives, and who might reach for stars to create new languages, new ways of being in the world. Then the teacher also thought she might be heading for a nervous breakdown. She came in early the next morning and put double the usual amount of bell work on the blackboard.

*   *   *

The family of Henry David Thoreau owned a pencil factory. He didn't have to go far to find a pencil. After his two-year sojourn at Walden Pond, which ended in 1847, he worked at the factory for a time. I wonder what his specific job was there. Did the pencils have a name? Had he jotted notes or written drafts for _Walden_ with these pencils? Were they painted yellow or some other color or were they bare wood?

It's conceivable, though unlikely, I'm told, that the prolific nature writer John Burroughs, who was twenty-three in 1860, once wrote with a pencil from the Thoreau family business. Chances may be better that he used a pencil made from graphite mined at Ticonderoga. I have a friend trying to determine these probabilities. My friend is a heavy drinker, however, so I'm uncertain about how diligently he's pursuing this investigation.

In 1911, Edgar Rice Burroughs owned a Chicago business, an agency that sold pencil sharpeners. Why it failed is anyone's guess, though it's likely it had to do with his salesmen not selling enough pencil sharpeners. When I was a grade-schooler, we had a pencil sharpener at home, mounted on the wall just inside the cellar door at the top of the steep, narrow stairs. It was my father's job to lean over that first step to turn the handle and sharpen the pencils when they needed it, and to empty the wood shavings and graphite dust from the barrel of the sharpener when it was full. If anyone else, such as my sister or I, had tried it we might have fallen down the cellar stairs. We could have broken an arm or a leg or even our necks. Sharpening pencils and maintaining the sharpener were dangerous jobs. Is it any wonder there was excitement associated with the pencil?

In 1925, William S. Burroughs was in, let's say, eighth or ninth grade, attending a private school. The name of this private institution was The John Burroughs School. It was there that William S. was observed aiming a pencil at other students as if it were a gun. It was an Eversharp pencil. There was no mention in the account of whether or not he pursed his lips and made percussive noises as he was aiming the pencil. Four years later he was enrolled in a Ranch School in New Mexico. This location was sufficiently remote that it was chosen by the government about fifteen years afterward for "military purposes," and the school was closed forever. This was Los Alamos, New Mexico, where Enrico Fermi, J.R. Oppenheimer, Edward Teller, and others gathered to work on the Manhattan Project.

About eight years later, William S. found himself in Mexico City. He'd gone to an apartment to sell a pistol to someone who'd expressed an interest. A couple of friends and his wife, Joan, had accompanied him. They were drinking. There may have been some drug use, as well, or just prior to the meeting. In any case, there were few strangers to drug use in the room. At some point, Burroughs said to his wife that it was about time for their William Tell act. Joan, as if they'd done it before, balanced a highball glass on her head, though at least one person said it was a six-ounce water glass.

Whichever it was, William S. aimed the pistol from a few feet away. It was a .380 Star automatic, which he knew shot low. Should we surmise that he made an adjustment for this in his aim? Perhaps he was so near that he believed an adjustment wasn't necessary. Whatever went through his mind at the time, when he pulled the trigger, the bullet hit Joan in the head and killed her.

He was charged with Criminal Imprudence and served thirteen days in jail. Whether or not the sale of the pistol was completed was not widely reported. *Junkie* was published, under a pseudonym, in 1953, and reissued under his own name eleven years later. Do you think William S. pointing that Eversharp at his classmates was a warning sign? Do you think early intervention might have helped here?

* * *

Does anyone have an extra pencil?

* * *

For a few months before I got out of the Army, I wore a uniform with PFC stripes on the sleeves and worked a midnight shift in a Receiving Center at Fort Jackson, South Carolina. I had qualified as a Sharpshooter with the M1 rifle and Expert with the carbine. There are three levels. Marksman is the lowest qualifying rank. The 1st Sergeant who'd run beside me in the combat exercise when I'd earned Expert pointed me out as a good example of aggression and deadly shooting. I was knocking those pop-up silhouettes dead. I was pretty good, huh? I thought so.

My job at the RC was to meet the busloads of incoming recruits, sometimes at two or three in the morning, make sure they had the proper paperwork, and send them on to their assigned barracks. If forms were missing, the recruits had to fill them out before they left the Center. I was one of the first people in uniform they saw on the base. I was the boss, their superior. They had to do what I said.

One night a young man stood across the counter from me who seemed to be refusing to fill out his form. There were about six years between us. I'd drifted from one job and place to the next until I got drafted. He'd enlisted, it appeared, as soon as he could. The room was about half full, nearly a hundred other recruits seated on folding chairs.

"Fill it out," I told him. "What you waiting for?"

He ducked his head low and moved the stub of pencil toward the paper, but didn't touch the point to the surface. The pencil point moved up and down like the beak of a shy bird getting ready to peck, but unable to bring itself to do it.

"Go ahead!" I said. "What's the problem?"

His head went even lower and he raised the pencil to his mouth and wet the point, then repeated the motion. He spoke as if addressing the countertop. "There's something wrong with this pencil," he mumbled.

I grabbed the pencil from his hand and scribbled in the margin of the form. "Nothing's wrong with it," I said. I tossed it back on the countertop near his hand and he picked it up, since it had seemed that's what I'd intended for him to do. His head still low, he said, "I can't write," almost in a whisper.

Right then I got a sinking feeling in my chest and knew I'd been studying to be an Expert Shithead. "Should have said so to start with," I said in a low voice to the top of his head. I took the pencil from his hand and inspected the point. "Hold on here," I said in a louder voice. "There is something wrong with this." I made as if to write, pressed until the point snapped, then tossed the pencil into the wastebasket. I took another one from the box of hundreds on the counter.

"Let me do it," I said. "It'll go faster." I asked questions and filled out two identical forms with his name and address, etc., on them. I wrote clearly when I signed his name, the Palmer way. I don't remember what his name was.

"This is your name," I said pointing. "Fold up one of these and put it in your pocket. The only time you'll have to do this again is when you sign your miserable Army paycheck. Trace it out. Copy it. Practice."

He started to brighten a little, his head coming up. "Yes, sir!" he said. "Looking forward to the miserable pay."

"Don't call me sir," I told him. "I'm just a PFC like you'll be before too long."

He nodded. "Yes, sir," he said.

"Oh, man," I said. "You're going to love the Army. Go sit down."

Then I ran the whole bunch of them out front on the blacktop under the spotlights and gave them the speech. "All right, men, you've got to police up this area or you'll be standing at attention here until the sun comes up. You all got off that bus flipping cigarette butts and dropping candy wrappers and shaking dingleberries out of your pant legs. Everything that's not blacktop and not moving gets policed up. Put it all in the butt cans on the porch here. Get those hands out of your pockets! Don't be walking and looking down with your hands in your pockets. You don't see something to pick up, bend down and pretend you're picking something up! I don't want to see nothing but asses and elbows out there! When I inspect the area, I find so much as a paper match, I'll dump these butt cans all over the blacktop and you'll start over. Don't be chasing those moths! Birds will police those as soon as it's light. Get it all up, now!"

I stood on the porch, leaning on the railing, having a smoke. The recruits were moving all over the blacktop, up and down, up and down, which was good, since if there were a quarter inch fragment of tinfoil or anything else there in the morning when I was relieved, the 2nd Lieutenant would have me out there doing it by myself. Not everyone had early advantages like a pencil box. I only had one myself for a couple of years.

Vietnam was starting to heat up when I got discharged. It's a good bet that recruit who couldn't write got sent over. I hope he found a pencil that worked and learned to write his name and got to come marching home again.

* * *

The word "pencil" once described a small, fine-haired artist's brush. It was spelled differently, too, as most words were, "pensel" in Middle English, for example, and "penicillus" from Latin, which means "small tail," or penis.

Some of you may wish to reread these little stories and observations about the pencil with this in mind. I wouldn't bother, though. It might spoil something. Sometimes a pencil is just a pencil.

* * *

Like an unnamed Bloody Run, the cut-up technique had been lazing around in the sun for thousands of years waiting to be discovered. William S. Burroughs, commonly associated with the cut-up technique of literary composition, credits artist Brion Gysin with its "discovery" and for telling him about it at the Beat Hotel, in 1959. This event was preceded, however, by Tristan Tzara (aka Sammy Rosenstock of Romania, and also Samuel Rosenfeld) who, while attending a Surrealist rally in Paris of the 1920's, proposed that he create a poem by randomly pulling words from a hat. Some of the crowd surmised that the hat was his and that inside were slips of paper on which he'd written words, but this was far from certain.

The rest of them were forced to acknowledge that words themselves, protoplasmic things, were squirming and crawling and creeping inside the hat, fuzzy, sharp-fanged, proud, soft-bodied, and shelled, crude, purring, vulgar, segmented, some glowing like fireflies, others nearly invisible, old and graying out, rare, obsolete, unsure of their own identities or nationalities, the silent ones, the loud, modest, blushing, clicking together like tiny castanets, all attempting to stretch their almost nonexistent necks upward so that they might be lifted into the daylight.

The possibility of a living language, especially contained by a hat from which Tzara had offered to pluck words and thus create a poem, proved to be too much for those assembled. They rioted, yelling and shouting, punching one another in their angry faces, breaking shop windows, shoving people to the ground, ripping up and burning manifestoes, damaging pissoirs – and Tzara was expelled from the Surrealist movement, in spite of having founded, with several friends, the Dada movement years earlier. His expulsion did not deter him from writing Surrealist poems until his death in 1963, dispelling any rumor that he was a closet realist.

Out of these tumultuous beginnings the cut-up method emerged. Burroughs and other enthusiasts saw its effects and possibilities everywhere, past, present, and future, in art, film, music, audio-tape, prose, poetry, computer applications, mixed media, and elsewhere. The cut-up literary technique involves cutting an original text into pieces and then reassembling it, usually by chance, into a new order. The resulting text can stimulate the creative impulse and, as its most profound result, decode the original text's true meaning. Beyond that, as if revealing true meaning isn't enough, the new text has the power to alter reality for the creator and reader, and the potential to serve as a method of divination. This last possibility is cleaner than poking around in a pile of chicken entrails with your finger and easier on the chicken, as well. Those of us who are skeptical of cut-up are likely to be converted into believers when the technology is applied to the Bible (King James' Version), the Encyclopedia Britannica, and the OED, decoding their true inner meanings.

In the meantime, if you are intrigued by the cut-up technique, it is something you can try at home. Cut up street and road maps of your city and state into three inch squares, shuffle the pieces and tape the maps back together randomly. You will have created a new place for yourself, a new way of being in the world. Go to bed with a smile on your face and sleep the sleep of the enlightened. Wake up to the sound of the phone. It's a friend with a warning. A man from your past and two of his henchmen, armed with shotguns, are on their way to your apartment to kill you. You've got a five minute headstart. Grab your car keys and wallet and leave the state, using the maps you've made the night before.

*   *   *

It's reported that the pen name "Tristan Tzara" was selected because it meant "sad in country," a living testimony to the cruel treatment of Jews in Romania. There is sadness in "triste," but no country in "Tzara," which seems to be one of those shape-shifting words, whose meaning assumes whatever definition its user is able to convince others it possesses. It might have been the last word hiding in a silken fold of the hat's lining.

"Tristan" is awash in a sea of associations. Tristan, or Tristram, is the very handsome hero of the medieval Tristan and Iseult cycle. He's described as a great warrior, musician, hunter, lover, dragon slayer, poet, and a wonderful storyteller, who some knew as a superb liar. Part of this cycle has been lost. Perhaps the last surviving manuscript pages fell victim to cut-up. The story continues in *The Book of Sir Tristram of Lyoness*, written by Sir Thomas Malory while he was in prison, completing it in 1469, a few years before his death. He'd been imprisoned the last twenty years of his life, during which time he wrote *Le Morte d'Arthur*, including the Tristram book, which grew out of the Tristan and Iseult tradition, and in which Tristram was a knight of the Round Table. Tristram surfaces again between 1759 and 1767, when Laurence Sterne's novel, *The Life and Opinions of Tristram Shandy, Gentleman*, was published in successive volumes. To say the book is digressive is understatement. The narrative veers and detours from one topic to the next, from relatives to opinion, to their characters and ideas – and so the title's promise to write about Tristram's life, as revealed by one event after another, never gets beyond a few years after his birth.

Sterne's interest in "the irrational nature of association of ideas" is a distant cousin of cut-up, and of Tristan Tzara, and in some measure speaks to the structure of this text, where memories and opinions have been allowed to surface in a stream of associations, but then nudged into a shaggy order. But method is of interest only to methodologists and to some individuals in writing workshops.

Tristan Tzara had no idea his offer to pull words from a hat at a Surrealist Rally had provoked a riot. He had no idea because it never happened. No hat, no offer, no riot. There's a hint of that in some existing versions of the story with vague references to "the twenties," when the event supposedly took place. Evidence of an event that did happen was Tzara reading his Dadaist manifesto, on 9 December 1920, at the Galerie Povololozky, in Paris. In "Dada Manifeste sur l'amour faible et l'amour amer," he provides instructions on how to make a "Dadaist poem." Words are to be cut from a newspaper article, placed into a bag, shaken "gently," and then pulled out "one after the other" to make the poem.

This blossomed into the Surrealist Rally, hat, words, riot – which, even if it didn't happen, should have. It's too good a story not to have happened. Imagination had struggled to become fact and almost made it. It was a nice try, though.

Meanwhile, cut-up survives, sometimes as "Cut-up" with a capital "c." Its latest reincarnation has been available in toy and novelty stores, individual words printed on strips of plastic that can be pulled out of a box, or hat, and stuck on the refrigerator to create a poem. Nearly a quarter century ago William Burroughs, Jr. referred to the term as "cut/up." A version predating these is "cutup," defined as a mischievous person, a prankster. Somewhere William S. Burroughs is smiling. Language is, indeed, a virus from outer space.

7.

Momentous events were in the news from around the world. An American president had earned high approval ratings for his assault on terrorism. Ecoterrorists had been blown out of consciousness by people who exploded their bodies to kill others. Discussions about who the real ecoterrorists were, those who burned ski lodges under construction and spiked old growth trees or corporations that poisoned the planet, came to an end. Freezing temperatures and cold rains penetrated the mountain sanctuaries in Mexico and up to 270 million monarch butterflies died. The first attempt to open the ANWAR to energy exploration failed in the US Senate. Another Earth Day came and went.

During this time, soon after David Suzuki had been the keynote speaker at Niagara County Community College, I had lunch there. Since I eat out infrequently, this was an unusual event for me. For a variety of reasons, eating out makes me uncomfortable, and knowing that others routinely enjoy this doesn't help. I always feel that I should be sitting with my back to a wall and sometimes contrive to do this when it can be achieved without drawing attention.

There were five of us around a school dining room table, three men and two women, all faculty or former faculty, together by chance. The table was located in the center of the dining room. Four of us were eating salad and pasta. I was working my way through a mound of wings, a large splash of blue cheese on the plate, a big bowl of chocolate pudding and a large Dr Pepper on the side. The wing sauce probably wasn't Slap My Ass and Call Me Sally, but it was good, hot enough to make my lips burn.

Then, having dispensed with Earth Day, David Suzuki, and the Mideast Conflict, three of the group suddenly discovered that they had the same proctologist. How the subject came up, I don't recall, but the coincidence seemed astounding at the time. I didn't consider the odds. I mean, how many proctologists are there per hundred thousand people? Conversation drifted to colonoscopies without benefit of sedatives. One of the women had endured three of them, before being offered something. "Oh, no!" said one of the men. "I want to be knocked out completely! I like that feeling just before you go under," he said with a smile.

I didn't contribute much to this conversation. Eating wings made it difficult and, besides, I was the one in the group who preferred to have his back against the wall. The younger of the women in our group was looking crestfallen, a little left out. All she had been able to do was ask questions.

"Don't worry," someone reassured her, "in another few years you'll be starting." Thus comforted, she related her experiences with mammograms, compressing imaginary breasts in the air with her palms, top to bottom, sideways. "Those can be very painful, too," the other woman said. Now three of us had nothing to contribute. It went quiet around the table for a few moments. "I have very dense breasts," she announced. This came out a little louder than she'd intended.

There was a pile of clean bones heaped up on my plate, with four crumpled heavy-duty paper napkins I had used wiping sauce and grease and blue cheese from my fingers and mouth. These napkins would not be recycled. I had the impulse to sing then, perhaps "When you wish upon a star, it makes no difference who you are…" flourishing a wing bone as a baton. Jiminy Cricket would have been proud of me. But then I thought of all the songs my father sang and one of his important rules: "No singing at the table."

*   *   *

Fifteen million buffalo roamed the western grasslands in 1800. This is an estimate, of course, and some say a conservative one, because the buffalo didn't often stand still or parade by in single file so they could be counted. Ernest Thompson Seton estimated at least a hundred million. Can you imagine just one herd about thirty miles wide and seventy miles long? A mature bull was six feet high at the shoulder and weighed well over a ton. In 1878, the last tiny surviving buffalo herd on the southern plains – fifty-two of them – was killed, wiped out by a hunting party. By this time the near extermination of the northern herd was almost over.

The largest number were killed in a short span of six years, during which time hundreds of thousands of buffalo carcasses sprawled continually over the southern Great Plains, putrefying in the sun. Rotting flesh can fill your nostrils with a stench that seems almost solid. You may have had this experience with a small dead mammal, say a road-killed opossum or raccoon that you encountered while jogging. At the apex of putrefaction, the odor is thick and nauseating, a warning to stay away. This may be an evolutionary defense for humans. We are subject to diseases harbored by rotting flesh. Other animals relish it as food. Turkey vultures do. They keep the summer roadsides picked clean across the Niagara Frontier. In fact, decaying meat was considered gourmet fare in Europe, in France, for example, where it was advised to "hang" the animal, without benefit of refrigeration, until a certain degree of rot was achieved before cooking. A duck, it was said, entrails intact, should be suspended by its tail in the pantry or back shed until the feathers pulled out, allowing the duck to fall. Then it was ready. The real gourmets suspended the duck by its head.

In America, we "age" sides of beef, hanging them from hooks in coolers from ten to fourteen days, and then cut them into steaks, roasts, and so on. During this time the cells begin a slow breakdown, entering the initial stage of a controlled decay. This makes the meat more tender. We don't call it decay, of course, because that would be poor marketing. It's "aging," as in what happens to fine wine and whiskey. I've been told that differences in degree are often more important than differences in kind. This may be an example.

* * *

Once, out rabbit hunting alone, I kept noticing dead field mice all day. It was late fall, no snow, and I was walking an old railroad line on the Niagara Escarpment, two hounds on the downside of the tracks. Rabbits tended to head uphill there when run by the dogs. When a rabbit crossed over the railbed, it was easy to see, an opportunity for a clear shot. Looking down frequently to keep from stumbling on the ties, I saw what was probably the fourth or fifth dead mouse.

This one looked perfectly alive, crouched there as if it were waiting for something. Why were they dying? I shifted my shotgun into my left hand, bent down and picked up the mouse. How long had it been dead, I wondered. I scooped it into the fingers of my right hand, fingertips sliding under its body. As I straightened up I experienced the sensation of the tip of my index finger sliding into its body, into a soft decaying underbelly. I flung it away in disgust. But could I have been mistaken? I lifted the fingertip to my nose and inhaled deeply. Do you know what the dry heaves are? I believe that mouse was a few days past ready, but since it hadn't been suspended by its tail in my pantry, I couldn't say for sure.

* * *

So you might sing about a home on the range, but the buffalo don't roam there anymore. They were shot to death and they rotted. Had there ever been, or has there been since, in the recorded history of the earth, so much flesh set to rotting in so short a time? Can you see the panorama, as was reported, of dead buffalo fallen so close together that you could walk on them for twenty miles without touching the ground? It is an American landscape not depicted by artists, dead buffalo stretching to the horizon, the sun coming up, the sun setting.

Most of them had no hides, but their great shaggy heads were still hair covered, the sun and moonlight glinting from mottled and bloody flesh in varied stages of decomposition. The shameful incense of their rotting must have risen miles into the air. Carrion eating birds, vultures, crows, condors, magpies, must have soared in from far off and stayed for years. The American Bald Eagle flared its wings in the skies over this scene and floated in. Prairie foxes, wolves, coyotes, bear, mice, and other creatures grew fat, increased in numbers. A humming drone of flies filled the daylight hours. Maggots by the wheelbarrow, by the dump truck full, writhed and shimmered in these carcasses. Smaller birds and other animals fed on them. Juices soaked into the earth. And everything that ate, shit, dispersing the energy of the buffalo herds over the plains. In some way the earth was enriched by this monumental aggregate of death.

*   *   *

Toward the end of June 2004, local Channel 7 news reporter Julie Fine visited a Western New York farm where a variety of unusual animals lived. I forget what most of them were – perhaps llamas, burros, miniature horses, a unicorn or two, etc. You know the sort of story. But among these creatures were a few buffalo, which seemed to have impressed her the most.

The spot ran its twenty or so seconds of film showing the animals, and afterward she remarked to her co-anchor, "But I mean like the buffalo were right there!" Yes, they were, Julie.

*   *   *

Final notes on things beginning with the letter "B."

Buffalo Bill Cody killed 4,280 buffalo in eighteen months while he was a meat hunter for the Kansas Pacific Railroad. This would have been dismissed as unremarkable by those who killed over two hundred a day for the hides.

Hide hunters, when they had time, scalped the buffalo for their curly head hair, which was used to stuff cushions and other furniture.

The blacks who fought on the side of the whites were called "Buffalo soldiers" by the Indians, because they thought the hair of their heads resembled that of the buffalo.

The 1960 *Encyclopedia Britannica* devotes eight sentences to the buffalo. Actually it's seven sentences and one fragment, which seems to be a stylistic characteristic of such reference books. We learn the buffalo belongs to the ox family and that one of its distinguishing features is that it has fourteen pairs of ribs rather than thirteen. It is also revealed that the proper name of this animal is "bison," the Latin nomenclature, B. Bison, but that in North America it is commonly called "buffalo." That seems the right name to me. It is probably the one Adam proclaimed. Bison Bill Cody doesn't cut it. You have just read eight sentences, counting this one.

Sanderson's paperback *How To Know The American Mammals*, published in 1951 by The New American Library, with a cover price of thirty-five cents, has nine sentences about the buffalo, one of them with sixty-three words. It also mentions the fourteen pairs of ribs.

Buffalo numbers, dates, etc.: In 1900 there were 25 plains buffalo in Yellowstone, 88 in Montana, 500 in northern Alberta, Canada. There were an estimated 60 million buffalo in North American before 1830. The Wood Buffalo National Park of Canada was established in 1922 for the protection of the remaining buffalo in northern Canada. It's about 28,000 square miles, approximately the size of Maine, home to 2,100 Wood Buffalo. There are about 260,000 buffalo alive today. That might seem like a lot, but 130,000 cattle are slaughtered in America each day. Forty or so years ago breeders put buffalo and cattle together to create an animal called beefalo. This sounds as if it might be a joke, but it's not. There may still be some of these around. Ted Turner owns about 55,000 buffalo, on a range of 1,284,000 acres spread across several western states, the largest private herd in the world. Being able to own buffalo may seem odd, but it's not – herds of buffalo and small numbers of buffalo are found on farms and ranches all over the nation. About 10% of the meat produced by Turner each year is sold in Europe and the

Far East. Speculate about how this could be a curious tithing. There are approximately 21,000 members of the NBA. This is the National Buffalo Association, not the National Basketball Association. Some of the above may be inaccurate. Don't quote me. Imagine you heard it all from some guy spouting off in a bar. Check things out for yourself.

Barbed wire was first patented in 1867. Seven years later it was being manufactured by machine. The West had already been changed forever, but this would slice up the open range with millions of points of sharp steel glinting in the sun. The form and function of barbed wire has remained the same for well over a century.

Western New York, August, 2004, *Buffalo News*: buffalo were in the news. A buffalo, having escaped its confines, was spotted roaming in Golden Hill State Park, about ten miles from where it started out. After a day of being pursued by members of various agencies, it was sedated and picked up by its owner. It had been free for about a week.

In a separate incident, near a town some thirty miles away, a woman was killed by one of the buffalo she'd raised. She'd bottle fed them when they were calves. The largest of the three weighed a ton and a half. They'd been enclosed by an electric fence in a "football field-sized" pasture the article reported, into which the woman had ventured. Her death was not witnessed, but the newspaper headline stated, "Trampling death raises issues."

The town dog warden said keeping the buffalo didn't violate any town law and that it was probable they'd be considered farm livestock rather than wildlife. This was confirmed by an officer of the Department of Environmental Conservation. A neighbor said the buffalo "should be destroyed or, at the very least, put in a zoo."

Both of these events involving buffalo took place on the 19th of the month, as an unusually rainy summer trailed into a stretch of unseasonably cool nights. Too much shouldn't be made of this. The Golden Hill buffalo had, after all, escaped a week prior to its being captured.

But even as coincidence, it brings to mind what happened annually for thousands of years, when triggered by some collective genetic memory, the huge buffalo herds began to grow restless, the urge to move pushing them into great flowing migrations over the plains in search of winter pastures. Some will conclude that we had two buffalo stories from the Niagara Frontier, mid-August, 2004, one ending in a park named Golden Hill, one in the death of a woman who loved animals, one happy ending, one unhappy. Others will say that both endings were unhappy.

* * *

From Buffalo, NY, on 19 October 2010, in a column published in *The Buffalo News*, Jeff Simon lamented the name of his city: "Our city's name is also the name of a large, comically shaggy-looking plains animal—a noble one to be sure in Native American culture, but for the rest of America, one of nature's most uncouth creatures."

* * *

Daniel Boone was known as a "mover" and a "long hunter," because he kept moving further into the wilderness and staying away from civilization for extended periods of time, a year or longer. He told the story of sitting around campfires with other hunters, west of the Appalachian Mountains, using large vertebrae as chairs. These bones are believed by some to have been the remains of the last hairy mammoths in North America. Indians had retold the story of these creatures. Pat Boone is the great-great-great-great grandson of Daniel Boone. He is known as a "mover and groover," and has been a singer and entertainer for many years, often remembered for his recording of "Tutti Frutti." This makes Little Richard scream even louder.

A nation of bones was left scattered across the prairies when the flesh of the buffalo had rotted away. For years these were gathered by bone pickers and converted to phosphates by fertilizer manufacturers. In a representative year, 1874, freight trains on the Santa

Fe Railroad transported seven million tons of buffalo bones. For decades afterward people ate bread made from wheat grown from the earth nourished by the bones of the buffalo.

About seventy-five years later, I picked up the shoulder blade of a deer in the Niagara Gorge. It had been bleached white by rain and sun, and was completely clean and odorless, except for the smell of the gorge, river water, stone. It was the shape of a tree drawn by a child, with the round top sheared off flat. A thin ridge arose from one edge of the reverse side. There were several ways that it felt comfortable in my hand. I carried it home with me where, for some reason, perhaps because its whiteness was so bleakly a testimony to skeleton or because I wanted its value to be signified, I painted it gold.

Here's another one for you, about another half century later, summer 2006: In Buffalo, New York, there's a bar called the Buckin' Buffalo Saloon. In this establishment there's a mechanical buffalo that patrons can attempt to ride. It's advertised as "the only mechanical Buckin' Buffalo in the USA." The buffalo head on this apparatus appears real, mouth closed, a resigned expression on its face, if such a thing can be imagined.

Half century measures – another footnote: By 2005 the last dwindling herd of the southern Plains buffalo, once numbered in the millions, was down to fifty-three. Inbreeding had been causing a high percentage of the cows to suffer miscarriages – or calves that were carried full term to die soon after birth. Predictions had it that the last of this genetically distinct group would vanish in another half century. By the year 2011, their number had grown to seventy-five, because six years before, Ted Turner had donated three of his bulls, distantly related to that earliest herd, to save them. Back from the brink, as they say.

* * *

The locker next to mine belonged to a career soldier, a thirty-year man, a heavy-set, American Indian. We had the same rank,

PFC, one stripe. He'd been higher, several times, First Sergeant even, but kept getting busted back down for one offense or another.

Standing in front of our lockers one midnight after drinking beer in an off-base saloon for several hours, he told me about his combat in Korea. During the evening he hadn't said twenty words, but now he was talking in slow, measured sentences. He'd been a machine-gunner. Mid-afternoon out in the flat, cold countryside, somewhere south of the 38th parallel, they were attacked by an enemy too numerous to count. The human wave, he called it.

Row after row of them materialized on the horizon about a half-mile away, hundreds, more than hundreds, running toward the squad's dug-in position. They could already hear them screaming. He could feel the hair on the back of his arms stand up, he said. There was no need for target detection here.

They waited until the frontrunners were about three hundred meters out before they started firing. A meter is a little under forty inches, so we are talking about three football fields plus nearly ten yards of an end zone. You learn these things in the US Army, when you are on the rifle range. You get so one hundred meters is a distance you can measure with your imagination.

Some of the frontrunners started to fall, but the gaps were filled immediately, those behind picking up the weapons of the fallen, firing and screaming as they ran. The screaming was louder now.

At two hundred meters, the ones behind could be seen clearly, leaping over the bodies of those shot down. At one hundred and fifty meters the squad laid down a continuous overlapping barrage of automatic rifle and machinegun fire and the dead piled up in heaps. Those behind clawed and climbed over mounds of bodies and pressed forward. They were fifty meters away when he ran out of machinegun ammo. He grabbed his pistol and started firing.

By the time he'd dropped two, the rest were an arm's length away and he killed a third at point blank range, who fell at his feet. It was then he realized the last of them had thinned out and those who remained were continuing to run, screaming in high-pitched voices, sweeping right past him, to the left and right of him.

They were Chinese, he said, many without a weapon of any sort, some with clubs and some few with pitchforks, eyes fixed on something far away. That's the way his eyes were when he finished the story. He was the only one in his squad to survive. The whole time he'd been talking, his hands had kept making small gestures, machine gunning, multitudes, pistol.

Now he ran his fingertips down the front seam of his shirt to his brass belt buckle, then fly seam, checking his gig line. "I was the lucky Indian that day," he said. "And there is no doubt in my military mind that I am the luckiest sonofabitch alive." He said that in a way that meant his dead buddies were luckier.

We continued to stand there talking by the lockers for a little while, him swaying slightly, then he ran both hands over his chest and stomach as if to check where exactly he was in that poorly lighted place, and said "Smoke if you got 'em," which was his way of saying goodnight, and we turned away from one another to go to our bunks.

* * *

Do you think it was bullshit, that story he told me? I have wondered about that myself and have decided the story was true. Some stories need to be told even if there's only one person listening. I've repeated it here to the best of my ability, without elaborating, just how I remember it being told. We know how memory is, though, and so you can make whatever allowances you have to for that.

Not long afterward, he got transferred to another base. The last time I saw him, he was in the company area saluting a tree over and over, while shouting, "Good morning, Sir!" A young Second Lieutenant stood a few feet away, one of those recent Officer Training School graduates referred to as Ninety-day Wonders. It was clear the Officer had thought his salute hadn't been quite crisp enough, or maybe he hadn't saluted at all. Now he was saluting a tree for practice, his arm going up and down, single PFC stripe bright in the sunlight, darker shapes on his sleeve where other stripes and patches had been.

I turned and walked the other way. I didn't want to be in a position where I'd be required to salute, and I didn't want my barrack mate to know I'd seen him there. I was also embarrassed and ashamed, and angry with myself because I didn't have the courage to kill the Second Lieutenant. I don't remember that PFC's name and I had been too ignorant to ask him what his tribe was. I like to think he was a Mohican.

*   *   *

The finest conductors in the world perform without recognition in the elementary schools of America. In one of these schools, in a third grade, let's say, all the children are lined up in orderly rows, facing forward, their eager faces awaiting the signal. The teacher holds the pointer aloft, this same pointer that had earlier located Greece and then China on a roll-down map, then lowers it swiftly to indicate the first column of children. "Row, row, row your boat," they sing, "gently down the stream" and the pointer descends to start the second row, who begin with "Row, row, row, your boat," while the first finishes with "life is but a dream," and starts over. By now the third row has begun, "gently down the stream," and the fourth begins, and the fifth, the medley of young voices mingling until waves of sound overlap against the stream banks, repeating and repeating, life is but a dream.

One of these young children will grow up to kill many people and then, one sun-filled morning, will wake up to find himself saluting a tree.

8.

I am not gripped by a fantasy that this book will be published, that it will attract a large number of readers. But there's a library, if I can find it, to which I will carry a handwritten copy some night, and that is the library described in Brautigan's *The Abortion*. Who wouldn't want a copy of their book on a shelf there? These pages will get passed around to family members and to a half dozen or so friends. I sometimes imagine them as I write, their heads shaking, and their smiling, but mostly I am telling these stories for the sake of telling them and because that is what the voice that came out of the dark asked me to do.

*   *   *

My Aunt Honey, who raised my sister and me after our parents died, told me on several occasions, "I love you so much that if you killed somebody I'd help you hide the body." She was from the Irish side. I don't know if that expression was an Irish declaration of love from the old country, passed down, or just Pennsylvania back-woods, peculiar to our family, or she made it up herself. I didn't doubt her for a moment, though. Another thing she said more often was "Pick up the yard! Do you want people to think we're Shanty Irish?" We lived on an unpaved road near an industrial area of Niagara Falls where trash blew in regularly – and there might have been a scattering of boards in the yard from one project or another.

Here's the yard: on one edge a one-car wooden clapboard garage, burn-barrel beyond that where the field met the roadside, one-room, clapboard summer sleeping cottage, a huge clapboard doghouse, former residence of a deceased Irish setter named Mickey, all buildings white with red trim to match the house, a clothesline with drying wash on it one or two days a week, a walk-in concord grape arbor, two short rows of white Niagara grapes, a twenty-five foot flagpole flying the American flag, metal fixtures aloft clanging against the steel pole in the breeze. The kitchen garbage disposal was the window over the sink, from which Aunt Honey flung pork chop bones and other plate scraps into the yard for the "poor stray dogs and cats."

*   *   *

Just last month, on a cold morning in April, I hurried down the long gravel driveway, carrying my blue recycling box to the road-side, worried that I might miss the pickup. Down the road I could hear the groan of the compactor on the garbage truck, so the recyclers wouldn't be far behind.

The plastics, newspapers, and tin cans in the box were separated, ready to save the world. If everyone did this, the elemental laws of physics could be repealed, oil, forests, and mining operations saved, saved, and stopped respectively. Head down, I positioned the box next to the garbage can just as the huge truck roared up, the air brakes hissing. The driver jumped out, because the company he worked for had cut their operating costs by requiring the drivers to also dump the garbage into the back of the truck.

"Dead fox," he observed, tilting his head toward the road edge. He flipped the lid to the ground and picked up the can.

It was a red fox, just several feet away, startling against the green grass of the yard. My target detection skills had failed. "Aw, shit," I said.

"Yeah," the driver said, tossing the empty can to the lawn, "poor little guy." He was already heading back toward the truck.

It was a big, healthy female before it was road kill, red fur, luxurious forelegs touched with deep black. Now it lay crumpled on its side, breeze ruffling the fur, mouth slightly open. The following thoughts surfaced: it had made it through the winter to die in the spring; if I hadn't allowed that sixty-foot wide hedgerow to stay wild the fox might have used some other corridor to approach the road and made it safely across; most of the small animals run down by cars could be avoided; some drivers try to run over them. I left it there until the next day, thinking its lifeless form might be seen as an accusation by whoever hit it.

I carried it, tape measure in my pocket, back across the road down the middle of the hedgerow about a hundred feet, and lowered it to a bed of leaves and mosses. It measured forty-two inches from nose to tail end. The full tail was eighteen of those inches. Its lower canines were three-quarters of an inch. The longest of its black whiskers were just four inches.

A week later, after a couple of heavy rains, it was flattened, almost gone, flesh melted so completely away it could have been candle wax, fur compressed to a thin layer, a few tufts of the undercoat scattered in the brush. The remains were almost difficult to find with the groundcover starting to leaf out. A different recycling process had been at work. The head was the most noticeable, an irregular lump smaller than a fist.

* * *

Did it occur to you that I could have picked the fox up by its back feet that morning and flung it into the back of the garbage truck? Would you have? Why or why not? This is an essay question.

* * *

Because I have been speaking to you personally and have been telling a story about a dead fox, there is something that needs to be cleared up, something I related previously that wasn't quite true.

You may remember the story of the two foxes, one chasing the other, gracefully, over and around a fallen tree. I wrote that I had spied on foxes... mating. As some of you undoubtedly knew at the

time, the fox is a member of the canine family and, as such, probably mates in a similar fashion to dogs. Once penetration has occurred, the male becomes "locked" inside the female and cannot
disengage until mating is complete. Many children have witnessed
this on the playground or on streets near the school. Investigations
will reveal that it was this sight that, repeated over time, led to
the first sex education classes. Witnesses to foxes thus engaged are
rare, but it is reasonable to assume that the same conditions prevail
during their mating. In reality, then, what I had described earlier
was inaccurate. If the female had been ready to mate, the scene
would have been different. Perhaps the actual mating took place
later that day or the next. What I'd observed was a prelude, the male
testing, the female not quite yet in heat.

So, I have spied on the foreplay of foxes.

The alliteration remains.

* * *

What does a fox being killed on the road have to do with weather, eighteen new houses within a half-mile radius, each with a two
and a half car garage and three or four acres of lawn, Indian Lookout, grazing cattle, garbage collection, Bloody Run, Shanty Irish,
being burned to a crisp, and the death of Joe Greene? I'll tell you
about it later.

* * *

Here's how the scene plays out. It's winter sometime in the
eighteen hundreds. John Burroughs is crouching by an old stone
wall in the woodlands of a northeastern state. He's hunting. His
exhaled breaths are showing white in the air. Inside his mittens cold
has numbed his fingers. He sees a red fox loping over the snow-
covered field in front of him, which he will later describe as moving
with "grace and ease." The fox is like a small flame flowing across
a field of white. He's so moved by the sight that he doesn't attempt

to shoot. Afterward, friends tease him about this when he tells them about it. He may have said something to them about not being able to get his mittens off in time. The part about him not shooting at the fox is true.

* * *

I wasn't referring to Mean Joe Greene, of the Pittsburgh Steelers. That's someone else.

* * *

In the spring of 2006 Loraine looked out a window into our backyard, that is the space between the house and the old smokehouse and outhouse, overgrown, bramble-strewn, where we pastured cattle for a few days each year, where the roots of a thirty-year old locust tree blown over in a storm reared into the air – and saw young foxes playing. They were brand-new, just out of the den, perhaps the first time out, plump furry little things, the color of honey in the sunlight. They tumbled over one another, made little forays into the grass which nearly concealed them, ran back toward the den under the big garden shed, came tentatively back into view.

Over the weeks that followed their golden hue gradually took on tones of red characteristic of the adults. Loraine discovered she could get closer in the attached garage, from the top of a cluttered workbench, where she knelt among the greasy bolts and old radiator clamps with a camera, ready to snap pictures through an opening in a window with a missing pane.

The mother fox showed up rarely, perhaps once a day, briefly, minutes only, wary and watchful in the extreme, thin, warning her kits not to stray far from the den. Loraine took pictures. I tossed road kill into the area, a gray squirrel, a red-winged blackbird, a rabbit, thinking these handouts would reduce the chances of the mother hunting near the road, or crossing it in search of food to support her growing young. All of these offerings disappeared quickly.

By late summer, the playing had stopped, the young foxes having assumed the shapes of adults and extending their range of exploration, seeking their own territories. Several times that summer, on the way to the barn or garden, we'd see the inquisitive face of a fox watching our passage from the tall grasses. By late fall and early winter, three of them had seemed to stick together, or perhaps they were the survivors. Several times they came down through the yard running swiftly, first one in the lead, then another, swerving over the light snow, running, it appeared, for the joy of it, visiting their old playground, our backyard and theirs. It was easy then to more completely understand John Burroughs, all those years ago, not being able to get his mittens off in time.

*   *   *

About a quarter century ago after the PFC and I parted company on that sun-drenched Army base in South Carolina, I crossed paths with Joe Greene. He sat in on one of my classes and wrote poetry. One poem he wrote was about a deer, seeing it in the woods. Try it sometime yourself to see how quickly you will be captured by deer cliché. This is already many years ago, but I still remember how much it wasn't a cliché, how it was about him seeing the deer and the deer seeing him, how they stood looking at one another. Later I was told the deer is sacred to the Haudenosaunee. I didn't know this at the time.

He wrote another about dead leaves being blown across the road in autumn. You may have seen this, too. It's an absolutely common sight, one I have seen thousands of times, usually at night in the car headlights. Joe took this common image and wrote about it in a way that invested the leaves with consciousness, that saw them not as shriveled leaves, but up on the feet of their curled points, scurrying with purpose, on a journey, going somewhere. Some readers may reject this as an anthropomorphic excess. A variation of this is called "pathetic fallacy." But that is literary stuff. There are other realities which acknowledge the spirits inhabiting the animate and inanimate world.

Joe loved word play, double meanings, riddles and puzzles. When he visited, appearing in the hallway long after he was no longer enrolled in classes, and I'd say, "Joe, what's up?" he'd answer, "Sky, clouds... " and keep smiling, gently pointing out the absurdity of some words. A few dozen of these exchanges taught me to say "Joe, how are you?"

He had left the Reservation to live in the city. I don't mention this as a value judgment, but as information. One night, getting out of a cab and heading up the stairs to his apartment, he was attacked by two men and beat over the head with a crowbar. They wanted to steal his money. They got twenty-six dollars. Days later, without regaining consciousness, he died. Do you think that autumn will ever come again when I see leaves blowing across the road in my car headlights that I won't think of Joe?

Before he died I would have thought of the poem. Now my mind slides quickly over the leaves traveling through the dark to the man who wrote about them. There's a poem by William Stafford, called "Traveling Through the Dark," about a dead deer found on the edge of a dark mountain road. The poet discovers that the deer had been pregnant. There's anthropomorphism in that poem, too, involving the automobile. The man in the poem hesitates alongside the road, thinking "hard for us all." A line in the poem says "Around our group I could hear the wilderness listen." He pushes the deer over the edge into the canyon. There's a lot of ways we're traveling through the dark.

Before Joe Greene was born, my father was pulling and boosting me up to the top of Indian Lookout. About this time in our lives we were riding down Indian Hill, and my father was telling me to watch for Indians. A few years after that I was picking up the shoulder blade of a deer from a trail in the Niagara Gorge. Joe Greene was a Tuscarora.

9.

Almost all contemporary poetry is boring. You may have written some of it yourself. I have. Boring poetry involves dull, unimaginative language, trifling, self-centered subject matter. You know it's true. Let's stop pretending otherwise.

Lawrence Ferlinghetti described it as "dead language" during an interview that I watched on video. When asked what he meant by "dead language," he seemed taken aback. What kind of question was that? The tracking was off and the top third of his head kept sliding off to the left of the television screen in an elongated blob and snapping back. Some people will see this image and direction as perfectly appropriate for Ferlinghetti, long time proprietor of City Lights Bookstore in San Francisco, publisher of Allen Ginsberg and other Beat writers, author of *Coney Island of the Mind*. What was happening to his head was so extraordinary that I imagined for a moment that his ability to answer the question was being impaired. As it turned out, it was my inability to ignore this distraction and to focus on his quick response that left me with just part of what he said, perhaps the important part. Exasperated, he replied, "dead language is... poetry without any *life* to it."

What's boring or not is sometimes subjective, but not to the extent that some people believe. The nature of something is not determined by your thoughts about it. Once upon a time, a professor Edmund Thomas, thirty minutes into a lecture on "Sunday Morning," by Wallace Stevens, detected a certain lack of enthusiasm in the face of a student who had not yet perfected the ability of feigning interest, or who simply didn't care. Abruptly breaking off his commentary, Thomas confronted the student, who said the poem was boring. Thomas gazed at the student dispassionately, replied dryly, "Some of the most important things in life are boring," and continued his lecture. A great lesson could have been learned that day, but probably wasn't.

The writing of boring poetry is necessary, providing fertilizer that gives rise to the occasional worthwhile poems, born of the writer's frustration and inspiration and plugging away waiting for the right moment.

Somewhere, there's a huge landfill where boring poetry ends up, shredded and torn and crumpled, moldering little mags and newspaper poetry pages, acid-free hardcover books disintegrating, poems about lost loves and dead grandmothers and sunny picnics in the park all atomizing into dust. The planting of trees on this landfill is forbidden, since it is feared their roots will penetrate the clay cap and lethal concentrations of boring poetry will be released into the air. Entire neighborhoods would have to be evacuated. No gasmask in the world could protect people against that shit.

Many years ago, at the dawning of the mimeo revolution in the little mag world, there was at least one poet in Niagara Falls, New York, a young man, filling page after page with torrents of poetry. Who can say if any of it was any good? Some days he wrote seven poems, a page or longer, during his lunch hour at the factory.

There had to be a high percentage of not very good or boring in there, but he wrote with joy and wonder and energy and enthusiasm, and he loved Kenneth Patchen's work totally, especially *Journal of Albion Moonlight*. He took Thoreau and Emerson and *New American Poetry* and other writers and books to work in his lunchbox. His wife took a dim view of all this.

I know these things because we were friends. One evening in his apartment, sitting at the kitchen table, he was delirious with the exciting possibility that he might get a poem published, or more than one, even a book! "What do you think," he asked me, "the title of my first book should be?"

"Why don't you call it The Book of Shit?" his wife said.

We all laughed, but the two of us could tell her remark had

only been disguised as a joke, and something alive in his face died a little. Over the next few months, whenever he mentioned poetry, she repeated this question or variations of it, such as "Oh, yeah, The Book of Shit." Can you tell they were not well suited for one another?

A year or so later, they were no longer together. I'll spare you the sad details of their parting.

Less than five years after that my friend was everywhere in the littles. That is a way of saying he had been widely published, dozens if not hundreds of poems in many small press publications. Editors wrote to him asking that he send poems. He started his own small press and then another. He corresponded with people all over the country. His first book of poetry had been published. Its title was *Dimensions of the Morning*. If it had been my choice the title would have been Connie, You Bitch, but he was more forgiving.

About ten years later he had dozens of book titles to his credit, and he finally published a book of poetry titled *The Book of Shit*. One of its poems was about what his wife had said that evening in their kitchen. His initials are DRW. He lives in California now, where he has been for many years, where the skies are higher and bluer than here, and where he is a fabrics artist, creating miniature tapestries, and teaches at the U. of Davis. He is still writing.

All during this early time I was writing, too. A few were good, I think, but most were not. One of them was exceptionally bad, not only bad, but boring, and it went on for pages and pages full of wise old men on park benches, and grandmothers baking pies full of love, friendly dogs, laughing children at play, a galloping white horse, birds singing, and so on. There was an entire boring town in there. I have forgotten the title, for which I am grateful. DRW, in his enthusiasm, mailed copies out to other poets across the country. My face heats up to think of it. I got a postcard from a poet in Cleveland, d.a. levy, across which he had written, "don't you have any death there?"

There was no question mark at the end of those six words, even though I have included one here for the sake of clarity. I wanted to send him a note back: don't you have any question marks in Cleveland? But I didn't, of course, and found out later that they probably didn't have any question marks in Cleveland because they'd used them up asking questions such as, when the Cuyahoga River caught fire did they pump water from the river to put it out? And why are the people from Shaker Heights, not that we wish to single them out, this is just an example, so full of shit? Questions such as these lead to other questions, and those questions lead to others, and etc., so you can see how a supply of question marks could get used up in a hurry. Cleveland had not yet begun its rebirth, so a lot of things were in short supply.

Levy was well known as an artist and poet in the littles across the country. He published a newspaper, *The Buddhist 3rd Class Junk Mail Oracle* and a journal, the *Marrawanna Quarterly*. Someone once snapped a picture of him in front of a huge billboard with words across it that read "It's Tough To Be A Good American."

Some time after that postcard arrived, he invited DRW and me to visit him in Cleveland and to read at an open reading called Poets at the Gate.

We met other poets and people there. One was Grace Butcher, who had been a miler for the US at the Olympic Games, and another was Robert Crumb, who went from table to table passing out mimeo sheets of his cartoons. He was just starting. Don't you wish you'd been there and gotten one of those? I'll bet you do.

I did not read my long boring poem. I read shorter boring poems, three of them, because the rule was "three poems or five minutes, whichever comes first." A timekeeper sat at the front with one of those bells that people used to hit to summon the desk clerk. When five minutes passed, the bell rang out and the reader abruptly gave up the mike and sat down, even if he or she was in the middle of a line. That was the rule. That way the audience couldn't get bored for any more than five minutes at a time, at least by the same person.

The first time we traveled to Cleveland, we walked with levy down to the corner grocery where he would buy three sirloin tip steaks to celebrate our visit. He had little money so this was very

d.a. levy
Climbing the turnpike fence to wonder at the wet mountainside wild flowers
1966, Oil on paper, 29" x 22"

generous. He did have a beard and long shoulder-length hair which, this particular evening, was not especially kempt. It was like those certain sections of the Oregon Trail.

As levy asked for the steaks, the butcher stared at him, expressionless. This was a time of unrest in America, the war protestors and the anti-protestors on opposite sides of the police line. Long hair and beards tended to be political statements then, not fashion choices. "Why don't you get a haircut?" the butcher sneered. Since the question had not been written out, I couldn't tell if the question mark were there, but it sounded as if it were. The butcher was a hoarder. "Because I like to eat steak," levy said. The butcher frowned as if this had gone over his head, but he didn't have a problem taking the money.

At that first reading at Poets At The Gate, a young poet who had recently attempted suicide had signed up to read. Both forearms were heavily bandaged. Levy was calling out the names. When this young man's turn came, levy said, "And now we have (and here he said his name), who's going to get up here and slit his wrists for us."

Those in the audience who weren't stunned into silence let out a collective moan. The young man went to the mike, head down, hair hanging into his face, read three very short, charming poems in a shy voice and sat down, long before his five minutes had expired. A gentle wave of applause followed him to his seat, sustaining itself for moments after he was seated, rising and falling in a soothing way that suggested it could go on for a long time, but then it tapered off suddenly and stopped. After all, as someone once said, that's what poets are supposed to do, open a vein and write. Wasn't that it?

* * *

Irwin Porges located a letter written to Edgar Rice Burroughs from a man who knew Geronimo. Burroughs was doing research on Indians for books he intended to write. The man told this story: Once Geronimo used a little stick from a pine tree, which he sharpened at one end, to cut open a small vein in his forearm. Then he used the blood to write his name on a photograph of himself. Do you think this photograph has survived and exists somewhere in the world? I know it does. Try to think about it the next time you pick up a pencil, a ballpoint pen, or sit down in front of your computer ready to do some writing.

*   *   *

When levy made a return visit to Niagara, we went to look at the Falls, of course, and then up to the University of Buffalo so that he could do a reading. In those days, poetry readings were commonplace, impromptu, slap up a few fliers or not, just stop in one of the wide hall corners, student union, lounge, and begin to read. The next thing you knew fifteen or twenty people had gathered to listen. There seemed to be two or three readings a day involving a wide range of poets, from those who wanted to try out what they'd written the night before, to writers in residence, to visiting poets and the internationally known. You couldn't possibly have gone to all of them. You'd probably recognize some names if I mentioned them, but I won't, since it's likely I'd neglect to mention a few and they'd get all bent out of shape because they were left out. You know how poets are.

I will tell you, the most famous ones were the worst. Maybe they were just doing it for the money or had to do so many per semester according to contract. If the reading were scheduled, posted, they'd always start late, as much as fifteen minutes, even when they were there. They'd chat and laugh with a cluster of friends at the front and finally look up, surprised. Oh, look! An audience! I guess they're waiting for me to read something! After a mumbled introduction by one of the friends, the poet begins a casual leafing through of a book (the poet had been *published*, you are supposed to notice) to find some poem that feels as if it should be read. This one? No. The pages turn. This one? Ah... maybe not. Oh, well, perhaps this one, even though....

And the audience waiting until the reading finally begins and after it begins they are still waiting for a poem that isn't boring. The poet fans the pages after each poem is read, searching for another poem, perfect for this audience, this day, this mood. Boredom wafts upward from the pages like an invisible fog. The landfill beckons. As the last poem is mercifully read, the audience melts rapidly away, having remembered they have only minutes to make it to the next reading.

What's with these people? Have you ever been to a poetry reading? More than one? Hands, please. Tell me your heart hasn't soared with joy at the words, "And the last poem I'll read this evening...." Something's wrong when those eight words are the most exciting ones you've heard all night, the best poem, really. Every poet should begin reading with those words.

In any case, levy didn't think much of Buffalo, the city or University. Back in those days, the world was younger, and people, places and events were evaluated according to their vibrations. Buffalo had bad vibrations, levy said. Even the traffic signs and signals had negative energy jumping off of them, maybe especially the traffic signs and signals.

It didn't seem too long after levy's visit that he was dead. The story was he'd put the muzzle of a .22 caliber rifle to his temple and pulled the trigger. The news traveled fast through the little mag poetry network. A couple days after his death, the phone rang at three in the morning, waking me from a deep sleep. "Hello," I answered.

"Levy's dead," the voice announced. It was Gerry Dombrowski, publisher of the literary mag, *Abyss*, calling from Dunkirk, New York.

"I know," I said.

What else we said that night I don't recall, but Dombrowski has since repeated that two sentence exchange to me on more than one occasion. Sometimes over the years I pick up the phone at night and say hello and it's Dombrowski, who says "levy's dead," by way of greeting. "I know," I say. Another poet bites the dust. We are whistling in the dark. One of Dombrowski's first jobs as a young man was that of "printer's devil."

One room away from where I am writing this, hanging on the wall, is a gift from levy, a painting that he did on heavy paper. Image and words, it's almost two feet wide and about two and one-half high. Most of the words curve across the top portion, a combination of block and cursive: "Climbing the turnpike fence to wonder at the wet mountainside," the cursive reads, with "wildflowers" in larger block letters to both sides. The paint is mostly black, dull, massive toward the bottom, lighter toward the top, a heavy smear of red overlaid down low, a light yellow in higher. Three heavy black stems, as wide as one-inch brush, rise from the base upward, in the same configuration you'd make if you held up three fingers. The blossoms, perhaps a dozen of them floating away from the stem tops, are also black, circular smudges made by thrusts of the brush against the paper. In the lower left corner are smaller words, "wild flowers," which escapes your attention initially because of the dominance of the massive stems. This is how it works in the world, too, most of the time. Your eye is first drawn to the obvious and then you see the less noticeable blooming away in its tiny splendor just as if it too had a right to make its little effort in the rain, no audience required. How lucky we are to notice!

The words at the top of the painting suggest a border, the turnpike fence, flowers below. When I look at it I often think of the railing I climbed to reach that portion of the Oregon Trail where I placed my hand in the wagon wheel rut.

I never answered levy's question. It was probably rhetorical, anyway. Perhaps they don't require question marks.

I once did a reading with three other poets, one of whom was John Logan, who was the heavyweight of the foursome, the big gun, the main event. I was one of the prelims. The reading took place at the Wintergarden in Niagara Falls, NY, a public glass-enclosed space holding a variety of plants, climbing vines and ferns, stone and pools of water, small trickling waterfalls. Bleachers and chairs and a PA system had been brought in for the occasion. About a hundred people had showed up. Before the reading started, John Logan came over and introduced himself, and we shook hands. This was a gracious thing for him to do, to make me feel at ease. He was past middle-age, a small, balding man, with a round face and glasses. He was wearing blue serge pants with cuffs, which were soaking wet halfway to his knees. He seemed cheerfully oblivious to his wet pants. I could say "he'd been drinking," but why get euphemistic here? I'd seen enough drunken friends and family members to know when someone has passed the "been drinking" stage and is drunk. Nevertheless, I decided he knew his shoes were leaking water and his pants were dripping wet, but he'd chosen to ignore this condition and this endeared him to me. He had probably stumbled or slipped into one of the shallow Wintergarden pools. He was amiable and smiling and he tilted his head back to look at me as we parted and said, "We'll have fun reading together!"

And, you know, we did, although what he read was a long, boring cataloguing of every meal he'd had with a friend during a four-day visit in New York City. When it was time for him to read, he squished up to the podium, adjusted the mike, and floated first the aperitif, then endless artichokes and bowls of bouillabaisse and baby shrimp into the green-scented air of the Wintergarden. All this was against the muted roar of the American and Horseshoe Falls in the background. I hadn't known that a menu, even with a liberal application of adjectives, could be a poem, and I'm still not sure about that, but Logan seemed to enjoy reading it, eyes on the paper, smiling to himself. No one knew, but this was toward the end of his life, and so we should cut him some slack on that poem. When François Mitterand, former president of France, was dying of cancer, he ate a last meal featuring tiny, protected song birds that had been drowned in wine to kill them before cooking. Should we cut him some slack, too?

After the reading I walked over to one of the other poets to compliment him on one of his poems. I said, "You may not regard it as one of your major poems, but..." and then a woman standing next to him interrupted. "All of his poems are major," she said coldly. He said nothing to disabuse her of this notion, but nodded solemnly as I lamely finished my comments, his nodding agreeing with me that yes, his poem was wonderful, managing somehow to convey the impression that the poem was far more wonderful than I could begin to imagine. The woman had turned her attention elsewhere. Granted, I had started my compliment in a clumsy way, but I'd no idea I was standing in the presence of someone who, each time his pen glided over the paper, wrote a *Leaves of Grass*, a *Wasteland,* a *Paterson*, a *Howl.* I promised myself to be more careful in the future. He'd been wearing new, tan leather work boots, the high-lace variety, unscuffed and dry. There was probably some real work he was going to do somewhere right after the poetry reading crowd broke up, or that's what he wanted everyone to think.

I hadn't shaken his hand, and didn't. But remember, I did shake John Logan's hand, so if you ever want to shake the hand that shook the hand of John Logan, just walk right up to me and stick out your paw. We'll pass it on, the good stuff.

Years before, I also shook hands with Jean Lussier, Niagara daredevil, who'd gone over the Horseshoe Falls in a rubber ball on the Fourth of July, 1928. I wrote a little poem about him called "Footnote," which I probably read that day at the Wintergarden. He had died years before that. Not everyone I shake hands with dies soon afterward, but it's something to think about.

*   *   *

Just recently, the Wintergarden was demolished. No trace remains.

* * *

The ghosts of deer keep flitting along the edges of my mind and I know I should get back to that shoulder blade, how it came into my possession. It's the only identifiable piece of that deer left now, except what exists in an old memory. Joe Greene's poem about another deer, my copy of it, has been misplaced, perhaps lost forever. A few years ago, during hunting season, someone threw the remains of a deer carcass into the roadside ditch near our house. It had been gutted and skinned, the head was missing, and the choice cuts, hindquarters and loin, had been carved away. The hide was still on the legs. Alive, the deer couldn't have been much over a hundred pounds, probably less. It may have been killed illegally or whoever shot it thought he'd take the good meat, not tag it, and then he could shoot another one. He got rid of the evidence in the ditch.

I picked it up and jammed its hollowed out ribcage down over a roadside fence post. The chickadees and woodpeckers and other birds could work on it all winter. By spring it had been picked clean, the ribs dropped away, the legs mummified and fallen off. Every so often I'd pick them up and balance them on the fence post and wires again, but they never stayed long. They were trying to go somewhere. People driving past would slow down, sometimes almost stop. You'd think it was the first time they'd seen bones. The spine and pelvis of that deer are still there, three years later, the individual vertebrae clearly visible, curved in a graceful clinging to the old fence post. Drivers don't slow down anymore. This is not where I got the shoulder blade.

The shoulder blade of the deer, also called the scapula, was sacred to some American Indian tribes. It could not be discarded carelessly after the venison was consumed, but had to be taken to the woods and placed in a low tree branch. When the killed deer came back into its new life, it would need its bones again. Those of us who insist on reconciling the spiritual with the scientific say, yes, of course, this makes sense, ecologically speaking, if we take the long view. The carbon and phosphate and calcium and other elements of that bone break down into the soil eventually and are drawn up by plants, saplings and brush and grass, which are eaten by deer, contributing to the growth of healthy bones.

I appreciate that, too, but still feel that something is missing. I'd like to believe it's the actual bone that's used, that the flesh of a reincarnated deer is resurrected around it. But that is a remnant of a belief system that has largely vanished, along with the people who lived in it.

Some traces remain in people who sense we are inextricably bound to the natural world, and these surface in poems like "Traveling Through The Dark," and in others, Richard Wilbur's "Death of a Toad," for example. I don't want to make too much of death. It doesn't need a PR person. Check out the nightly news for a week. But I'll mention three essays with the word "death" in the titles: "Death of a Moth," by Virginia Wolff, "Death of a Pig," by E.B. White, and "Reflections on the Death of a Porcupine," by D.H. Lawrence. The writers are meditating. The idea that death is part of life is only true in the grand scheme. For the individual it's an obscenity. Death is part of life only when someone other than you or someone you love is doing the dying.

After my death, and a certain interval during which time such a thing will become available, I want someone to take one of my shoulder blades and carry it into the woods. This shouldn't be a big deal, no ceremony, or fussing. Just jog in there a couple hundred feet, put it in the low branches of a tree, then jog back out to the car to get on with your grocery shopping or to make your doctor's appointment on time. Don't paint it gold and don't look back. Make sure it's not a woods that will be turned into a shopping mall, a housing development, or a golf course. That would really kill me.

If you do this right, it will give you a poem or a little story to tell. Some late rainy night you'll find yourself lying up in a bed or sitting in some gin mill, telling about it. Try not to get too metaphysical. Remember there's a lot of poetry in the world. Some of it's written and some isn't. Some of it's people walking around in the dreams of their lives. It's up to you to find it.

Summary: 1) Be selective about whose hand you shake, especially if you mean it. 2) John Logan once stepped into water that had come down the Niagara River, heading for the falls. 3) The deer is sacred to some people. There are enough people on earth so that every animal, every living thing, ought to be sacred to someone. 4)

If you're not going to write with blood, don't bother.

*   *   *

Why do you think Geronimo sharpened that stick of pine to cut open a vein in his arm? Why didn't he cut the vein open with the knife he used to do the sharpening? When Geronimo signed his name in blood on that photograph, did he sign "Geronimo" or "Goyathlay?"

10.

The elderly who lived in the nursing home were often outside in all kinds of weather. They sat on benches in the hot sun, slumped forward, staring at the ground, smoking, drinking coffee, and walked long blocks to one of the stores in town where they redeemed can deposits to buy snacks, soft drinks, and more cigarettes. They ignored light drizzling rain. Some routinely wore ill-fitting, off-season clothing, heavy coats and wool pullover hats in summer, thin pants, shirts, blouses, and sweaters on a cold winter day.

When I recently stopped at the pharmacy just behind the nursing home, I was approached by one of the residents. "Sir!" he said, "Sir!" as I got out of my truck. He walked toward me until he was a foot and a half away. He fixed me with his glittering eye if you know what I mean. It was summer. He was dressed appropriately, slacks and a short-sleeved shirt. In one hand he held a Styrofoam cup, finger hooked over the rim, with a half inch of cold coffee sloshing in the bottom, the stub of a dead cigarette between the free fingers. The other hand held a new cigarette, already lit, which he nevertheless repeatedly lifted to his lips and puffed on it gently while holding the end of the dead butt to it. Ignoring that he had the process reversed, performing this with the Styrofoam cup in his hand was quite a trick.

Satisfied he had it going, he spoke quietly in a matter-of-fact voice. "There was a fire here this morning and I was burned to a crisp. I'll tell you about it later."

"Well," I said, "You look pretty good now."

"I'll tell you about it later," he said.

There was a meeting of the minds there and so I excused myself and went into the pharmacy.

*   *   *

The large sign in front of the nursing home, "Senior Meadows," suggested the old folks had been put out to pasture. This was either someone's idea of a joke, or had simply gone unrecognized. Since the nursing home was, after all, located on the northern edge of the town where rows of houses abruptly gave way to farmland, you can understand where "meadows" might have originated. In any event, after some years, the name was changed. You can speculate about the new one. What would you name such a place?

*   *   *

Years ago there was a boarding stable named LaValley's on Porter Road, Niagara Falls, New York. A half dozen or more young men hung out at the stable during the evenings. Some of them boarded horses there. After chores, the men scrunched up around a small table in the tack room and played cards for hours, trading insults, making up rude nicknames for one another, telling jokes. This is called camaraderie. They would have liked this word had they thought of it, because it sounded like something gauchos might shout at one another while riding horseback over the pampas, whirling bolas over their head in wild abandon.

There was Dale, Moose, Jay, and Whipper of the names I remember, or changed, and a horse named Eagle in one of the closest stalls. The horse's name has not been changed, though it probably should have been. Who'd name one animal for another? But cars are named after animals, aren't they? Two or more were even named for horses.

Eagle was an old, gentle creature, rumored to be part Appaloosa. There were a few faded spots on his rump. He belonged to Dale, who rode only on weekends. The previous owner dropped by once a week or so to peer critically into Eagle's stall. "You feeding this horse?" he'd ask Dale. "Looks to me like he's losing weight." He'd shake his head, mutter, "That horse was round as an apple when I sold him to you." While the faces of those within earshot were turning to hide their smiling, Dale would go to inspect Eagle, maybe give him an extra scoop of oats. It took him a long time to catch on.

But this was a man who'd been in the eighth grade before he'd learned that zippers were designed to prevent inadvertent unzipping. Because he'd continually gone around with his fly half or all the way open, a friend had sarcastically informed him that the zipper tab, when pulled all the way up and pressed flat, locked in and stayed up. Dale laughed aloud. "Damn!" he said. "What won't they think of next?" He tried it and kept checking to see if the zipper stayed up.

These men were responsible citizens, however, make no mistake about that. I don't know if they voted, probably not, but most of them had families of their own, full time jobs, paid taxes, and cut their lawns regularly. One of them had told the others a story about how he'd held up a little plastic horse and repeated the word "truck" several hundred times when his young son had begun to talk. When the child began to reveal the new word he'd learned, his mother hadn't thought it was very funny. She believed names were important and she repeatedly called her husband some, the most frequently occurring ending with "hole." Thus, he'd been properly admonished, but privately still believed it was funny – almost as funny as the other new word his son had learned from his mother. Did you ever see a man laugh with his mouth closed? It's a pitiful sight.

One evening the group realized they hadn't seen Jay for a few days. Moose had just commented on his absence and was taking a last drag on an unfiltered Camel when the door to the tack room began to open very slowly. Moose's eyes went to the door, his lips pursed, thumb and forefinger pinching a stub of cigarette so tiny it appeared to be a burning coal he was attempting to extract from his mouth. If this sounds dramatic, it can't be helped. This is the way things happen sometimes. Not all drama is made up. Some of it comes from real life.

The door opened wider and Jay shuffled into the room. Moose

grunted, exhaling, and crushed the stub in an overturned jar lid. This left a little smudge of burnt tobacco and a piece of white cigarette paper about three times the size of a piece of confetti. He always smoked them to the end.

"What the hell's the matter with you?" Moose asked. Jay was bent over at the waist, his eyes directed toward the floor, his steps short and hesitant. "It's my back," he said. "I hurt my back."

"Thought you lost something," Dale said.

"Funny," Jay said, making an effort to stand straighter and failing. "Real funny." Then he told the group about his misfortune.

He'd been in a bar having a few drinks with a woman who ended up inviting him to her place. They rode in her car, a short distance to A or B Street, one of those named during a time when the city fathers had been short on imagination, but still able to remember the alphabet. They probably believed this was clever – when in doubt, remember the alphabet, a rallying cry that would immortalize the Niagara Frontier as "Remember the Alamo!" had for the Texas mission where Daniel Boone had died.

Jay refused to tell the woman's name. He said it wasn't important, dismissing the question with a wave of his hand, which caused him to wince. Of course, her name was important, though, or he'd have told it. He did say the woman's husband drove truck for an outfit called Boss Linco, a name that was a source of fear to him. He'd imagined being beaten to a bloody rag doll by a hairy, three hundred pound truck driver and then dragged by his ankles helplessly into the street where his head would be wedged under a front tire. How long had he known the woman? He wouldn't say. It could have been the love of his life, which the guys would have loved to find out, because it would have been a lot easier to agitate him with their crude remarks.

The woman lived in a small, one story house, and her husband was on the road, not expected home for two days. Jay and the woman sat on the narrow front porch for a while, having a drink behind the screen of the trellis, which was covered with a broad-leafed vine of some kind. A little after midnight, the two of them having gone inside, Jay's amorous preoccupations were interrupted by the deep rumble of a big truck pulling up in front of the house. Now his heart was really beating.

The bedroom was in the back of the house and the woman leapt naked from the bed and to the doorway, then back. "Quick!" she said. "It's my husband! You've got to go out the window!" She scooped up his clothes, wadded them up around his shoes and shoved the bundle into his arms. She threw the window open. "Hurry!" she said, and Jay put one foot up on the sill and launched himself into the pitch-dark night, a leap of faith into the unknown, and crashed, twisting, full force into a picket fence. Crumpled on the ground, stunned, he heard the window close. After a few moments he could see the sturdy white pickets, a line of pale ghosts, none of them broken.

At this point in the story he paused, because his friends were laughing so hard. He seemed to have expected them to congratulate him on his close call, or to express some sympathy for his injury.

"I was in horrible pain!" he said.

This made them laugh harder.

"You have no idea!" Jay said. "I had to crawl on my hands and knees through two backyards before I could put my clothes on!"

"Scared of getting caught bare-assed?" Moose asked.

"No, it was the pain! And it was worse the next morning! I couldn't even bend over to tie my shoes!" Now he was indignant. "My wife had to tie my shoes so I could go to work!"

When fresh laughter burst out, Jay turned angrily and shuffled out the door, which he managed to slam. None of them would ever think of vine-covered cottages with white picket fences in the same way again. Okay, so it's rose-covered cottages. Close enough.

* * *

About a year later, I got a phone call from Jay. He had a litter of coon dog puppies for sale and I could have first choice for twenty-five dollars. When I got to his house, Moose was there, and the pups were in a cardboard box in the living room, fat, furry, pointed-ear, shepherd-looking, piling over one another, scrabbling on the sides of the box. I looked at Jay and Moose to see if this were a joke. It didn't seem to be.

"These aren't coon dogs," I said.

"What do you mean, not coon dogs?" Jay said. "Sure they are."

"Coon dogs," Moose said. The phrase seemed amusing to him. He took a drag on his Camel. Maybe he was in a state of perpetual amusement over the name of the cigarettes he smoked.

"They're not coon dogs," I said. "Is that the mother?" I gestured toward the long-haired, mixed breed shepherd in the kitchen doorway.

"Yeah," he answered.

"Well, that's not a coon dog, either. Where do you see any hound in her?"

"The father was a coon dog," Jay said. "From down the street."

"Maybe," I said. "But these aren't coon dogs."

I got up and headed for the door. He followed me out onto the porch. "How about ten?"

"Jay," I said, going down the stairs toward my car, "they aren't coon dogs."

"Well, can't they learn?" he called after me.

"I don't think so," I said over my shoulder.

By the time I got in my car, he was back inside the house. I could imagine Moose in there, smiling a little, taking a drag on his cigarette, letting the smoke drift out, saying real slowly so he could feel the shape of the words in his mouth, "Coon dogs."

* * *

In a well known painting of a buffalo, large loops of its intestines are hanging out, a condition evidently caused by a severe spear wound. The spear is long and slender and appears to transfix the body, with an entry point just beneath the tail, exiting through the abdomen. What may be a splintered piece of the spear is on the ground. The buffalo's tail is curled upward in rage or pain, or both.

Directly in front of the buffalo is a man, more than a stick figure because the body is an elongated oval, but not as detailed as the buffalo. He is either stretched out on the ground dead, having been killed by this animal he has wounded, or is being propelled backward by the tremendous blow delivered by the buffalo's lowered horns. His penis is pointed straight out from his body, almost as long as his feet, which are close together, heels dug into the ground. His face is nearly featureless, with a dot for an eye, and two trailing-off lines which can be seen as suggestive of a bird's head. His arms are flung wide. The hands, as those drawn by some contemporary cartoonist, have four fingers each.

Near the man is a carving of a bird on the end of a stick. A broken piece of this stick is nearby. The bird's beak is represented by two lines, upper and lower sections that do not meet at the end, similar to the lines used to create the man's head. Speculation says this bird may be a totem, a sign of the man's tribe or clan.

If he survived his ordeal, the man in the painting may have been the artist. If this is unlikely, he may have recreated a scene that he observed – or he may have been told the story of what happened. Many people would be very much interested in speaking with the artist. This is impossible, however, since the painting was found on a stone wall, deep inside a cave in what is now called France, and is believed to be over 15,000 years old.

* * *

Almost a year has passed since I began writing this. I haven't been writing regularly. It is the first day of February, six to eight inches of snow on the ground, temperature 38° F. We've just come out of a three-week deep freeze – forty-eight hours ago it was zero when I awoke. This morning the space shuttle Columbia burned up on reentry. Pieces of it fell to earth across Texas and into Louisiana.

Driving to town, away from repeated television images of debris contrails and talk about the seven lost crew, the fields are vast and white, winter wheat under snow and stubble poking up from last year's corn. At the far edge of the fields the woods are blurry with fog hanging over the still frozen ground. I pass a light blue pickup pulled over on the roadside, door flung open, no one inside.

Out in the snowy field about a hundred and fifty yards, a coyote is running parallel to the road. We are both heading south. When I slow down to watch, he stops, looks in my direction, starts off again. He runs an uneven lope on three legs, his right back one held up. He is slowly covering ground, but is out there in the middle of nothing, a quarter mile to go before the brushy growth along a creek will swallow him up. He is the only warm thing out there, moving, the focus of my attention, and perhaps others, with rifles or shotguns, along the edge of the distant woods. I scan the line, but see nothing. The trees are indistinct as if seen though gauze.

Nearer town another pickup has stopped, huge, black, running gear high up off the pavement. We're going in opposite directions. I pull over and roll down my window. The driver wears a bright red jacket and billed cap, the baseball variety so commonly worn. He has a neatly trimmed white moustache.

"That's a big one," he calls over. "The biggest one I ever saw!"

"He's running on three legs," I say.

"I've got a gun in the truck," he says. "I'd sure like to get a shot at him!" He glances over his shoulder at the two houses, double garage, and side-by-side lots that have come down the road beyond the village line. The coyote had stopped to stare at us and is now moving again. He's tired, is what. In a few minutes he'll be behind the houses. "But I don't know any of those people," the man says, meaning the residents of the homes.

We drive slowly away from one another. By the time I cross the village boundary and look back, the coyote has vanished.

*   *   *

When pieces of the Columbia came streaking down out of the sky across Texas, first reports had it the vice president was hunting there. It's a big state and so he didn't get hit. But what I want to know is: What was he hunting? And what kind of shotgun or rifle was he using?

One of the first shotguns I owned was a Riverside Arms, double barrel, 12 gauge. I paid $15 for it. With the safety on, both triggers snapped when the butt of the stock was bumped on the floor. I took it apart and found two stamped metal dog-leg shaped parts that were bent. I hammered them flat and that corrected the problem. What odds will you give that the vice president wasn't hunting with a shotgun like my old Riverside Arms double?

I went on to own a Winchester Model 12 and a Remington Deluxe, 870 ADL. The Remington had a 24-inch barrel, a Simmons rib and a Polychoke. It was a heavy brush-mobile rabbit gun, but good for other stuff, too. Odds here? The failure of my imagination can only extend to a Browning, maybe an over under, or a fine old Parker double for the vice president, engraved with pictures of game animals, silver or gold inlays.

It seems beyond irony that while the culmination of the highest technologies the world has ever known comes hurtling back to earth, unsuccessfully this time, at eighteen times the speed of sound, the vice president of one of the most scientifically advanced countries in the world is hunting. He is undoubtedly descended from the man depicted on the cave wall, in the place that came to be known as France, the one who put the spear through the buffalo so many thousands of years ago. We all are, aren't we, directly or indirectly?

No, no, I hear you thinking, I'm descended from the artist, the one who painted the picture on the wall. And I'm sure you are. But remember the possibility that the artist and the hunter were the same person.

A few days later, Dr. Sally Ride, the first woman to travel to outer space, was being interviewed on television. She sat relaxed, looking directly into the camera, a fire burning merrily in a fireplace beyond her left shoulder. Was it winter outside the room, the fire providing comforting heat, or was it merely elemental reassurance, or was it a prop, in spite of its being a real fire? In our most sophisticated, high-tech homes we keep a place for fire.

She was talking in a serious, committed way about our "drive to explore," and the necessity of "human space flight." It was, she said, her tone indicating its inevitability, "extending human presence in the universe."

A song written by Sir Mack Rice as sung by Wilson Pickett applies here. The Niagara Frontier used to be the frontier, and in some ways it still is. As a child I looked from my bedroom window and saw the fires from the open hearth furnaces in a local factory lighting up the night sky. I believed they were the Northern Lights.

*   *   *

Old-time buffalo hunters often set up a shooting area from a knoll overlooking a grazing herd. The first shot fired would purposefully gut-wound a nursing cow. This injured animal would begin to wander in pain and distress, but wouldn't go far from her calf. The smell of blood made the herd restless and it would begin to mill about, presenting new shooting opportunities for the hunters. They then began to kill the bulls and bigger animals. The killing went on for hours. The shooting was so constant that rifle barrels grew smoking hot and the hunters pissed down the barrels to cool them off, then continued the killing. When we say buffalo "hunters," we use the term loosely.

*   *   *

Norman Mailer's *Of a Fire on the Moon* reports the consequences of waste-water dump from Apollo 11, on its way to the moon. Even this slow dribbling discharge throws off the trajectory of the craft. This requires corrections. The fine droplets of liquid float in space, slowly dispersing, but catching the light and showing up as a myriad grouping of stars on some instrumentation. They are in their own slow orbit around the moon, in vast, shimmering descent. Waste-water is a euphemism for urine, of course.

I have pissed in many places. I have pissed in toilets, urinals, sinks, showers, bathtubs, outhouses, swimming pools, in the woods and fields, against trees and rocks, off back porches, front porches, side, out of windows and doors, alongside and in streams, rivers, lakes and oceans, on beaches, in parks, parking lots, and in flower beds, on sidewalks and roads, off balconies, bridges and cliffs, and so on. I have written my name in the snow. I have pissed my pants, my bed and, probably more than once, on my own foot. I pissed upwind until my father taught me better. I don't think I'm different from most men.

I would like to say I have never pissed in outer space or on the moon, but I have, by proxy. This is called extending the human presence in the universe. Like any dog, and this isn't necessarily meant as an insult, we're marking off territory. Planting a wire-stiffened American flag on the moon is one thing. Pissing on it is another.

I don't think about this all the time. But some nights when that old yellow moon is up there modestly smiling, I can't help it.

It's that same old moon in disguise that has followed me through the years, lopsided, hiding behind clouds, silver and sliced, golden and pale and wearing a halo of blood, that followed me home from the movies as I walked through the city, the same moon my mother and father must have looked at and all the people I've loved and still love and people for thousands of years around the world turning up their wonderful and awful faces in the night.

This is the moon that cast light on the slow stone growth of the pyramids, on the waters of Bloody Run the night after, on the My Lai Massacre, on the bare flesh of skinned buffalo across the Great Plains.

It's the earth's silent companion, accompanying us through the millennia in our long sweeping journey around the sun, coaxing the tides and the menses, measuring our calendars, reflecting sunlight from opposite sides of the earth, promising to us in the darkness that the sun will roll into view again.

Certain young children, the skin of their faces still tender, before it is toughened by wind and sun and other of earth's elements, can lift their faces to the moon and feel the faint heat emanating from it, that bounce of sunlight from over 93 million miles away. These children are among those who can spread-eagle themselves on the ground and feel the earth's slow revolving and, simultaneously, here in Western New York, its rebounding, too, from its compression of thousands of years under ice. We call these children imaginative. They have imaginary friends. We are secretly relieved as they grow older when these friends move away to unknown area codes, and the universe-sensing abilities of these children are lost or forgotten as their attention turns to collecting baseball cards or comic books or playing soccer.

But yes, at the end of all these things, I sometimes think of that haze of urine settling onto the moon, across the Sea of Fertility, across the flat empty plains, across the craters and across the Sea of Tranquility.

And I also think of Apollo 11, named after the ancient Greek sun god, who no one believes in anymore, who is also the god of poetry, incidentally, from which the three astronauts detached in a smaller craft to descend to the surface of the moon, and what words came back to earth to commemorate the event. I'm not referring to the Mother-May-I remark so well suited for PR, bumper stickers and posters, but the other: "The Eagle has landed!" That too was calculated, but simply so, to make us think of the American eagle, America, and it does, but I also think of Benjamin Franklin and Winston Churchill, and of an old horse named Eagle that at one time occupied a stall in LaValley's stable on Porter Road, Niagara Falls, New York.

11.

D.H. Lawrence once wrote, "Everyone says, porcupines should be killed; the Indians, Mexicans, Americans all say the same." He was setting out to justify his killing of a porcupine, an act he'd carried out at the urging of a female companion referred to only as "Madame." Who was this woman?

It wasn't my Grandmother Baxter, who wouldn't have wasted time urging Lawrence to do anything, especially if he were going to whine about it later. She would have killed the porcupine herself, something she did once in Canada, on a wooded shore of the Lake of Bays. She clubbed it to death with a tree limb she picked up in the woods. My Grandfather Baxter told the story, laughing, proud of her, and pointed out where, the previous year, she'd killed it among the trees on the mountainside, just off the dirt road leading to their summer cabin.

Later, I went back there, scuffed around in the leaves and found a few bones and a sodden patch of quills. I was probably nine or ten, and had no idea why she'd killed it, though there'd been some vague talk at the time of a porcupine having gnawed the lower board at the rear of the outhouse. It had been after salt left by the urine.

The outhouse board had been marked with a delicate lacework of shallow grooves scrolling across its surface, no deeper than a sixteenth of an inch, a curious scrimshaw of secret messages left by a porcupine's incisors. A lower corner of the board, about a half inch, had been gnawed away. It was easy to determine that another ten years of this unacceptable nibbling might have resulted in the board having to be replaced.

There was no way of telling that the porcupine clubbed to death had been the one guilty of the chewing. But if a porcupine chews on your outhouse, even a little bit, the best course of action is to kill them all, wouldn't you agree? Up north past the dark waters of Lake Muskoka to the shores of the Lake of Bays, it's cottage country now, the lake is motorized, and septic tanks probably outnumber outhouses. The trace of flavoring that long-ago porcupine sought out is less available. But the lesson still applies: no odd woodland creature has a right to the salt from your piss, even though some might feel it's little enough to ask. As Lawrence said, "Things like the porcupine, one must be able to shoot them, if they get in one's way."

He probably would have said the same about the buffalo. "Things" like that get in the way, don't they? Being things, they're not alive at all, but furniture in a doorway. The Indians, might have disagreed with him about that. Then there's his formal use of "one" that distances the speaker from content, that wants to put an aristocratic monocle on the lunacy. One must be able to kill things like the porcupine, must one? And how many things *like* the porcupine does one know of? One admires his progression, though: from entire populations of ethnic and national groups who all say porcupines should be killed, to "one" must be able to kill them and, finally, to his using the first person. By now he's given himself general permission to kill.

Lawrence did a lot of writhing around in that essay about the death of a porcupine. He went into great detail about how it happened, how the porcupine had tried unsuccessfully to escape while he was going about killing it. But it had deserved to die: porcupines killed the tops of pine trees by browsing on the tender twigs; he had a short time earlier tried to help a dog that suffered horribly with a muzzle full of quills; porcupines are ugly; they move with a "bestial, stupid motion" and bring a "touch of squalor" to the moonlight.

All living organisms live by killing, Lawrence says. That's the design of things, he's figured out. The rule by which some life forms have the right to take the life of others involves which is more "vividly alive." He provides an absurd list: wren over alligator, snake over insect, dandelion over fern or palm tree, etc., etc., and himself over the Mexican hired to drive his wagon. Those beings less vividly alive are happy to serve. The horse with a man on its back or pulling a cart is happier than a wild horse. It didn't occur to him to put porcupine over pine tree, obviously. The pine tree should be happy to serve. Even rabbits kill. They kill grass. Check it out, he tells us. Rabbits are mostly guts, designed to digest devoured grass. But he didn't eat that porcupine he killed.

Then this whole world view is intertwined with "existence" in relationships with the sun and the Holy Ghost, the kingdom of heaven within, and his lament that humans are losing their potential to be vividly alive because they pay too much attention to money. "One must be able to shoot," he says. "I, myself, must be able to shoot, and to kill." The essay "Reflections on the Death of a Porcupine" is wonderfully demented.

*   *   *

John Burroughs was never able to shoot a hummingbird, though he tried, probably repeatedly. It was the only bird he hadn't shot and the only one faster than a loon, he said. Those of us who've heard the loon have memories of its wavering cry echoing over mountain lakes. Its numbers seem to be declining and its haunting voice is less heard these days. Rumor has it they don't like civilization much.

Taking advantage of the bird's natural curiosity, Burroughs once lured one to swim close enough to his boat that he could take a shot at it. How he did this, I don't recall, but he may have tied his handkerchief to an oar and waved it slowly until the inquisitive loon swam near. Then he shot at it with his pistol, but missed. The loon is a diving bird of great ability. When it surfaced it was probably a hundred yards further away, popping up in an entirely unexpected location. That was one that got away.

The loon he killed was a "magnificent specimen," shot with a breech loading rifle. Burroughs speculated that the loon had been able to dodge bullets fired from the old muzzleloaders, but wasn't used to the "new species" of rifle. It's a curious choice of words. For D.H. Lawrence, in one instance at least, living creatures are "things," and for Burroughs, a technological advance in firearms is described as a new life form. The old blurring of the animate and inanimate world continues. A man teaching his young son to talk holds up a plastic horse and repeats the word "truck." This is intended as a joke, of course, but years ago the horse was a truck, and still is in some parts of the world. Even today, over a century since the internal combustion engine began to propel automobiles, the strength of these machines is still described by horsepower equivalents.

*   *   *

John Burroughs lived in a time when it was common practice for naturalists to kill birds so they could study them up close. This may account in some measure for his not being particularly concerned with the slaughter of millions of buffalo. It's not that he believed they were being studied, but there were so many of them, like the birds he shot. And yet the passenger pigeon all but disappeared from the earth during his lifetime.

The abandoned nests of passenger pigeons were still in the trees in 1869 when Burroughs and a friend named Orville camped in the wooded mountains along the Delaware River, near a stream called Neversink. They were trout fishing. Richard Brautigan would have approved of Burroughs' description of streams, their character, water quality, purity, and the fish within them, almost a worship.

One night the trout fishermen were disturbed by the shrill grunting of a porcupine, which Burroughs said was its way of "cursing" their campfire. So they searched for it and found it in the dark woods, where Orville shot and clubbed it with a rifle. It was then trying "harder than ever to escape," Burroughs reported, with nearly all of the quills shot or beaten "off the poor creature's back." Since the porcupine, which Burroughs referred to as a "porky pig," was still "trying to crawl off into the darkness," he pulled his Smith and Wesson pistol from his pants pocket where he carried it and finished the wounded animal off with a couple of shots to the head. Then, Burroughs said, that both men watched or, in his words, were "witness" to a glorious display of northern lights before lying down to go to sleep.

*   *   *

Early in 2005, culminating eleven years of work, two Canadian linguistic scholars announced they had finished deciphering the curious curved lines found cut into the underside of a granite overhang in the Laurentian Mountains of northern Quebec. They delivered a paper entitled "Implications of the Protolanguage Laurentian Recordings," at the annual Beyond Sanskrit Conference (BSC) at Berkley on 31 March of that year. Many of the rows of markings appeared "unfinished," but what had intrigued these dedicated anthropologists was that several of the individual characters were identical to fragments recorded by others in widely separated locations.

Because the bulk of the translated notations was devoted to the taste and nutritional values of various species of tree shoots, both coniferous and deciduous, and other plants, there was speculation among the interns and student assistants. Most of them thought that the information could be attributed to a disappearing population of a vegetarian religious cult of the nineteenth century, secretive in nature, given to speaking and writing in code. The translators themselves indulged in no such speculations, which they regarded as fanciful and unscientific, if mildly amusing. What interested them most were the following translations: "Thou shalt not scrape boards in search of salt. Thou shalt not complain about campfires in the black woods. Thou shalt not get in the way. Thou shalt not dishonour the moonlight." These were puzzling admonitions. Naturally, the translators had many questions, but answers were not forthcoming. They could not begin to imagine, of course, the answers to other questions they had no hope of ever formulating.

We leave them to their pondering while we ask questions that are far easier to answer. What do Grandmother Baxter, John Burroughs, and Lawrence have in common? What is the title of a J.D. Salinger short story that uses the word "squalor" in a meaningful way? What is the connection between D.H. Lawrence and Snoopy?

* * *

Some stories keep going. That pelvis with its curve of vertebrae I had slid down over the fence post? It disappeared in its fourth year, a few days after hunting season opened. My first reaction on seeing the bare, weathered fence post was one of disbelief. The rib cage with its curve of vertebrae was gone, as absent as if it had been dreamed. Someone had obviously taken it. Long grasses at the base of the fence post had been crushed down as if someone's feet had stood there while it was lifted.

Who would have taken such a thing? And for what purpose? Georgia O'Keeffe might have. She'd been known to gather bones from the desert of New Mexico, around the Ghost Ranch where she often spent summers, once shipping a barrel-full of them to her studio back east. Otherwise, she'd have set up her easel in the pasture or the roadside ditch, and begun to paint. The scene was a study in contrasts, the deeply fissured wood, sun-whitened bone, rusted barbed wire, the tall fern stems of wild asparagus, its scarlet red berries appearing to be suspended in air around the post. O'Keeffe loved bones for their shapes, their architecture, which might seem to be an extreme artistic specialization. All form – no origin, no function, no narrative?

But O'Keeffe isn't so easily cornered. Even a casual awareness of her wide range of paintings indicates as much: she's painted "Tent Door at Night," a series of barns, nude watercolors, "Black Cross, New Mexico," other crosses in the Laurentian hills of Canada, "Green Apple on Black Plate," clouds, skyscrapers, "Slightly Open Clam Shell," "Jimson Weed," "Red Hills with Pedernal,"

"Pelvis with Distance," "Fishhook from Hawaii No 1," "Brooklyn Bridge," "Patio Door with Green Leaf," a dead rabbit next to a copper pot, and on and on. She loved flowers, too – which is a comment akin to saying Andy Warhol loved soup. So you'll check out her work for yourself and realize that deer rib cage of mine could have turned into two wide, diffused bars of white in the background of a canvas dominated by a luminescent red globe, the sun, a wild asparagus berry.

She painted skulls of cattle, deer, ram, horse, often accompanied by the blossom of a flower floating in the sky over a desert wasteland. "Summer Days" is a deer skull floating against a cloudy sky, its empty nose cavity poised above a bouquet of wildflowers also floating there, all above a narrow and ragged strip of blue sky with a barren red mountain range in the distance. Judging from the antlers, it's a mule deer, a six-pointer. She once said that bones were as beautiful as anything she knew about, as being "strangely" more alive than the living animals walking around.

A skull she found in the desert on the D.H. Lawrence ranch was immortalized in "Horse's Skull with Pink Rose," though the horse might have preferred an immortality that involved walking around. Another painting was "Horse's Skull with White Rose," and yet another, "Cow's Skull and White Calico Roses." Probably more well known than these is "Cow Skull – Red, White and Blue," an oil painting about 40 by 30 inches.

Technically speaking, there's no documentation that these horned cattle skulls were cows. They could have been steers or bulls. This is one of those category notations, where all cows are cattle, but not all cattle are cows, a distinction that may seem of little significance to some, but still. "Bull's Skull with White Calico Roses" would put a different lens in front of that painting.

That aside, "Cow Skull – Red, White and Blue" is a painting with the horn tips of the skull nearly touching the edges of the canvas, the skull in the upper portion of the view, in front of, but not precisely centered on, a vertical black strip that reaches from the top to the bottom of the painting. This black strip could be a post or a two-by-four from which the skull hangs, but it's also part of a crucifix, the horns forming the cross bar, though it's probably a mistake to think of if this way. Red stripes run down the edges of the canvas and the tips of the horns protrude into these. The center portion, behind the black post, appears to be a draped fabric, a flag of sorts, blue in the wide middle part, fading to white on either side, next to the red stripes.

Words can't recreate, obviously, the experience of the painting, not a thousand words, not ten thousand. It's still worth knowing what O'Keeffe said about it, though. She said the painting was a response to other artists blabbing on about writing the Great American Novel, the Great American Play, and so on. She also said it was created in reaction to those whose paintings suggested America was a place of poverty and decay, rundown shanties, and so on. She knew America as a rich country, cattle drives that went on for days, for example, their unending silhouettes moving across a hilltop against the sky. Her painting, then, was "in a way" kind of "a joke."

A joke in 1931 has become, through the passing years, an embodiment of patriotism, positive, then critical, a crucifix, kitsch, an icon, and finally accumulates layers of meaning that eclipse whatever after-the-fact remarks the artist articulated. Or anyone else's comments, for that matter. It would, therefore, be a romanticist misperception to glimpse the westward sweep of Manifest Destiny thorough the eye socket of a cow skull, an expanding vision of the thousands of animals that replaced the buffalo herds across the plains – though I am tempted to do so.

For the record, O'Keeffe also said, "A pelvis bone has always been useful to any animal that has it – quite as useful as a head, I suppose." This may be dry humor; a blend of wit and cynicism; a recognition that the pelvis bone is the bone portal through which many of earth's creatures emerge to their lives; an endorsement of the sensual over the intellect, because the comparison is pelvis to "head," not pelvis to skull; or a subtle pornography; or transcendent simple-mindedness; or wisdom, or all of these.

Georgia O'Keeffe was much photographed. There were hundreds of Georgia O'Keeffe stills taken by her photographer husband Stieglitz, many nudes, partial nudes, in front of her work, hand studies, and so on, and others, taken by others, more candid, spontaneous, revealing. Out of these photographs I've seen, a snapshot of her taken in the desert, very likely near Ghost Ranch, New Mexico, is the most striking, compelling.

She's wearing a dark shirt, buttoned to the neck, a black, unbuttoned jacket, a low-crowned black Stetson, and jeans with once-turned cuffs. In her right hand she's holding up at waist level a thick stalk of vertebrae from which long ribs sprout, perhaps a three-foot cluster of them splayed out, an upended bone flower, rib-blossomed. In her left hand, held by one horn, is the head, not yet a skull because it's still covered with a parchment of hide, the bone beginning to show around one eye where the hide was shrunken. She is smiling.

Ansel Adams, I believe, though I'm not certain, took this snapshot, and at least one other, a variation on the same day, in the same place, same subject. Other than the subject matter and the famous painter, anyone you know could have taken it. There's a shadow from the brim of the Stetson cutting across the top of O'Keeffe's face. But to hell with all of that and lighting and other photographic concerns, Adams might have thought. He wasn't passing up the chance to catch O'Keeffe smiling.

When Georgia O'Keeffe died, there was no funeral service, no memorial, in accordance with her wishes. She was cremated and a friend scattered her ashes over Ghost Ranch from the top of a mesa, a north wind blowing. The first time she'd traveled to the ranch, she missed the turn-off road. When she stopped to get directions she was told to go back the way she'd come and to turn at the skull. It's a pity she hadn't provided instructions that after death her remains be left far out in the windswept desert, where years later her sun-bleached skull, and vertebrae, rib cage, and pelvis might have been found, so that some future artist might smile and hold up her pelvis to frame the desert stars.

O'Keeffe died in 1986, nearly twenty years before the ribcage and vertebrae were stolen from my fence post, so she could have been ruled out as a suspect from the start. But it could have been one of her admirers, imitators, or a protégé. They are, I've been told, legion, though the person who said that was drinking a double shot of Jack Daniels at the time, his sixth of the evening, and smoking, his cigarette held deeply jammed between the second and third paint-stained fingers of his right hand, with which he kept lifting the shot glass to take a sip, and so he could have been making a joke.

* * *

It was a hunter, then, I think, who stopped his vehicle, most likely a pickup truck, right in the road, a common enough practice in these parts, and walked with shortened steps down the steep ditch bank over to the fence post on my property. He has stolen my bones which, after all, belonged to me, did they not, being on my property and all? They are now on his fence post should he have such a thing, or hanging from a garden shed or in his den near a neon beer sign.

He might have been driving the roads at night spotting deer when his sweeping cone of light revealed the medley of bones embracing the fence post. On impulse – there were no other vehicles approaching as would have been indicated by headlights – he took it. Or perhaps the onset of hunting season and the theft were unrelated, and a young man driving by had stopped to take the bones so that he could play a joke on his friend, or girlfriend, and pelvis and vertebrae ended up propped near a front door or positioned on a porch chair.

Of course, I've forgotten the possibility that the deer resurrected itself around those bones, blood vessels and nerve endings growing, flesh swelling into functioning muscle; until it eased itself down from the post, got its feet under it, shook its head, and walked off across the frosty pasture, unsteadily at first, then with increasing strength, taking experimental little leaps, and snorting, looking around at its new and half-remembered world, the moon reflected in the orbs of its eyes. But when faith is at its lowest ebb, the concept falls too easily into wishful thinking.

12.

The photograph was taken of a place that has vanished. This doesn't make it unique, of course. Undoubtedly you know of many places that no longer exist, where the sun shines on vanished landscapes only in your memories. This may be the story of earth.

The world captured in the photograph was a reflecting pool alongside the Niagara River just above the rapids and waterfalls. It was actually an inlet, the water continually refreshed as it moved toward the brink, but moving so slowly that it appeared still, the surface unblemished, reflecting sky, drifting clouds, and the gentle motion of leafy tree branches. The word "refreshed" may have misleading connotations here, since the water was continually contaminated with industrial wastes beyond our imaginations. Some of the industries were nearby along the upper river and others were far off, as far as Duluth steel mills, where the lake bottom was a dull red, the color of new rust, everything, pebbles, sand, stones, submerged tree trunks. Even the minnows were a drab red there, their tiny scales like flakes of rust. All the discharges from all the industries, agricultural runoff, leaching landfills, malfunctioning sewage treatment facilities, and straight-pipe septic systems around four of the Great Lakes eventually cascade over Niagara, today as it did then. I think about this when mist from the falls blows in my face.

*   *   *

But let us pretend otherwise. Let us imagine the water is so clean and cool and fresh that on a sweltering summer day you can scoop out an old graniteware dipperful of it and drink and drink and drink. The rain and snowmelt gathered from a large part of the continent fills all the cells of your body. You can see your face reflected as you bend over the pool and the sky and the clouds above you and all of nature around, and the rim of the dipper is cold against your lips, pure water spilling over your chin and down the sides of your neck as you swallow great gulping mouthfuls one after the other as if you could never get enough. It was that way once, you know, not all that long ago.

*   *   *

On the Straight Arrow card "Danger Signals," is the following: "These Indian Danger Signals are still used today... Straight Arrow wants you to use and recognize them... you may someday save a life." One of the five dangers on the card can be noted by this: "Two cross-bars with a stone suspended from the top bar means... 'All nearby water is bad drinking water... or even poisonous...' This diagram drawn on the ground means the same thing... but Straight Arrow says 'Use the cross-bars as they will not wash or wear away.'" (These are sticks, two driven into the ground a few feet apart and two others, an upper and lower, lashed across them. The diagram scratched in the dirt is a square, lines passing one another at the corners, with a round mark in the center.)

Let me say that a stone suspended from a framework of sticks lashed together with strands of rawhide (or sturdy twine, if rawhide is hard to find – would Straight Arrow suggest using an old boot lace?) wouldn't get it here.

At Niagara I suggest one-inch rebar, set in concrete three feet into the ground, below the frost line, the cross bars welded in place. A stone about the size of an infant's head, granite smoothed by the glacial scouring thousands of years ago, with a hole drilled though it, should be suspended from the top bar by a stainless steel cable no less than ¼" in diameter. The rebar should be painted a rustproof chrome yellow or red. Do you think one of these every hundred feet along the entire length of the river would be sufficient?

This would put a lot of people to work, surveyors, operating engineers, laborers, ironworkers, cement finishers, welders, stonemasons, and painters. Niagara River Greenway money should be available to pay for this. Individual citizens could "adopt a stone" to help out.

* * *

The finest reflecting pool will always be Walden Pond. What Thoreau reflected on there as he lived beside it will never be equaled. He saw the pond as eternally renewed, its purity unsullied in spite of industrial intrusions, ice cutters, woodchoppers, the railroad and, perhaps at some level of awareness, even himself.

With his borrowed axe (his "economy" precluded buying one?), implement and emblem of the woodchoppers, he felled "some tall, arrowy white pines, still in their youth," at Walden Pond to use in the framing of his cabin. Most of the other boards he obtained from disassembling an Irishman's shanty, which he purchased for $4.25. So the shanty Irish are directly linked to Walden's history far beyond the one hundred Irish ice cutters that worked on the winter pond, and we wonder if some current family named Collins has traced their history back to James.

Years later Thoreau decries the loss of the woods surrounding Walden Pond: "But since I left these shores the woodchoppers have still further laid them waste, and now for many a year there will be no rambling through the aisles of the wood, with occasional vistas through which you see the water.... How can you expect the birds to sing when their groves are cut down?" he asks. Yet a half dozen sentences later he soars into a transcendental optimism that excuses and forgives: "Though the woodchoppers have laid bare first this shore and then that... where a forest was cut down last winter another is springing up by its shore as lustily as ever...." The woodchoppers of the present, huge lumber companies, may discover these "springing up" lines and use them superimposed over glossy green, full page ads showing plantations of little white pine seedlings, row after row.

The ads would be almost religious, all the little Christmas trees replacing the forest and saving the world, dreaming their little dreams of becoming 2 x 4s. How disappointed they will all be to find out there are no 2 x 4s anymore. They will end up as 1½" x 3½" pieces, which is nowhere near as romantic, and as piles of chips for sheets of particleboard.

* * *

Thoreau's relationship with the axe is ambivalent. He borrows an axe, though he could have afforded to buy one, as if ownership would be an admission that he, too, was a woodchopper, to be identified with the destruction of forests. He takes pride, however, in returning the axe to its owner sharper than when he got it, and also repaired, the head more firmly fixed to the handle with a wedge fashioned from green hickory, driven in with a stone, and then soaked in the edge of the pond to swell the wood.

This wasn't the first association between Thoreau, an axe, and Walden Pond. As if there's no memory of the borrowed axe, Thoreau tells the following story: In a winter "Many years ago" he had chopped several fishing holes in the ice of Walden Pond. As he reached the shore, he "tossed" his axe back onto the ice (why he did this is open to speculation) where it slid about seventy-five feet, as if directed by an "evil genius," straight into one of the holes.

Stretched out flat on his stomach, Thoreau peered through the hole in the ice. Twenty-five feet below, the axe rested on the bottom, head down, wooden handle buoyant, pointing up, "gently swaying to and fro with the pulse of the pond." He observed that if the axe were left undisturbed, the handle would have eventually rotted away. He didn't say that the head, too, would have over time become a useless fragment of rust. The disintegration of the handle alone would have effectively rendered it harmless, no longer the tool of woodchoppers. But none of this was to happen. Thoreau took pains to retrieve the axe. Using an ice chisel to cut another hole directly over it, fashioning a slip-noose and, with his knife, cutting down the longest birch he "could find in the neighborhood," he snared the axe and lifted it back to the surface.

He never mentioned the axe again, and had seemingly told the story to illustrate the clarity of the water in Walden Pond. There he was, over a century and a half ago, stretched out on the frozen eye of Walden, staring into its depths to locate an axe. He had no glimpse of his own face reflected that day, at least not that he reported. He saw no glimmer of the struggle to preserve Walden Pond and its wooded shores these many years later. He couldn't have foretold the plan to sell "naming rights" to Walden Woods in the 21st Century to make up for low tax revenues. He probably thought names were important. We love Thoreau, don't we? We forgive him, our most ardent of naturalists, for comparing the calm surface of Walden Pond to a mirror, an artifact of manufacture, after all, however ancient, not a thing of genuine nature, but a copy of it. Better to compare Walden to the looking glass that Alice went through. If even he couldn't stay clear of axes and mirrors, what hope is there for the rest of us?

*   *   *

A house once stood several hundred feet out in a field west of Hyde Park Boulevard about a half mile from Indian Lookout. Though it is close to the Niagara Gorge, a person who stood at this location wouldn't know it. Hundreds of feet from existing roads, it was just a short distance from the National Carbon fence, which was topped with strands of barbed wire, and the looming, dark factory building inside and the mountains of soft coal stockpiled for the furnaces. The land was flat, low lying, most likely at one time the site of marginal farming, and part of the Bloody Run watershed.

By the time I was ten, nothing of the house remained except the cellar, the rest so completely gone that it must have burned generations before. It was about ten by fifteen feet, undoubtedly not a "full" cellar, the house that once stood on it having been larger. I found out while writing this that if my memory of its size is accurate, then the cellar was the same size as Thoreau's cabin.

In the spring, snow melting and rain filled the cellar almost to ground level, and it stayed that way most of the summer. The foundation walls extended less than a foot above ground, except where one side had partially collapsed inward. The water was of varying depths, no more than six feet at its deepest. In one corner a set of stone slab steps descended below water to the cellar floor.

When the sun grew hot that year, I'd go there, indirectly, down this cinder road, then that one, across a field, then through the hedgerow of thorn bushes and turn, finally, into the field that concealed the cellar. I'd been forbidden to go there, of course. I'd sit on the top stone step, sneakers and socks off, pants rolled up, my feet resting on the first underwater step, spindly little shins made crooked under there. The water was clear to the bottom. Water skimmers raced on the surface near the grasses overhanging the foundation edges, though I never questioned how they got there. I thought about the people who'd lived in the house. Had they moved away? Had they perished in the fire that I'd imagined? Had they been burned to a crisp and would they find a way to tell me about it later? Or had they just grown old and died?

It wasn't long before I took off all my clothes, leaving them heaped on the top step, and slowly walked down the stairs until the water reached my neck, then pushed off. I could swim, dogpaddle, and I did, to the other side and back. Then I sat on that sun-drenched slab of concrete, sluiced water from my body with my hands, and waited until I dried off so I could put my clothes back on, looking around, a skinny, pale salamander, taking the sun.

There were dragonflies swooping and hovering over that little rectangle of water, and motes suspended, pinpoints of light beneath the surface, reflections. I remember once, crouched there, watching a water-beetle just a few inches down, coming up near the top, I imagined, because the water was warmer there, when suddenly I was unable to see it, but saw in its place, the reflection of my own brushcut head. There was underwater, and above water, the dragonflies, the field, and world around, and what was reflected on the surface that was different than the world around. The smokestacks in the reflection weren't the same as the ones a short distance away.

*   *   *

Before the summer was over, an older boy and his younger brother followed me to the cellar. The older boy had a bow and arrow, a new one, store-bought, bright and shiny with varnish. Standing at the edge of the cellar, he leaned forward, lowering the drawn-back bow until part of the arrow stuck into the water. Inches beneath the arrow point, was a toad on a ledge of collapsed foundation. The boy released the arrow and retrieved it in one motion, holding it high in the air, water dripping. It had pierced two toads during their mating, one on top of the other's back, and they were stuck together on the arrow. He laughed and said something dirty, but I don't remember what it was, just the feeling I had of everything being spoiled as I walked away from them.

*   *   *

So whatever happened to that axe Thoreau pulled out through the ice at Walden Pond? Is it still in the family? Is it one of the authentic artifacts on display in the replica of Thoreau's cabin at Walden? Did it go in a garage sale about 1952? Has it showed up on eBay? He went afishing and pulled out an axe.

*   *   *

A reflecting pool is a body of water, the surface of which is so smooth that it reflects images of what is nearby. If the scene it reflects is one of natural beauty, it's a doubling of that beauty, sometimes in motion, changing with the light and seasons. Does blue sky, nothing but blue sky and those few scudding white clouds shine up from the pool? Where are you in the picture, standing or sitting tentatively near the edge, staring down?

The pool should be a place of quiet, where solitude might be sought, where an atmosphere of serenity is cultivated, a place that encourages reflection about the ways of the world and our relationships in it, meditation, prayer.

Park benches might be found on the shores, but not picnic tables. No vehicles should be allowed within sight of the pool. It's free of commercial exploitation, sports or recreational activities, entertainments such as fireworks, kite flying or wet t-shirt contests, races of any sort, beer blasts, musical or theatrical productions, "it's-for-a-good-cause" events or walks, concerts, turkey or hog calling competitions, dog shows, circuses, carnivals, mud wrestling, mimes, or jugglers. No restaurants, food courts, vending machines, or souvenir shacks. No religious or political rallies or ceremonies. Some of these are worthwhile. That's fine. Do them elsewhere.

*   *   *

Limits on the size of a reflecting pool, though impressively broad, do exist. Lake Ontario, for example, is too big, even if it is extremely calm and smooth on occasion. From what vantage point could a person view reflections there? A drop of water is too small. It has been demonstrated with special photographic equipment, that drops of clear water, curved, clinging to a leaf, for example, may reflect extraordinary and beautiful perspectives of the natural world, foliage, flowers, curious and colorful insects. Because these views are not available to those without esoteric technologies, however, the CRPR (Committee for Reflecting Pool Review) has determined that drops do not qualify as reflecting pools. Walden Pond, it may be argued, like Lake Ontario, is also a body of water too large to permit reflections to be viewed from a vantage point, which is true enough, but the quality of inner reflections generated there more than makes up for this.

*   *   *

The ideal reflecting pool is smaller, rather than larger, let's say one to five acres, irregularly shaped, deep enough to suggest mystery and to sustain schools of minnows or other small fish so that these may be observed in the shallows, but none of a size to encourage fishing. It should have a natural bottom.

Ferns, wildflowers, and grasses should be permitted to grow unmowed on some of the shore, trimmed grass in other areas. At least one natural stone bridge should span one of the irregular fingers of the pond. Mature trees, native to the region, not nursery ornamentals, should also be left to grow on the shores, establishing groves or small forests. There should be no artificial lighting.

*   *   *

So whatever happened to all of our reflecting pools? Perhaps there never were that many to start with. It's simplistic to say they were backfilled and turned into parking lots, highways, malls, and other commercial developments, but in many cases that's probably exactly what happened. Reflecting pools don't normally have high economic potential. A reflecting pool with hundreds of people tramping its shores isn't much of a reflecting pool anymore. Sadly, that was the experience of the pool at Niagara for much of the year, where horse and carriage rides and, later, automobiles traveled a dirt road just a few feet from the water's edge and drove over the stone bridges. Other photographs reveal this road.

If it existed today, tour buses would be stopping one after the other. The tour drivers would speak to disembarking tourists over a PA system. "Okay, folks, we've got ten minutes here. Get over there and reflect! But seriously, it's a lovely place, really, Niagara's Reflecting Pool. Make history by seeing your reflection in it! See you back here in nine minutes." Most of them would return in five. Some wouldn't get off the bus.

Maybe it's better the pool is gone altogether, evolved, mutated, surviving in other forms. A flier recently delivered with the newspaper advertised, "Sale, 90-Gal. Pond Kit, 79.99, Includes 19-gal.

Pre-formed pond, water course, pump, bubbler and bell fountain."
Everything diminished. They couldn't even spell out "gallon."
Ninety gallons is only about twice as much water as was held by
one of those old-fashioned, high-sided bathtubs.

The world is full of hot tubs, now, and in-ground pools and
above-ground pools. What's more unnatural than above-ground
pools? Underground clouds? This is not to say these pools don't
suffice for some people. Lots of reflection has probably gone on in
hot tubs and, at twilight, there's often a solitary man out with his
leaf skimmer at the backyard pool who hesitates a moment at some
surface intimation that flickers and is gone. In over one hundred
nuclear facilities across America blue sky nothing but blue sky is
emanating from spent fuel rods in the cooling pools, that Cheren-
kov radiation blue glowing like weak neon.

The $820 million twin rover mission to Mars has sent streams
of data back to earth, nearly all of it attempting to answer this question: Is there now, or has there ever been, water on Mars? According to an Associated Press article, reporting a news conference held
at a Jet Propulsion Laboratory on 26 February 2004, scientist Ray
Arvidson said, "Water is the elixir of life, and if we come up with
the conclusion that water has been involved [on Mars]... at some
time in the past, then I think the probability that... life could have
gotten started goes way up." Some time after this it was, in fact,
concluded that water once existed on Mars.

*   *   *

I know of another planet where water has been involved for
millions of years, and still is, in rains, in clouds, fogs, dew, in mists,
and ice, and in effervescent seas, and where multitudes of life forms
have gotten started, many of which, evolving in a slow and marvelous explosion, exist until the present day. I will tell you where it
is. Bloody Run is a tiny piece of evidence. Mars is not the only red
planet.

*   *   *

He and his friend were deep in the "primitive" woods is how John Burroughs described it, on an extended search for trout streams. They were on a quest for streams of perfection, flowing with sweet, pure waters, suffused with oxygen, bathed in sunlight splashing through the foliage. These streams should have been unvisited by other fishermen, blessed with deep pools, remote, beating with the pulse of trout. For early Christians, the fish was a symbol of Christ, and for many fishermen, the trout is the prince of fish. So Burroughs and his friend prowled the stream banks and stepped into them carrying their poles and lines, hooked trout and lifted them from the sparkling waters into the air. This was long before catch and release was widely practiced, of course, and so they ate those trout.

They were living in the woods, and had only what they could carry in and the fish they caught to eat. A few pounds of beans and cornmeal disappear in a hurry. They didn't pack that cast iron frying pan in with the camping gear for extra weight. At its highest level of expression, catching trout might have been a spiritual experience, but it was also an exercise of man's dominion over one of the creatures of the natural world, and at the practical level, something to eat. Perhaps they said grace before meals. Burroughs' friend, after all, was a man named Aaron.

Some of those days spent fishing in the mountain streams were remembered by Burroughs in *Locusts and Wild Honey,* published in 1879. Here he told the story of having hooked a trout he couldn't bring to land, even after long struggles, because of his fishing line running awkwardly over the trunk of a fallen tree. He was in a fever to land that fish. He thought at one point that he'd jump into the water like Sam Patch and wrestle the fish in its own element. He'd heard of Sam Patch, obviously, Niagara daredevil, who jumped from high places into rivers. His motto was, "Some things can be done as well as others." The fish escaped the hook finally and Burroughs regretted not thinking of the pistol he had in his pocket, saying that if he had, he'd have shot the fish "through and through."

Later, his disappointment subsided and he came to think of the struggle and the fish going free as a wonderful experience, providing a memory that catching it wouldn't have. In spite of this conversion, you know his earlier impulses were the real deal. If the Aaronic consecration of the trout stream fails, shoot the sonofabitch.

It's well known that friends and men off in wilderness environments talk to one another in very unguarded ways. Cowboys talked around their campfires. Lewis and Clark probably shared stories. Most of these conversations are forever lost. John Burroughs and Aaron talked and parts of what Aaron said was remembered by Burroughs and later reported. Some of this was in *Locusts and Wild Honey* in the "A Bed of Boughs" section, which refers to the cedar boughs stripped from trees to make soft, fragrant camping beds in the woods.

Seemingly out of nowhere, Aaron asks, "Remember that pretty creature we saw seven years ago in the shanty on the West Branch, who was helping her mother cook for the hands, a slip of a girl twelve or thirteen years old with eyes as beautiful and bewitching as the water that flowed by her cabin?"

Burroughs did not reveal the nature of his response to Aaron. He might have said, "Do I ever!" and he didn't want that known. Would a twelve or thirteen year old girl have been a trifle young for these middle-aged guys? Given those years, we might make some allowances, since it wasn't uncommon for young girls around that age to start families of their own, and there was then a general belief that childhood ended abruptly and adulthood began at the onset of the teens. But really. This young "slip of a girl" was still with her mother. John and Aaron, however, instead of being attracted to the mother, were captivated by the young girl. Is "captivated" too strong? Maybe not strong enough. It had been seven years since they saw that girl and she was still in Aaron's mind vividly enough for him to ask the question, and eloquently, too, and a significant enough memory for Burroughs that he remembered it clearly and wrote out Aaron's words. If the description and eloquence weren't Aaron's, then they belong to Burroughs. Who's putting words in whose mouth, here?

Aaron's question didn't harken back to a one-time incident, either. When they came across a homesteader's cabin in the woods, they'd approach the door to inquire whether they might obtain some milk. This would relieve a steady diet of fish. Or perhaps they wanted it for their coffee? Burroughs readily admits that seeking milk was subterfuge, that they'd often inquire at a shanty where there was no evidence of a cow or goat. What they sought was the opportunity to linger on the doorstep looking at a "backwoods maiden," as Burroughs described her, who might be inside. In the land of milk and honey, if they couldn't get the milk, at least they had a chance at the honey. For Aaron it was a tonic. He said he "refreshed himself with the sight of a well-dressed and comely-looking young girl," and that "all his perceptions and susceptibilities quickened." He described another young girl as having "a slightly pale face... strong and well arched, with a tender wistful expression not easy to forget."

The girl he'd remembered for seven years, however, had in the end lost his intense admiration when she spoke. The sound of her voice, he said, reminded him of "pots and pans." What he meant by that is open to speculation. Did her voice have a nasal, metallic tone? Was it discordant, her speech hitting hard on the consonants as if pots and pans were clanging together? That pots and pans comparison is suggestive, though. Aaron was in his mind a woodsman, frontiersman, a wild man, rejecting anything that sounded a note of the domestic, the pots and pans of a settled life.

Somewhere today there's a young girl in middle school, a soccer player, perhaps, who plays with abandon, totally oblivious to the notion that her great grandmother at her age had been the focus of such sublimated lust and yearning from John Burroughs and his friend Aaron. That had been in another century. She probably wouldn't be surprised, though, if someone were to tell her about it. If John and Aaron were alive today, the two of them might be found standing side by side on a sunny afternoon, fingers hooked in the cyclone fence, watching her chase the ball across the playing field.

13.

I walked right up to death without knowing it. Isn't that the way it is most of the time? There it was at my feet, but I hadn't stepped on it. It was busy inhabiting the carcass of a deer, not that it was so preoccupied that it wasn't elsewhere around the world doing exactly the same thing in millions of bodies that used to be alive, from insects to whales to hundreds of thousands of people, but I hadn't thought of that at the time. I was about twelve.

I'd been walking along a trail in the Niagara Gorge, an old railbed, and was upset by the deer because it was dead, but also because I should have spotted it from far off, should have noticed the body in the trail, that irregular shape that didn't belong, that inert hump of brown on the shale, with sheer cliffs rising on one side, broken stone sloping down to the river on the other.

Where had my mind been? Daydreaming, probably, eyes fixed on the ground in front of my feet instead of scanning the entire landscape, aware of the scene flowing before me.

I'd failed Straight Arrow, my teacher, who'd been trying to instruct me about the natural world with those lessons printed on Shredded Wheat cards, how to recognize tracks of wild animals left in the mud or snow, the ways to use fire, campfire, Indian roaster, how to lash sticks or logs together for an Indian Bull Shield or an Indian raft. I would never learn these skills because I was not an American Indian.

I would never be Straight Arrow, as much as he was worthy of admiration. He was tall and athletic without being muscle bound, graceful in buckskin breeches and vest, which he probably crafted himself. His long hair was held back with a headband at the back of which two feathers pointed up. He was gentle and considerate in his instructions. He wrote, for example, when revealing that the Indian lacrosse ball was carved from cedar, that "perhaps it would be a good idea for readers to consider using an old tennis ball." He could foresee a striped croquet ball being flung like the crack of doom into some little white boy's forehead.

* * *

Some years later I had learned to be cynical and rejected my old childhood friend. What kind of name was "Straight Arrow," anyway? Weren't all arrows supposed to be straight? So what was the big deal here? He was named for having straight arrows? Everyone else had crooked ones?

* * *

Back in one of my old neighborhoods there was a boy, about seven or eight, younger than us by ten years, whose legs were crooked, some disarrangement that might have originated as high as the hips, his feet splaying at odd angles. He couldn't run fast, but propelled himself awkwardly, arms pumping, his torso leaning forward in a parody of haste. He was a good, happy kid, enthusiastic in all things, but perpetually "it" in games of tag. One of his friends nicknamed him "Swift Turtle." Do you think it's possible Straight Arrow is that kind of name? Did he have the same kind of friend?

* * *

The Straight Arrow story: he was an orphan raised by white people, says one source. Another says he was "born an Indian," and publicly lived the life of a white rancher, but privately, in his other life, came riding out of a secret cave of gold astride a palomino named Fury "on the trail of justice."

*   *   *

What's this "found" stuff? You just don't find babies, do you? Or perhaps you do, if a stork delivers one to your front lawn along with a plywood silhouette of itself to announce the arrival, or if your culture has taught you to look for babies under cabbage leaves.

The Straight Arrow card that describes how to make a papoose carriage suggests one possibility. The first six drawings on the card consist of instructional diagrams: "Select 6 light but strong sticks and with cord tie them together like this." The last two drawings are of a woman, one with the papoose carriage on her back and one of her near a tree, having removed the carriage. She is slim-waisted, shapely, and attractive in fringed buckskin shirt and leggings, a single feather standing at the back of her headband, posed gracefully, feet together, one heel lifted slightly, one hand extended palm down, while the other places the strap of the papoose carriage over the stub of a broken tree branch. "When the papoose is not moving around with his mother he is hung on a tree or hook like this," the printed words say.

Could this be what happened? Straight Arrow's mother left him for a few minutes, while she slowly moved some distance away, picking berries, for example, and white settlers "found" him? Can we imagine her heartbreak when she returned?

So is this the way to find a baby? His parents "lost" him? He was an orphan? Let's tell the truth here. White people probably killed his parents, don't you think?

Another question: "found" at a young age, how did he ever come to learn all the "secrets of Indian lore and know-how" in the first place? Setting all this aside, we have something in common, Straight Arrow and me. We were both raised by white people.

*   *   *

At the Boston Tea Party, whites disguised themselves as Indians. After the party they probably ditched their Indian clothing and went to the nearest pub and knocked back a couple of ales and had a couple of laughs, while the water of the Boston Harbor was steeping the biggest cup of tea ever made in America. Straight Arrow disguised himself as a white man to raise cattle. He'd sneak into his secret cave as a white man, probably looking over his shoulder, then emerge an Indian riding the palomino, Fury, golden horse, from the gold-bearing earth, galloping off to do something right.

*   *   *

In the Niagara Gorge, I'd looked at the dead deer as carefully as I could. I'd almost stumbled on the body before I saw it, but at least I knew how it had died. She had a broken front leg, bone protruding at the knee, which was bent under her body. There was no blood on the ground. Her mouth was nearly closed, eyes open, dull and glazed over, no depth to them at all. In the corners of the eyes and along the line of her lip were white specks, very tiny, about the size of the white space enclosed by the small letter "e" in the words of a regular newspaper column. These might have been grass seeds, I thought.

Long grasses swayed over the edge of the cliff far above us. It had fallen from there, I decided, or had been chased by dogs. I checked up and down the trail in both directions. There were no deer tracks or even scuff marks in the shale that might have been caused by hooves leading up to the body. The upper edge of the gorge was unstable, chunks of the cliff often falling off without warning, sometimes in winter because of freezing and thawing cycles, sometimes after heavy rains. Because I spent a lot of time in the lower river gorge, I knew the walls were continually falling, and had been for thousands of years. These weren't huge and dramatic rockslides, but the gentle pattering of shale fragments, some smaller than a shirt button, every few minutes within earshot, the irregular ticking of a deep stone clock.

With this slow motion disintegration of the gorge walls and unstable rim, it was easy to imagine the deer losing its footing at the top, especially at night, or in an effort to elude pursuing dogs, attempting a leap from one crumbling outcropping to the next and not making it. In panic, could it have leapt into the dark space of the gorge? Indians, after all, used to stampede Buffalo herds over cliffs, didn't they? Something similar had happened to the deer.

Later that week, I discovered the white specks I'd thought were grass seeds had been blowfly eggs. They'd hatched into small maggots. In days they had grown as large as grains of rice, and were moving, soft bodies pulsating as they fed on the soft tissues already in decay, the eyes, mouth, and broken leg. The deer was bloated now, the stench drifting on river breezes. I avoided that section of the gorge for the rest of the summer.

The following year, as soon as school was out, I went back to check on the deer carcass. Only a few patches of sodden hair were left on the shale. The bones had been widely scattered, in some instances hundreds of feet away. The skull was gone, and I imagined a dog lugging it home to his front yard, where his owner took it away and threw it in the garbage. A few clean and bleached ribs were in various locations, and a short row of vertebrae, still stuck together, was wedged at the base of a rock on the slope down to the river. Turkey vultures and raccoon and opossum probably all had a share of the deer, dragging bones away through that previous summer and fall and some of them into the winter. The largest remainder I found was a shoulder blade. I may have been the last animal to carry a bone away.

*   *   *

At home, down in the cellar, I pawed around on the paint shelf until I found the little jar of gold paint. It was about twice the size of the coffee creamer containers used in restaurants today, with a rusted screw lid and only a shallow puddle of paint left in the bottom, swirly and oily. The brush was from an old watercolor set, bristles worn, stiff with dried paint. It worked more like a swab than a brush, but I used it to stir the gold paint and it loosened up some. Then I painted the shoulder blade, hanging it from a string to finish the last part. I dropped the empty jar and ruined paintbrush in the garbage. My fingertips were smudged with gold. Straight Arrow had his palomino and secret cave of gold and I had my golden shoulder blade.

*   *   *

Later that summer, at almost exactly the same spot in the gorge where the deer's body had been, I found three more deer, all in a sprawled heap. Partially on top of them was a dead dog, a boxer. My idea about how the first deer had died was confirmed. The dog that had been chasing them had also gone over the gorge cliff in the dark. This time I had spotted them from quite a distance away. I did not go back to witness the slow deterioration of these bodies.

*   *   *

Somewhere in the lower river gorge, perhaps wedged in the rocks under the rapids, or carried off by the current and settled into the bottom-silt of Lake Ontario, there were once buffalo bones. Some remnants may still be buried there, preserved in the cold airless dark. These are bones that the bone collectors didn't get. This was before the great buffalo slaughter began in earnest, but not so long ago that they were bones from the wood's bison, which roamed along the river before white people arrived. Those bones have also undoubtedly disintegrated in the soil of what would later be called the Niagara Frontier.

A single buffalo went over the falls in 1827, as an entertainment, September 8th, to be exact. This was sixty-four years and six days after the Devil's Hole Massacre if anyone's keeping count. Dates are important in history, aren't they? To say the buffalo "went" over the falls is misleading, suggesting a willingness. The buffalo was actually "sent" over. Some of Niagara's early entrepreneurs arranged it. I wrote about this in a poem called "Looking For

Niagara," which I'll paraphrase here, so the story can be told again.

The following information appeared on handbills around Niagara about one hundred and seventy-five years ago: The schooner Michigan with "a cargo of ferocious wild animals" will be floated "over the falls of NIAGARA 8th September 1827 at 3 o'clock," after "the greatest exertions... to procure Animals of the most ferocious kind, such as Panthers, Wild Cats and Wolves; but in lieu of these, which it may be impossible to obtain, a few vicious or worthless Dogs."

On the day of the spectacle, this turned out to be a buffalo, two bears, two raccoons, a dog, and a goose. Twenty-five thousand people, who knew what entertainment was when they saw it, lined the riverbanks, cheering and gasping. The buffalo lowered its head, got into a defensive posture against the roar of the water, hooves splintering deck planks as it heaved to stay balanced, and then went down, swallowed up, far from the prairie, but cheered by the crowd.

* * *

We don't want to forget that worthless "Dog," do we? Or the two bears, and two raccoons, either, for that matter. (The goose was the survivor who lived to tell the tale.) We wonder how that Dog ended up there. Was it a stray, or an old Dog that hung around some tavern, or some kid's buddy that got snatched up and pressed into service? They put a rope around his neck and led him to the ship, where he was introduced to the entertainment business, bewildered, for a one-time performance. What was the Dog's name? Do you think it was Lassie? Then you choose a name for this Dog. The river's attending to a lot of bones, that's for sure, deer and Dog, bear and raccoon, and buffalo, and people, too, not that we intend to add them as a footnote.

* * *

Newspaper stories of deer crashing through the glass patio

doors and thrashing around in the breakfast nook before they bleed to death in the family room grow increasingly commonplace. There are just too many deer. But the idea of purposefully killing healthy suburban deer to reduce their numbers is abhorrent to many.

Sanderson mentioned this deer glut over fifty years ago, writing "they have become so over abundant in several areas in recent years that they have had to be declared pests for their own protection, lest they eliminate their natural food, and die of starvation or pestilence." It's not clear that making a "pest declaration" solved anything. Sanderson's book was published about the same time I carried off the shoulder blade.

Eighteen years later, the pestilence he'd predicted arrived. A disorder involving loss of balance and extreme malnutrition leading to death had been discovered in deer in Montana. It is called Chronic Wasting Disease, similar to mad cow disease in cattle. In twenty years the disease had moved at least six hundred miles, perhaps over eight hundred, from Montana into the forests of Wisconsin in a concentration heavy enough to cause an extreme response. Plans were made to kill at least 15,000 deer in one area, the killing to be done by sharpshooters, hunters, farmers, and others. Speculation says the carcasses will end up in secure landfills.

This drastic thinning of the herd, it is hoped, will eliminate, or at least slow, the spread of the disease. If this doesn't happen, it will network through the woods, infecting the deer of the east all the way to the Atlantic, spreading most rapidly where their numbers are highest. You can estimate how many years this will take. It may also travel in other directions, of course, including into the human population. It's not known if the disease can do this in its present form.

* * *

Hundreds of thousands of deer were killed, along with the buffalo, in the latter half of the eighteen hundreds. If you wanted a buckskin shirt, jacket, or leggings, that was the time. Five or six inch fringes? On sleeves and pant seams both? No problem. These were believed to aid in the wicking away of water during rain or wet snowfall. Getting wet was buckskin's only drawback. It soaked up water readily and didn't dry quickly. Afterward, it had to be "worked" to restore its original body and flexibility.

In 1873 Levi Strauss patented Levi's, those heavy cotton pants with riveted pockets and seams. They dried out just fine. Over the next quarter century, miners, loggers, prospectors, and the aging remnants of the frontiersmen all went to Levi's. Fifty years later there were many different brands of denim pants, shirts, and jackets. Some of the beats wore them, and then more of the hippies, with lots of colorful and sometimes unneeded patches or big holes at the knees, this to suggest they'd been worn out doing honest hard work. Thus, wearing clothing that signaled a rejection of capitalism, the weekend hippie emerged, sandpapering the knees out of new jeans during weekday evenings to have appropriate wear for weekend partying. Somewhere in these years pre-faded jeans and jackets hit the market, clothing with an instant past. They'd been around, those old jeans had.

Preceding all this were the actually poor, for whom the jeans iron-on patch caused a vague shame. They didn't know their holey clothes and iron-ons were actually holy, thin badges of honor for the knees. They had clouded feelings that they were losers, failing to prosper in a world of money. All this, of course, is generalization, speculation, oversimplification, and distortion. History works that way a lot.

*   *   *

Items in *The Buffalo News*: a little over a hundred years after the slaughter of the great buffalo herds, a dozen fiberglass replicas of buffalo, painted black and brown for realism, and mounted on concrete bases, were placed along the State Thruway, near Buffalo, New York. These were part of the herd that had escaped being decorated by artists some time earlier. Now they were being used to

celebrate the completed construction of an eight-lane Thruway section, the first in the western part of the state. The project manager
said, "it's so classy having four lanes in each direction, it seemed
appropriate to add the bison.... I think daily commuters will get an
upbeat feeling from it."

There'd been plans to plant "ornamental" prairie grass around
the buffalo replicas, but when I recently drove by, the grass around
them appeared to have been cut short, and the small herd had already scattered, five in one area, three in another. They tended to be
distracting as some officials of the Thruway Authority had feared,
standing motionless in grassy areas alongside streaming traffic, un-
derpasses, overpasses, but all the migrating vehicles stayed on the
highway, and I resisted the impulse to pull over, to climb the railing to search for those missing ruts of the Oregon Trail. It would
have been appropriate for realism's sake to add enormous heaps of
buffalo bones to the tableau, skulls and so on, also of fiberglass,
painted white, fused together so they couldn't be stolen, and some
replicas of dead Indians, too. What do you think? Too distracting?

* * *

Genuine buffalo bones may be available for those of us who are
interested. According to a *U.S. News and World Report* article of
9 June 2003, 25,340 buffalo were slaughtered in the United States
for meat in 2003. These had been raised for consumption in a hu-
mane way, we are reassured, as were other "exotic meats," including camels, lions, and zebras. Toss in an aardvark or two and it's
exotic meats from A to Z.

We have the MGM lion, the Cowardly Lion, The Lion King,
and lion steak at about $35.00 a pound. In ancient Rome, people,
especially Christians, were thrown to the lions and devoured. Now
we're getting even. Is there, or has there ever been, a creature on
earth, mythological or otherwise, that humans would refuse to eat?
Unicorn would be $1000 a pound. We'd deep fry angels if we could
figure out a way to net them.

Mitterand eating those song birds doesn't seem so vulgar now, does it? But the image persists. Him with his head and face draped under a white linen cloth, according to custom, chewing away. It is said this drapery intensifies the gustatory experience, isolating the diner from distraction while concentrating the odor of the cooked birds, which are eaten whole and undressed, and permitting the taste buds an unhindered focus. It also involves such private moments that the look of exquisite pleasure on the diner's face shouldn't be witnessed by anyone. But such heads and faces should also be covered out of shame.

* * *

Just last week the newspaper supplement *Night & Day* ran a feature about the Allentown Art Festival in Buffalo, New York, discussing the work of photographer Cliff Burch and his wife, who take pictures of animals in their natural environments. Reproduced in the article is a photograph of a buffalo taken at Yellowstone National Park. It's a massive creature, taking up two thirds of the picture, humped back and cape looming above the broad head and horns. It's just standing there, halfway between directly facing the lens and being broadside, sparse grass to its knees. Its picture has been snapped thousands of times at Yellowstone and it's allowing it to happen again. It's relaxed, but in a posture suggestive of explosive energy, shadow of horn on its shoulder, genetics going back to its ancestor on the cave wall.

The caption under the photograph says this "wild buffalo" has been captured on film. There's another kind of buffalo? It's tough enough to imagine the 25,340 buffalo, docile, heads down, shuffling into the slaughtering chutes, but maybe it does happen that way.

* * *

In the *Buffalo News* classifieds there's an ad under "Miscellaneous for Sale," beneath an icon of a buffalo in side view, in black ink, its slightly elevated tail making it just over a half inch long, tiny horn and eye in white. The words are, "Herd About Buffalo: Full-sized, unpainted fiberglass buffalo," followed by a phone number. The ad, which I first noticed in April of 2004, has been running continuously for over three years. The original decorated buffaloes were displayed in 2000. Today is 14 September 2007, the two hundred and forty-fourth anniversary of the Devil's Hole Massacre, and that little silhouette of the buffalo is still in the news.

*   *   *

People have to eat. The messianic among us are vegetarians. The rest of us are flesh eaters. Those in search of a personality eat lion as a conversation starter. I once wrote a long poem entitled *Hunger*. It wasn't very good. Perhaps you know of a poem by Stafford, "Written on the Stub of the First Paycheck." The second to last line is "Every dodging animal carries my hope in Nevada." I love that poem. Bing Crosby is mentioned in it. I'd like to believe that deer of mine leapt into the dark air of the Niagara Gorge thinking it would touch gracefully down onto a rolling, grassy plain, with patterns of young saplings sprouting along a river bottom, visible in the moonlight all the way to the horizon.

*   *   *

A year or two after I imagined the deer soaring over the gorge edge, a news brief appeared in a local paper, one of those filler items, ten sentences, located in the margin of the page. This was December, 2005, about two weeks before Christmas. It was a well-written little AP piece, full of symmetry and irony and death, fact-primed for an urban fairy tale. In Ranson, West Virginia, five deer, all does, leaped to their deaths from the top of a five-story parking garage. A woman saw the deer falling and called the police. Their bodies were found on a service road for the Charles Town Races and Slots, next to a security van. The responding police officer also discovered deer hair and "scratches" on the fifth floor. We'd guess the "scratches" were hoof marks on the concrete, wouldn't we? Trees were visible in the distance from the top of the garage and the officer speculated the deer had been fooled by the trees, "mistakenly thinking they were close to home."

*   *   *

This story grows around six sheets of paper just slightly larger than the Straight Arrow cards. These pages survive from years ago when DRW published *Hunger*. Some of the story may be dream, arising from these pages. But I have a golden memory of DRW sitting at his kitchen table, in the very same room where the words "book of shit" were first spoken, his head bent earnestly over an old wooden and stained California Job Case. He is selecting letters carefully, little lead-type elements of the alphabet, and lining them up, putting them together to spell words. He is determined to publish *Hunger,* a poem that simplified the world into two kinds of people, the "eaters" and the "eaten," as a chapbook – and this would be real printing.

This was years before "desktop publishing" would become a common phrase. This was the era of mimeos, of carbon copies. This was long before tons of "arts" grants were available for such activities, when those who did such things did so because they loved to do them. This was years before DRW became widely known as "DR," said aloud as "Dee-Are."

Well, he did it, sweating over the pages, coaxing an old contraption of a roller press with cheap, stamped-metal wheels and a hand crank to work one last time. Where did he even get this stuff? At a rummage sale, garage sale, or at a St. Vincent de Paul thrift store, where it was jumbled behind the sun-streaked glass or on a countertop among dusty table lamps and used toasters? He did a press-run of one hundred and twenty-six copies, I recall, under the imprimatur of Press:Today:Niagara. Already it would be press yesterday. The cover stock was dark gray. The twenty-six collector issues were hand lettered "a" through "z." DR had an instinct for producing a rare book. I know that not all of this is dream because I have a copy of *Hunger* around here somewhere. DR must have kept one. And there is a copy in the Poetry Collection at The State University of New York at Buffalo, where some small part of me will continue to exist, to survive, as long as the library continues to do so. Just today I emailed to check if it were there and a young woman named Susan assured me that it was, and doing fine. She answered questions about it. One of the questions I asked was if it smelled musty. She said yes. That shows the power of the email. If you ask the right question a young woman miles away will delicately sniff your chapbook. It is satisfying to imagine that she actually did so, rather than answering "yes" because all the books there were musty – though even that would reveal something about the state of poetry today. The thought of her sniffing the chapbook is almost better than the thought of her reading it.

But what I really want to know is: what happened to the other one hundred and twenty-three of them? They'd be collector items today, worth lots of money, wouldn't they? I wouldn't sell mine at any price, for obvious reasons. But if you have one, or know someone who does, and are without emotional attachment, I am in the market. Depending on condition, I will offer up to, say, a dollar... or if it is in excellent condition, up to a dollar a page. I will pay the postage. Does that seem fair?

14.

My grandfather McCoy often crawled in through our back door on his hands and knees. This was my mother's father and we all called him "Pa," including my father, as if in some way he was the father of us all.

I never saw this myself. It took place when I was too young to remember. It's in my mind vividly, though, because I heard the story later and because where we lived is so clearly there, the long wooden-floored porch at the back of the house, the old screen door leading into the tiny pantry and then the doorway into the kitchen.

Pa and my father regularly went out drinking together. They'd go out on a Saturday afternoon to pick up a few groceries, to see a man about a dog, or on some other errand, and get back after dark, having "tied one on," as the expression went. That was a common expression during those days, although the 1,528 page *A Dictionary of Slang and Unconventional English,* by Eric Partridge, makes no mention of it. If someone locates the origin, there will be a reward. If it doesn't turn out to date back to a time when the whiskey jug had a handle and the drinker would literally tie it to his belt or around his neck, I'll be disappointed. But I will buy you a beer sometime when you're in the neighborhood.

We'll find some old saloon with worn linoleum on the floor, where it's dim even on a bright summer day, where a ceiling fan turns lazily overhead, and the first dollar is taped to the streaked mirror behind the bar. "Draw two," I'll say to the bartender, gesturing to the selected tap. We'll carry the beer over to a scarred little table and sit down, take a swallow, tell one another some lies, then think long and hard about all things past and future. It's tough to say in which direction most of the thinking will focus.

So here's how the story with my father and Pa proceeds. It's dark and the old Ford comes crunching slowly down the cinder road and turns into the driveway, parks. The car doors open and close. There are footsteps on the back porch, the old, wooden screen door creaks open and slams shut and my father comes into the kitchen, goes to the stove where the drip coffee pot is always on low, pours himself a cup, sits at the kitchen table with his head in his hands, bowed over the coffee, and begins to cry. He's trying to say something, but the words are unintelligible, blurred by his drunkenness and sobbing. He keeps talking and crying, blubbering. Who's he talking to? What's he saying?

Then the screen door slams again and after a few moments Pa crawls into the kitchen on his hands and knees. All this time he's been crawling up the steps and along the porch in the dark. He's so drunk he can't stand up, but he's talking, making absolute sense, every word clear and distinct.

They are perfect drinking companions. One can walk, and one can talk. What could be better than that? Well, you might say, they could both be sober, but if that's your attitude it's easy to see you are a self-righteous prig who has no sense of humor whatsoever.

*   *   *

The chuffing locomotive was an American Flier. Its tiny sound was an echo from locomotives racing over the plains while passengers shot buffalo, from the locomotives pulling freight cars laden with millions of tons of buffalo bones and from locomotives that pulled trains through Niagara Falls, New York, during WWII, soldiers looking out through the dusty passenger car windows at waving schoolchildren.

*   *   *

Take two: buffalo all but gone, cattle drives become cattle cars on the Hannibal and St. Joe and on the Northern, Union, Canadian Pacific. Chinese suffered those iron rails down over the dead, the sleepers. John Henry is in there, steel clanging on steel in mist and smoke, Jack Kerouac is riding along, Underground Railroad, Freedom Road, a thousand songs and stories, gandy dancers, bindle stiffs, and Sandburg's poem, "Limited," where a passenger train pulling a thousand people in all-steel coaches hurtles "across the prairie in blue haze." It was crazy motion rushing ahead, roaring, flailing, erasing and leveling place before highways, moaning and wailing, and fading – new generations already here and coming on that won't have trains running through their dreams.

*   *   *

A man walks into a bar. This is in 1983, in Amsterdam. This isn't Amsterdam, New York, but in the Netherlands, so this is a location with mythic possibilities. There's another man already standing up at the bar, drinking. The man who walks in is William S. Burroughs. The man standing there is Richard Brautigan. This is called a chance encounter.

They are introduced. Brautigan is wearing a tall crowned felt hat with a wide, drooping brim. You may have seen him wearing a similar hat in a book cover photograph. Actually, it may have been the very same hat. Who could say now? Brautigan is extremely intoxicated, inebriated, under the influence, that is to say, drunk. He has, in effect, tied on a good one.

The conversation between the two is limited, not an easy give and take. In some circumstances, I read somewhere, Brautigan was not a loquacious conversationalist, anyway. So Burroughs says a few things, maybe mentions a place of dead roads, and Brautigan makes elliptical replies, empty wine bottles in the old corral, etc. This may be all he's capable of at the time or all he's willing to offer.

Finishing his drink, Brautigan politely excuses himself, then gets down on his hands and knees and crawls away. Some of this is imagined, but not the location, not the chance encounter, and not Brautigan's method of exit from the bar. All these, on good authority, are absolutely true.

* * *

That American Flier was my yearning, my face up close to the department store window, fall-to-sleep wishing and hoping. Pa bought it for me out of his meager pension, I realized when I grew up. It's true he regularly spent money to get crawling drunk, but he didn't have to buy that train. It pulled a boxcar with sliding doors, a tank car, a flatbed for logs, a passenger car, and a caboose. Around and around the base of the Christmas tree it went, little puffs of smoke rising from the smokestack, doing its very serious business.

We lived with railroads, north south, and west, all within ear-shot, one just two small fields away. Night after night while I was in bed the distant slamming of boxcars and ore cars being put together to make a train came in the open window, the huffing of the engines, screeching of wheels on rails, the hissing of released steam. Later, often deep in the night, the hoot and wail of a train whistle rising and falling, sometimes floating on the wind, two short, one long on the way out of town, going somewhere far away. These were calls to be going also, to be riding along, sitting in an open boxcar door, legs dangling, off into the wide world beyond home.

In the appropriate landscape, when the filmmaker wants to create a mood, there's that long mournful train whistle in the distance. Someone's leaving and never coming back.

The coal burning steam engines are all gone now, of course, aside from those museum pieces or curio lines run for tourists, railroad history buffs, nostalgia addicts. Perhaps I'm one of the latter. But if you want to hear those sounds today, you must purchase one of the recordings that are available. Then you can pour yourself a cup of coffee, put on your striped railroad cap, turn up the volume, and close your eyes. It won't be as good as having lived next to the railroads, of course.

*   *   *

Incidentally, Sandburg's "Limited," isn't as good as it used to be, either. Its first line, followed by the rest of the poem, has been ruined, deconstructed by the drug scene. If you are capable of intense concentration, you may be able to reclaim the original poem for a brief time. You might also be able to restore the wilderness and the prairies this way.

*   *   *

During this time of commenting on actual railroads, the little electric train, the American Flier, has continued around the base of the Christmas tree in modest, unceasing pursuit of its manifest destiny. The tree itself is a major element in our scene, shabby in some way, but also resplendent, appealing in its homely detail, an amalgamation of Christmases past bravely maintaining a tradition for Christmases to come. This was in one of the immediate post-War years when the effects of rationing were still felt, when those home on leave wore their service uniforms in public and out to the saloons, and gold stars were still displayed in the front windows of homes.

My father always bought our tree a day or two before Christmas. It was then prices dropped to almost nothing, especially for the lopsided castoffs, the ones that would clearly be leftovers on Christmas day. Our tree came out of that pile.

Home in the living room, the air filled with the fragrance of pine and methodical cursing as my father sawed off a few inches of the trunk so the fresh cut would encourage water absorption, and two or more of the lower branches that would be in the way of the holder. The saw was dull, the pine sap sticky, and the tree flopped around on the carpet like something wounded. My father was not really angry, but felt swearing was a sort of incantation that helped with this kind of work, a belief I've adopted and maintained until the present day. With coat hanger wire he fixed the severed branches into the tree's empty spots, then hammered the spike at the center of the tree holder into the base of the trunk, and righted the tree. Would it stand upright? It had damned well better.

Even so, the tree was never perfectly vertical, and so it would be positioned close into a corner of the room, with the slight lean toward the corner, just in case. A tree in the house, after all, its trunk in a three-legged stand the size of a large soup bowl, couldn't really be trusted. It had already shed a scattering of short needles everywhere in an effort to take over.

Decorating the tree: my father strung the lights, one string of the heavy outdoor variety, the indoor having been in short supply because of the War, he was told, and the rest the old double-wired type, where one loose or burned out bulb put the whole string out, with frayed cloth wires and red, green, and white bulbs. Standing on a chair, he whittled at the topmost branch of the tree with a paring knife until the thin glass base of the spire fit onto it. Then he was done. He might sit down and have a beer. The rest of the family took over.

Others had stars or angels for their tree-top ornament. We had a painted spire of glass from the 1800s, we believed, as old as many of the ball ornaments. These decorations were fancy, fluted, some with one concave side, delicately painted, more fragile than egg shells. Some of the paint had dulled, turned powdery, or flaked away. My mother draped on the garlands, fronds of tarnished gold, some lengths of which had nearly thinned to rope, and the newer, a thin reddish and white plastic mix.

The application of tinsel, the last decoration to be put on the tree, was the source of great contention among both the immediate and extended family. It is worth noting here that tinsel in those days was actually strips of very thin metal which, judging from its weight, had some lead content, and not the strips of synthetic film sold today. There were two methods of tinsel application: 1) the careful and precise placement of a single strand or, at the very most, several strands, onto the tree branches with frequent episodes of standing back to view the effect from all angles. This could take hours. 2) standing back several feet and tossing or flinging the tinsel at the tree. Wherever it landed and hung is where God wanted it to be and it was fun. It was spontaneous, magic, chance. Who knew where it would land or how it would look? Everyone could join in, including the children, and so what if their handfuls of tinsel resembled gobs of silver spaghetti caught in the branches? This was Christmas.

Aunt Honey was of the toss-and-fling school and Aunt Deedee a strand-by-strander. Arguments broke out, but then the adults struggled to be civil because of the season.

The tradition during those years was to do rounds of visiting to exchange gifts, have a drink or two (it was Christmas) and to see one another's decorated trees. At Aunt Deedee's, the tree was festooned with tinsel, long graceful strands from every branch and twig, artfully placed so that the illusion of icicles had been created. It was a glimmering, glittering cone of tinsel with a glimpse of pine visible here and there and lights all of one color, one year blue, the next white. A fluffy white material swirled at the base of the tree, heaped to resemble snow drifts, which it did. There was no electric train. We weren't allowed to approach this tree, but had to admire it from about five feet away, where we stood, hands at our sides, awestruck.

At our house the tree was a phantasmagoric vision of decorations old, new, and homemade dangling from strings, inserted Christmas cards, multi-colored lights and short chains made of construction paper strips draped from one branch to another and stopping abruptly. The tinsel was draped and tossed. I believe my mother rearranged some of the tinsel clots after my sister and I went to bed.

When everything was ready, we had the lighting of the tree. My father inserted the plug into the wall socket, and I was allowed to turn the transformer switch to start the train circling. We all stood back to see how beautiful it was, turned off all the other lights in the room to see Christmas in the corner, as good as any department store window.

*   *   *

It was the night before Christmas when the end of this story took place, and all through the house were family, friends, and neighbors, tree brightly lighted in the corner, train going around. The adults were having a drink. Crackers and cheese might have been set out, the milkweed floss serving tray having been pressed into service. There was a lot of laughter and general merriment. The radio might have been playing. Snow had been falling heavily since mid-afternoon, big flakes whirling in the wind, drifting over the cinder road on which we lived. It was going to be a white Christmas.

Then, from the snow-filled front porch there arose a muffled thumping and stamping. No one exclaimed that it must be St. Nick and, when my father opened the door, in came Uncle Bill, and Uncle Earl, known as Pee Wee, accompanied by a blast of cold air and wind-flung snow, both in their Navy blues, and both stinking drunk. That they were drunk didn't surprise anyone, since they were known to be drinkers, so there was look what the wind blew in, close the door, come in, come on in, close the door, Merry Christmas, and have a drink, as if they hadn't already had enough to float a battleship, as if they weren't already three sheets to the wind, to keep this Navy motif going.

Uncle Bill was his usual self, drunk, and though he was Pa's son, walking, and smiling and snarling and cursing all at the same time out of the corner of his mouth. Pee Wee was on his feet, too, but struggling, leaning backward, catching himself at the last moment and regaining his balance, then swaying to one side or the other until he lifted an arm into the air and his equilibrium returned. He hadn't gotten rid of his sea legs yet. He walked across the living room floor as if it were the heaving deck of a ship, one hand extended to accept the shot of whiskey my father had poured. Uncle Bill had already tossed his shot into his mouth, which served as a funnel to his throat and stomach. "Down the hatch," he growled. Then, although he had little use for family activities, meals, holidays, birthdays, funerals or much of anything else, he appeared to realize it might be appropriate to say something about the decorated tree with the electric train chugging around it. "Well," he said with a twisted smile, looking at it from across the room, "ain't that the cat's ass!"

This caught Pee Wee's attention. Spotting the tree, he went in a straight line toward it, not wavering or staggering at all, though it seemed he had to concentrate to accomplish it. He looked good, hair slicked back, his Navy blues well-fitting and pressed, undoubtedly tailored. The whole family had always remarked on Pee Wee being a smart dresser. He came from the side of the family that applied tinsel strand by strand, however, where all the lights were blue, and our tree was obviously one that could be approached.

He got up real close, his gleaming shoe tips only inches away from the train track. As if mesmerized by the multi-colored lights, he spread his arms wide to embrace the idea of Christmas and fell slowly forward into the tree, crushing it into the corner of the room. Now he was really embracing the tree, clasping it to his chest for support. His feet hadn't moved from their original position. With a convulsive effort he attempted to stand up straight, but overcorrected, and slowly, legs rigid, went over backward, still clutching the tree as if it might save him, down to the floor with a great crashing, the sound of a fighter hitting the canvas, tinsel flying into the air, glass decorations popping, lights snapping out, needles scattering, train derailed, tinsel across the tracks sparking and smoking.

The entire episode was over in just a few seconds. No one had been close enough to catch him, though a few hands had probably stretched out in hopeless gestures from across the room. There had been a collective gasp, a sucking in of breath as he started over backward. Now, in the instant after Pee Wee had hit the floor, just after all the flung tinsel had settled, three or more people shouted simultaneously, my father's voice the loudest, "Jesus Christ!" The true spirit of Christmas had come to our house. This would have been a perfect time for someone to have said, "We'll look back and laugh about this in years to come," but I don't recall that anyone did.

*   *   *

Well, I'd like you to know that I'm looking back and laughing all these years later, anyway, perhaps not laughing right out loud, but when I think about it I get a big, goofy smile on my face and that giddy feeling in my chest that should come out as laughter. Of course, I may be the only one left alive who was there that Christmas Eve, so there's no "we" to laugh with. Only I am left to tell the tale. I am become an ancient mariner. Do you think this story has a chance of making it into an anthology of *Best Loved Christmas Stories*?

*   *   *

There's a picture in my mind from the early sixties, a still life, of a hand-sized Hitachi radio in a cream-colored leather case. This radio hangs from the wrought ironwork of an old floor lamp, just below the shade. The lamp casts a mellow, diffuse cone of light. The picture means Vietnam.

The lamp and radio are in an apartment into which I have moved after getting out of the Army. I'm cleaning, painting the walls. It's after midnight, I'm alone, and the radio is playing, station fading in and out. I'm standing there, head down, thumb on the tuner wheel, slowly adjusting, but what I'm hearing isn't static. It's percussive, tiny sharp noises, one two, the next four closely together, and then a string of them too close in succession to count. For ten or fifteen seconds the noises continue without the pattern repeating and then a voice comes out. What I'd been hearing had been transmitted over the open mike of a war correspondent, the sounds of rifle and automatic weapons of fighting in Vietnam. America had advisors there and the voice went on to say where exactly the fighting was taking place and how many advisors of ours were there, but I've forgotten. We all know how that turned out.

Several weeks before I'd heard Vietnam on the radio, I'd been riding a train from South Carolina home to the Niagara Frontier, wearing khakis so heavily starched the shirt and pants seemed to be cardboard armor plate, bending only at elbows and knees. I'd ended up sitting with a past-middle-aged black man who lived somewhere in the south. I didn't know where exactly, or where he was going, or his name. He didn't know my name, either, or where I was going, except up north. He wasn't going that far. He has a son in the Army, a career man. We get to talking and telling stories. We talk coon hunting and hounds. He's partial to Redbones, Treeing Walkers second favorite. I favor Black and Tans, or a Redtick. He's got some good stories and right in the middle of one about a rattlesnake swimming across a creek (which he called a "branch") holding up its rattles to keep them dry, he reached down into his valise and pulled out a quart jar of moonshine. It's early afternoon. We start passing the jar back and forth. It was the second time I've had moonshine, the first a sip from a PFC in my barracks. The man was smiling and showing me how to tell if it's good stuff – when you give the jar a little shake, it beads up on the inside of the glass. All I'd known about moonshine before this I'd learned from Robert Mitchum in *Thunder Road*.

So there we were, racing through the countryside, with the clickety-clack of the railroad track, car swaying a little side to side, past mile after mile of pine woods and fields, sipping moonshine and telling stories. It couldn't get any better.

An hour later words that came out of my mouth were getting tangled up with my tongue which made the man smile. His words were still rolling out as smoothly as ever. Then he nodded toward the window. We were traveling through a long unbroken stretch of fields, no house or barn visible anywhere.

A short distance from the tracks, a man stood facing the train, pants dropped around his ankles, vigorously masturbating.

He wore a long sleeved shirt and a big, floppy, wide-brimmed hat, brown, if that matters, and it was clear that the train was the object of his rapt attention and furious activity.

When he passed from view, the man asked, "You seeing things yet?" We laughed and laughed and laughed. We continued talking and sipping moonshine. After dark the conversation tapered off and he dozed for a few minutes, then roused himself to say quietly, "Just a poor old crazy man is all he was." I nodded. He closed his eyes again.

I have grown to more fully appreciate over the years that his comment was meant to tell me, a young man, after all, inexperienced in the ways of the world, that this was not the way the world was, that what we'd seen could be set aside, dismissed. While he could have been also reassuring himself in some measure, I believe the remark was for me, the oblique advice of a good old grandfather.

*   *   *

Obviously, I was incapable of accepting that good advice and recently, thinking of trains, the event resurfaced. My American Flyer days far behind, I concluded that the masturbating man in the floppy hat had not been excited by the sight of the train. Nobody loves trains that much, do they? It's far more likely he'd discovered a spectacular outlet for his exhibitionist compulsion. While he probably had to walk some distance to meet the train on time, he avoided being apprehended in a nearby small town or other local venue. Furthermore, he had the reward of being able to expose himself to multiple people in one performance, a serial exhibition to a virtual film strip of shocked and gaping faces streaming by framed in the passenger car windows of the train.

And how would his audience, as offended as they might be, complain? Who would they complain to, the conductor? They probably couldn't even say for sure in which jurisdiction the offense occurred. All that remained for him after the sound of the train faded away was to pull his pants up over his thin pale shanks and start the lonely trudge through the fields back home. For all I know, of course, it might have been a triumphant stroll, back to his kitchen where a train schedule was taped up over the sink, but that's not how I imagined it.

*   *   *

Please consider that a Masturbating Man in Floppy Hat card should be added to the Tarot deck. It might signify one of the following: 1) Gratification will be yours. 2) You will have a large but fleeting audience. 3) Beware of overexposure. 4) The train is leaving without you. Choose one of the aforementioned or make up one of your own.

*   *   *

The image of the masturbating man in the floppy hat has stayed in my mind for a long time. I haven't thought of him very often, perhaps every few years or so when the word "moonshine" gets mentioned or when the subject of train rides comes up in conversation. Now the image is in your mind, too. Don't say I never gave you anything.

*   *   *

One more thing: By this time I knew that Indian Lookout, which I had always imagined to be a natural upcropping of Niagara Gorge stone was, in fact, evidence of commercial intrusion, a remnant, a leftover chunk of gorge wall left standing when a slot for a railroad bed had been blasted away years before. While down below the river flowed, others had imagined a chimney, a castle in the air.

*   *   *

And speaking of rivers, we might live near the Niagara and it may splash and roar in our dreams, hard, glittering, wearing brass knuckles, exhaling chlorine, committing suicide twenty-four hours a day – but it's an imposter, after all, a footnote to the misi zibbi, the Big River, the Great River whose watershed nearly reaches us on the Niagara Frontier.

That river, the Mississippi, belongs to Mark Twain, and cannot be repossessed ever, draining the guts of a continent, where ghost steamboats churn eternally, run aground by the railroads, where the cotton barges floated, where the raft carrying Huck Finn and Jim will swing into the current a thousand times a day and into the evenings gently floating. Mists swirl around them, but the moral vision of Twain is not dimmed. It is powerful and shimmering still, because of the age in which it was formed, because the wound it probed is not yet healed.

Twain is twelve feet deep, and twelve feet tall, as well, though he traveled west, removing himself from the immediacy of the bloody Civil War, afterward pausing long enough to write a brief narrative about his visit to Niagara, in which this great humorist, man of understanding and sorrow and love and compassion blinked, faltered, as he simultaneously mocked the Irish and Native Americans.

What was happening there, Mark Twain? Were you having a bad day? Were you hung over, having tied one on the night before? Did someone cheat you out of ten dollars? Did they sell you a chunk of "Niagara spar" and tell you it was petrified mist from the waterfalls? Well, that is part of what we do here. We will break your frigging heart. What you wrote was not funny, Mark, not funny at all. We will continue to honor you for what you wrote later, when you were more grown up.

15.

Eighth grade metal shop was a primitive little grotto in North Junior High School, on the ground floor, rear of the building, designed to prepare us for the factories or the trades to which most of us would graduate after high school. There might have been a single power source, one huge electric motor whose energy was distributed around the shop by horizontal shafts and levers that engaged an assortment of lathes, drill presses, milling machines, band saws, and other machinery by pulleys and long leather belts that at least in one place ran to a pulley at the tin ceiling, twelve feet above us. Gas flames pulsated bright orange from a series of small kilns that cradled the blunt heads of soldering irons ready for use, handles protruding over the bench. Against one wall were racks holding lengths of cold rolled steel in varying diameters, sheets of galvanized tin, shimmering new tin, other steel stock. There were dozens of unsafe conditions, in plain sight, but OSHA hadn't been born, so they'd have to wait twenty years to be violations: exposed gears, sharp edges and corners waiting to slice thighs and wrists open, to gouge eyes out, tear fingers off, soldering irons just a few degrees below red hot, able to burn to the bone, leather belts whirling, blurred, waiting to grab a pants leg or shirt sleeve and run a limb around a pulley.

By all rights, we should have gone limping into ninth grade with eye patches, with crooked and scarred fingers, singed hair, puckered burn scars, the still pink rat tracks of newly healed forearm stitches. But we did not. We came through unscathed. We loved it there in metal shop because we were in the eighth grade and we were immortal.

Mr. M., the shop teacher, who wore a suit, white shirt and tie, imagining he was the foreman, or the teacher, which he was, routinely said, in a gravelly voice, "Okay, boys, keep working. I'll be back in a few minutes." This meant at least a half hour, since he was off to visit a woman who taught in one of the upstairs classrooms. This was the signal for us to start chasing one another with hot soldering irons, to spit on torn scraps of paper and stick them onto the racing leather belts, and for one or two of the adventurous to grab hold of the belt speeding to the ceiling pulley, and rise up, letting go at the last instant to drop back to the floor. They were grabbing it before it grabbed them.

We all put in a lot of time doing our milling assignments, band sawing, and knurling exercises, and into soldering little deformed sugar scoops together from patterns we'd cut from tin and bent according to directions. These scoops our mothers dutifully plunged into the sugar containers at home, in spite of the lumpy solder and beads of hardened flux stuck like amber on the internal seams. That is, all of us but one of our classmates, Bill L., who once he discovered he could turn out ball-peen hammer heads and handles on the lathe, went at it as if he were on piece work. No sugar scoops for him. If Mr. M. was out of the shop for forty-five minutes, Bill L. could make a ball-peen hammer, beautiful, perfect diamond knurling on the handle, the whole tool emery-clothed to a silver sheen. He made about a dozen of these, different sizes, during our metal shop weeks.

The last of these was a fourteen incher which he smuggled out of the class by shoving it handle first down inside the front of his pants, the head hooked over his belt, his untucked shirt hanging over it. This last one he revealed to several of us as we walked home together after school, extracting it slowly, still keeping it partly concealed by his shirt. We all greatly admired the perfect gleaming workmanship of the hammer, the nerve it took to keep making them under Mr. M's nose and Bill L's successful thievery. We never told anyone, of course, since we were all from the same tool-poor neighborhood. I'm only telling now since so many years have passed. Bill L. and I lost touch shortly after Junior High. He went on through school to become a Math teacher, I heard, of all things, and has since died. He's beyond all prosecution, now.

I sometimes wonder what became of his collection of ball-peens. Were they passed on to his children? Did he have any children? Did the hammers go in a garage sale for fifty cents each? Did anyone know their history? Do they languish still in a dusty toolbox somewhere? Rust has certainly dulled them, which might have started even weeks after they were made, since the steel we used was especially susceptible to the slightest moisture.

* * *

Whatever their fate, I still think of Bill L. whenever someone asks me, "How's your hammer hanging?" The "g" on "hanging" is never acknowledged by a real speaker of American English, naturally. It's "How's your hammer hangin?" And if you're now beginning to think that I'm gradually working my way around to telling you how my hammer's hangin, you've got, as my father used to say, another think coming. That's my business.

* * *

I will tell you, however, the creation of the most enduring and valuable memory from eighth grade metal shop was incidental, conveyed by a curious little icon of American advertising that is still with us today, all across the nation, unhappily spread widely and grown large. But the message was the thing, after all, perhaps the most important thing I learned in Junior High or in any school thereafter, not that I realized it then, or have followed its guiding light since. Nevertheless, I look back to recognize the tiny doorway that opened to a different path, even if I've failed to walk it. And there's no reason I shouldn't pass it on.

High on the shop wall, about six feet to the left of where Mr. M. had positioned his desk, was an example of sheet metal work that some earlier student had made – or since it was especially well done, perhaps Mr. M. had crafted it himself. He never pointed it out to us, but we passed it each day as we entered the shop and again on our way out.

It was a model of a billboard, the edges folded to make a frame, about eight inches long and five high. From the top edge, supported by gracefully curved steel rods as slim as pencil lead, two small metal cones about half the size of thimbles pointed their wide ends at the face of the billboard. They were supposed to suggest spotlights, which they did, and had been neatly fashioned with one solder joint each, though they had not been wired with actual tiny bulbs. The tin of the entire piece had darkened over the years. Across the top of the billboard were words, the letters formed of melted solder, which read "Thought of the Week."

The face of the billboard had been cleverly slotted so that a piece of paper could be slid between them and held. On this paper the "thought of the week" would be printed. It could be easily changed. During the months we spent in metal shop, however, the words remained the same, printed in ink on paper that had yellowed with age. The words were "Read Good Books." They may have been placed there with the best of intentions when the billboard was brand new.

The students who noticed made fun of it because it never changed. We didn't realize that of all the "thoughts of the week" that could have been there, "Read Good Books" was clearly the best, even if the paper had yellowed and a fine dust had settled over it all. The dark and empty little spotlights were appropriate since the words themselves provided the illumination. If you followed their advice you would have your own thoughts of the week, or the month, or year for all the years of your life and there'd be no need to be rushing up to the billboard each week to see what the oracle had left.

So there you have it, and you can blow off this "thought of the week" on your own, for being obvious, commonplace, mundane, etc., even while you affirm its wisdom. Of course, you say, Read

Good Books, everyone knows that. Well, then, I have a question for you. If you believe Read Good Books is such a great thought, then why the hell are you reading this one?

* * *

What? You're going to try to squirm out of it by noting it doesn't say Read Only Good Books? Shame on you.

* * *

Thought of the week on billboards: they are visual pollution, omnipresent blotches along the roadsides and byways of our nation in growing numbers that could be nearing the three quarters of a million in the near future. There was an estimated 500,000 of them in 1997. Some of us have trained ourselves not to notice them at all, like floaters in the eye, some find them a distraction, and others see them as intrusive, demanding attention and blocking what might otherwise be a more natural view. It's time for them to go. Pass the necessary laws, arrange reparation for the billboard corporations and put thousands of people to work dismantling, transporting, and relocating them.

We've got enough billboards to build a wall one hundred feet high along the remaining 1300 of the 2000 miles of the United States-Mexico border. What's this half-hearted 700 mile effort? Aren't we the most powerful nation on earth? There's the Great Wall of China, the Berlin Wall, the wall that Israel is building, though some call it a "fence." We deserve to have our own wall, our own national monument of embarrassment and shame. When we fail to solve human problems of national, cultural, and economic complexity, then we should build a wall, an actual world representation of the invincible walls in our minds, and a damn big one, too.

A hundred feet high and 2000 miles long seems about right – it'd be visible from outer space. It'd be a tourist attraction. Loudspeakers spaced every five hundred feet could blare out Pink

Floyd's "The Wall" continuously, twenty-four hours a day, louder on holidays. Terrorists would no longer have free passage in or out of the United States. It would inspire drug smugglers to new levels of creativity. We could sell naming rights to the wall. Since its components would have already been designed for such use, we could sell advertising space on it. Job listings could be posted on the Mexican side. The spotlights could be rewired and illumination of the whole wall achieved with solar panels and wind generators. This would provide a wonderful testing and demonstration site for the companies that manufacture such alternative energy devices.

Thousands of people would be employed in the wall construction: design engineers, carpenters, masons, concrete finishers, iron workers, electricians, laborers, and others. Agreements could be forged that would result in the hiring of a significant percent of Mexican workers with union membership, wages, and benefits, of course. Even before the wall was completed it would be slowing the influx of immigrants by providing jobs on the border. Robert Frost, whose 1914 poem "Mending Wall" says that good fences make good neighbors, may have said it best, don't you think? Or is it possible you have misunderstood the poem? You haven't read it? You've forgotten Read Good Books already? "Mending Wall" also says that something doesn't like a wall.

In any case, the billboard wall would be one of those win, win, win, win, win situations we keep hearing about. You can probably think of dozens of other benefits.

Perhaps the most significant, however, would be the opportunity it would provide for the President of Mexico, who, at a media conference in 2087, would stand in front of the wall, faced by cameras and microphones to intone, dramatically, imperiously, cunningly, self-righteously, petulantly, and demandingly, "Estoy hablando al Presidente de los Estados Unidos. ¡Tira esta pared!"

* * *

The total elimination of billboards from American landscapes will probably never be achieved. To reach compromise between the opposing groups that will inevitably arise, such as Burn All Billboards (BAB) and Save our Billboards (SOB), provisions will probably have to be made for some of them, say 1000, to continue to exist. A newly formed governmental agency, Federal Exemptions for Billboard Art (FEBA) would make final decisions about which will survive based on historical significance or exceptional artistic value. One or more billboards on Route 66, for example, might qualify on the basis of location and time in service. This was the route, after all, where millions got their kicks, and some recognition needs to be paid. All the billboards that remained would be required to fit into two categories with regard to their displays: 1) public service announcement, or 2) reproductions of fine art, traditional or contemporary. Citizens would be able to petition FEBA with recommendations.

None of this will happen anytime soon, of course. Children entering kindergarten this year will be collecting Social Security checks before this plan gets underway. I have, nevertheless, started a rough draft of a petition to FEBA, to recommend the preservation of a billboard I favor.

It's located on the right side of the I-190 in Niagara County, New York, as the driver heads south toward the Grand Island Bridge. It's mounted on a single high pedestal in front of the remnants of a woods where I used to hunt years ago. There are no words on the billboard, nothing blatantly advertised. It's high enough for the sky to be a backdrop in the driver's vision and the billboard itself presents a background of blue that on a good day matches the blue of the real sky. White clouds shaped like buffalo drift across the blue of the billboard. The memories of all the vanished buffalo have been reborn, resurrected there from the artist's vision.

You probably remember how, when you were a child, the clouds took on shapes of fantastic and wonderful creatures, faces, outstretched arms, dragons that transformed themselves or fell to pieces as you gazed. You remember how mare's tails swept across the sky. You haven't got time for that shit anymore, do you? You're all grown up now. You'd plunge off the highway at 70 mph, still gazing, late for work for sure. That's why we need that buffalo cloud sky billboard, to remind us of what we've lost. We need to preserve at least a quick look at that mystical rectangle of sky, that doorway in the real, imagined, remembered world.

* * *

The house is ticking and sighing as old houses do in the dark, hours past midnight. After a century and a half, it has the right to do so. I am stretched out in bed, unable to sleep, wondering what Straight Arrow would think of this billboard meditation, and how the trinity of Burroughs, Edgar, John, and William, would react. Straight Arrow would be with me on this one, I believe. He'd sneak with me through the night to the cloud buffalo billboard and, because he knows how to make rope to do things with the right sort of knots, would fashion a sling to pull me up to the face of the billboard. Suspended in the glare of the spotlights, I'd spray paint a broken black spear into the biggest of the buffalo, and descend soundlessly to the ground again as gently as the fog gathering there, clouds the earth has captured, blurring familiar terrain and easing us into dreaming.

We pass the Burroughses on the way home, each drifting through the fog alone and looking straight ahead, lost ghosts. They don't appear to notice us. It's a long walk home. We avoid roads as much as we can. The long grasses of the fields are wet with dew and our feet are soaked when we get there.

* * *

You are going to end up working in a factory, just like your old man. It's going to be hotter than the ungreased hubs of hell in there during the summer, and as cold as it is outside during the winter. You're going to be breathing foul dust all day and you'll be so filthy at the end of the shift that when you go home your own kids won't recognize you and will begin to cry. But there is another place. If you can get a job there, working in a factory won't seem so bad after all.

Employees will get an hour for lunch, and up to four fifteen minute breaks a day. Meals will be served to employees in a dining room where men will be charged ten cents per meal and women will eat for free. This factory will have a roof top garden, a library, a large auditorium, and marble-lined baths and showers for employees. There will be so many windows in this factory that people will call it "The Palace of Light." A rich and pleasant aroma will permeate the air inside. The owner will say it is necessary for the factory to be "a temple of cleanliness to have the purest and cleanest of foods."

You may spend all of your working life in this place. But because nothing lasts forever, you may only be there a few years, or even months, before the doors close for good.

This factory actually existed in Niagara Falls, NY. It housed the Shredded Wheat Company, which started in May, 1904. When it began to close over a half century later, the newly formed Niagara County Community College took over the administration building. Eventually, the college was to be housed in a brand new campus, but some old timers still refer to it as Nabisco Tech.

* * *

Out of high school I went to work at International Graphite Electrode where they manufactured graphite electrodes for arc furnaces. Think of them as cylinders of the same material used in lead pencils, only bigger, some of them six feet long and about thirty-two inches in diameter. So that these electrodes could be continuously fed into the arc furnaces as they burned away, the ends were made with tapered, threaded sockets. They could be joined using other threaded graphite pieces that weighed about eighty-five pounds each and were known as nipples.

These were the largest nipples I'd ever seen, but this did not make the factory a sexy place to work. It was low paying, sour smelling, and dirty. Graphite dust floated in the air, settling on equipment, machinery, and other tools, underfoot, making clothing black, even shiny on often touched surfaces. An hour into the shift, hands and faces were smudged or solid black. The only areas of visibly clean skin were the lips and around the mouth where workers had been unconsciously licking, and sometimes eyelids, around the eyes, something to do with blinking. Unless you took soap and a stiff brush to them every day, the whorls of your fingerprints remained clearly outlined with embedded graphite. You could get hammered in some bar, then hold your fingertips up a few inches from your face and say, "Yep. It's still me."

* * *

Remove the graphite from a couple thousand No. 2 pencils and put it all in an old dishpan. Plunge your hands into the pieces and swish them around for five minutes or so, breaking the graphite into yet smaller fragments. Do this in the hot sun. Now rub your hands over your face and go look in a mirror. You will get some idea of the job, nowhere near a full understanding, but something.

* * *

At noon I'd take my bag lunch out on the loading dock with J. Burke. That probably wasn't his name. He might have been Birk, or Berch, or Berk, but he was six or seven years older than I was and knew how to make the best of things, walk on the sunny side, etc., an attitude I've often admired.

The loading dock was a long massive block of concrete, the end level with the factory floor, the length extending outside, high enough so that a tow motor could drive straight into the boxcars on the rail line that was right next to it. We'd sit on the edge, legs dangling, or on low stacks of pallets that were on the dock.

Instead of a lunch, J.B. always brought a quart thermos full of cold beer. Out on the dock one day, under a blazing sun, he stripped his shirt off, revealing a pasty torso, with some gray half-tones where graphite dust had worked its way through. His hands and face were black. He unscrewed the thermos, poured himself a capful, drank it down and slowly refilled it. I was eating a peanut butter sandwich, the graphite from my fingers smudging off on the soft bread. J.B. looked all around, at the goldenrod and thistle growing along the railroad track, at the big tin-covered factory buildings, rusty, with broken windows high up, and at the sun-filled, blue sky, a few white clouds drifting.

"All the comforts of home," he announced. "Sitting in the sun and having a beer."

I gave him a look and kept eating my sandwich.

"Well, it is a little dirty," he admitted, "but what the hell, you can't have everything."

*   *   *

The old-timers at International Graphite said I'd never last and they were right. I worked there for nine months, long enough for something to be born, and then quit – just in time to make the first day of hunting season. In fact, I may have asked to have that day off, and decided to quit when the request was turned down. Opening day was pheasant season, a short season to begin with, so I shouldn't have to say more about that. I remember all my opening days with happiness, even joy. Nine months at the factory gave me a handful of moments worth remembering, but in the end, the best memory I have of the place is walking out through the gate for the last time, the feeling of absolute freedom, that anything was possible. I mean, isn't your work supposed to be your happiness?

Most of these so-called old-timers were only in their thirties and forties, maybe a few in their fifties, with too much time in to quit, too many families and mortgages and too much seniority accumulating day by day, every week to be thinking of some other path they might have taken. Those paths had all grown in by the time I got there. So there was some toughness associated with the recognition, and perhaps resignation, that they were in it for the long haul and some pleasure in pointing out to the new kid that he didn't have it.

When they'd see me sagging halfway through the morning they'd start in with out drinking too late, huh, chasing them women, closing them bars, which was true, and finish up with "You don't know what work is. You ain't going to make it here."

"You're right," I'd say. "I'm just here gathering material for a book. Keep messing with me, I'll put you in it."

This, for some reason, used to really piss some of them off. So, naturally, I kept it up. Now I was the one having the fun, and so after a while we just put in our shifts and went home, waiting for the next hire to pick on.

Six memories from I.G.E. that stuck:

One. Riding to work with the good humored Roger B., who'd pick me up on Hyde Park Boulevard across from Brunette's Groceries and we'd roar down the Boulevard, up over the railroad tracks on Hyde Park Bridge, down Porter onto New Road, which was cinders and might actually have been new once, and streaking through the factory gate, skidding in a cloud of dust to a stop at the time shack, where I'd launch out of the car and run to punch us both in while he parked. I don't remember being a minute early or a minute late. The time clock always read <u>exactly</u> on the hour, the beginning of the shift. A couple of years later, Roger B. was killed in a intersection accident when somebody ran a stop sign and nailed him broadside.

Two. The guy who, shortly after the shift started and the foreman handed out the day's assignments, routinely grabbed a newspaper and headed for the bathroom. He'd go into a stall and close the door, emerging about an hour later, just in time for the first break. Others had to work harder to pick up his share, but what really got to us was he'd spent all that time in there pretending he could read.

Three. The big six-foot electrodes come out of the furnaces over specs on diameter. They're electric-chainfalled into big lathes where they are sanded down, gauged until they meet acceptable tolerances. Little skinny-ass guy from West Virginia leaning forward with both hands on a full sheet of sandpaper, back and forth on that spinning cylinder, clouds of carbon spewing off until his upper body disappears. His family probably worked in the coal mines for generations. This is child's play to him. His voice comes out of the cloud of graphite, singing a Hank Williams song about seeing the light and no more darkness, no more night.

Four. Two of us are asked by the foreman to work through lunch. It's a question that requires no answer. One hundred and seven nipples have to be boxed for shipment. There's a tow motor operator waiting to load them into a boxcar. It seems an inappropriate number, but an order's an order. We've got to assemble the boxes, lower the nipples into them, close and tape the boxes, stack them on pallets, and metal strap them down. If a nipple is lowered into the box off-center and one of the thread catches an edge of the box, the cardboard crumples and the foreman, who's watching, demands a new box. This happens eight or ten times. We're sweating.

The guy working with me is slightly built, from Hungary. He's told me he had a better life in his homeland, where he was some kind of professional. Here, his left safety shoe has a loose sole and the seam down the back of the heel is broken open. This slows him down. He's got to half shuffle and step carefully to keep the shoe on his foot. We are required to buy our own safety shoes and he doesn't want to spend the money on a new pair to have them ruined by graphite. He's tied the sole up, but the string keeps slipping off and finally he just puts up with the flapping sole, which is loose all the way back to the instep. When we finish boxing the nipples, he's bent over and straightens up very slowly, flexing his blackened fingers. The foreman says, "Okay, you can go to lunch now. Take your time."

As soon as we're out of sight, I stop. "I'm having a smoke," I call over my shoulder. "He said take our time." The guy from Hungary is a little way behind. He catches up, his left foot sliding, the sole flapping with a popping noise in his effort to hurry. He glances first one way and then the other to make sure no informer is eavesdropping, then leans close. "Dis is hell," he confides in a lowered voice.

Five. The heavy paper tape used to seal the cardboard boxes is about two inches wide, bright orange with the letters "IGE" printed in heavy black every few inches on one side and glue on the other. It comes in rolls about six inches in diameter, which fit into a dispenser about the size of a four slice toaster. This contraption holds water and permits a length of tape to be pulled and torn off against a serrated edge. The glue gets wet as it's pulled. It's like a big scotch tape holder with water added.

We also use the tape for mending holes in our blue jeans, which are usually worn out or ripped at the knees. Two or three strips around the leg seals up the hole for the day and keeps the graphite dust out – guys walking around with bright orange tape and IGE, IGE, IGE on their legs as if this were the most normal thing in the world.

There's one of these tape dispensers in the entire factory and it's in rough shape, the serrated teeth dulled, the tape spool bent. If it's needed in more than one place, arguments break out.

Suddenly, one Monday morning, a brand new tape machine appears. Four of us assigned to a box-making job get the new one and we're in good spirits. We're all standing around smoking, the machine sitting in our midst on a stack of pallets.

Then somebody says, "Here comes Vince!" He's about a hundred feet away, eyes fixed on us from behind his horn rimmed glasses, scowling, coming fast. He's never been caught smiling and he's really looking enraged now. His shock of black hair is bouncing as he comes. He swoops into our group, snatches up the new tape dispenser, and tucks it under his left arm. "I've got seniority!" he screams. He stands there a moment, glaring at us. No one says anything. He walks away, the dispenser clutched tightly against his body. No one laughs.

Six. Spinning a threaded aluminum ring gauge down over each nipple was a required test. But every tenth nipple had to be tested by screwing it into the end socket of an electrode. This was to check if it threaded in smoothly and went in to the required depth in an actual simulation.

Do you like that "actual simulation" phrase? Well, we didn't screw on another electrode to the protruding half of the nipple, did we? What we did, however, was demanding enough. The eighty-five pound nipple had to be held level, cradled in hands and balanced on forearms, as it was inserted into the socket, then turned evenly until the threads started. Obviously, after it was turned all the way in, it had to be unscrewed.

Once, as I was unscrewing a nipple, it jumped a thread and caught the tip of my left index finger, pinching a blob of flesh nearly off. A small portion did leave my finger, maybe a chunk a third the size of a pencil eraser, and the rest was piled up and hanging on the very end, blood, blob, and graphite, as much black as red. Surprisingly, it didn't hurt that much. I pushed the blob back in place and wrapped a paper towel tightly around it. At home, I unwound the towel and put on an adhesive bandage. There was a lot of graphite mixed in with the flesh. I could feel my heart beating in it that night. The place that had revealed my fingerprints had now taken one of them back, I thought.

I kept it covered for a couple of weeks, never washing the fingertip or even looking at it directly when changing the bandage. More graphite worked in under that bandage every day. I knew the end of my finger would be graphite black forever.

When the healing was done, I was witness to a tiny miracle that had taken place on the end of my finger – the blob had grown back as if it had remembered being a fingertip, the graphite had disappeared and my fingerprint was miraculously reappearing. Today, that finger end is slightly thinner than its counterpart on the other hand, a scarcely noticeable difference, and I hadn't thought about it for years until I stirred up memories of I.G. while writing this. Some little part of my flesh and blood went into an arc furnace somewhere and blazed up in light as bright as the sun, molten steel flowing. I'd like to think it ended up transformed, incorporated into a molecule of bridge girder, an axe head, or a shotgun, rather than some long ago junked car body or refrigerator door, but chances of that are probably very slim.

16.

When we last saw Pee Wee, he was under the Christmas tree. This gives a new meaning to "Oh, look what's under the tree!" As he slowly toppled over backward, tree following him down like a compliant lover, someone should have yelled "tim-ber!" And this might have happened in some other home, in some other gathering where they were inclined to make a quick joke about such occurrences. At our house, however, with Christmas Eve poised on the brink, a half dozen or more people leapt to pull it back.

Someone yanked the plugs for the tree lights and train out of the wall and someone else pried Pee Wee's arms from around the tree and repositioned it in the corner. "Who hit me?" he asked, still flat on his back. "I'll kill the sonofabitch!" Two people hauled him to his feet and he watched others wipe up spilled water, refill the tree stand, re-adjust light strings and garlands, tighten loosened bulbs, put the American Flyer and its cars back on track, and pick up fragments of broken ornaments. He remembered then and mumbled something about the tree falling on him.

Many hands plucked tinsel from his uniform and tossed it back onto the tree. Pee Wee himself located a few strands on his sleeve and stepped forward, with support, to carefully hang them onto a branch. Some family traditions refuse to die.

They left then, Pee Wee and Uncle Bill, and not to overdo this, but what actually happens is sometimes over the top, and so it must be reported that Pee Wee plunged off the railingless front porch into the snow-mounded shrubbery. Unhurt, he was extricated by a couple of men from the house, and helped into the car. They drove off and we watched them go, taillights like two fading Christmas tree lights as the car moved slowly away, plowing through the drifting and falling snow, probably toward one of the bars at the end of the block. "Merry Christmas!" some of us shouted. Inside the house, the tree lights were working again and the little train was going around and around.

Today, of course, we are all sadder and madder, with heightened awareness about drinking and driving. This was a different time, however, and the War and the millions of dead were millions of reasons for servicemen and women and everyone else to get drunk and stay that way. All those people who could never again have a shot and a beer for themselves needed others to have one for them, each and every one. And fallout from Hiroshima and Nagasaki had blanketed the earth and was undoubtedly falling gently over the Niagara Frontier in the snowflakes that Christmas Eve.

*   *   *

When I was young and even more foolish than I am now, my friends and I decided our goal would be to have a beer in every bar in the city. Certainly we weren't the first to think of this, though we may have believed we were at the time. It seemed a noble pursuit to us. Each night we started out with the best intentions, but when we'd hit the third or fourth bar, someone in the group would suggest we have one more before moving on. That one would lead to another and then another and that would be the last place we'd drink in that evening. It was an elemental lesson on how the excessive consumption of alcohol prevents the realization of life's goals.

But we got to drink in a lot of bars over a year or so, many times walking from one to the next as our numbers dwindled and the only car owner in the group made the decision he no longer wanted to chase unattainable goals. Some nights just two of us were out there trying to keep the vision alive.

There should be a thousand memories and stories that come out of this journey to the bars, but guess what? Most of it's fogged out, hazed into a smear of impressions, bars with great jukebox selections, Hank Williams, Ernest Tubb, and other country, Bo Diddley, Chuck Berry, and "I Only Have Eyes for You," "So Fine," and all that still of the night doo-wop, and those dim little neighborhood bars where, when you walked in and asked for a beer, all heads turned at the sound of a voice they didn't recognize, and places with gallon jars of sausages in brine sitting up on the bars, and that one saloon on a forgotten street where Hoagy Carmichael's half-brother, who'd taught Hoagy everything he knew, had decided to spend his life in anonymity – every evening descending from his rented upstairs room to play the old rinky-dink piano for hours, for a handful of drinkers and his own entertainment.

Did I make that last one up? There was such a place, I believe. All the people in the bar knew who he was, but only remarked on it casually. It was no big deal. The guy's name was Douglas. Dougie, everyone called him. Play "Stardust," Dougie. And there were all those great, long, and funny conversations, too. If we'd been sober, of course, the conversations would have been irredeemably stupid, but who wanted to admit life was like that?

During this time, I thought later, I might have stepped up to one of the same bars where my father and Pa had leaned, like twins, one foot each on the brass rail. But none of the old-time drinkers had said to me over those months, "Hey, ain't you...? I knew your old man."

* * *

I did get recognized once and that memory is very clear. It was going on midnight. The bar was long, narrow, only about five feet between the bar stools and booths along the opposite wall. My friends and I were in a booth drinking pitchers of beer. The place was packed as it was every night, loud jukebox music, loud din of people talking and shouting, laughing, cursing, people constantly shouldering their way along the bar, edging toward the restrooms at the back, looking for an open spot, returning to seats. Should I say the place was a dive? Is a beer joint one rung up the ladder? All right, then. We were tying one on in a dive.

Our booth is about halfway down the bar and I keep glancing at the people going by and then the flow stops and when I look up there's a guy about my age looking at me. He's swaying slightly, reminiscent of Pee Wee, and he's tilted his head to one side the way people do when they're attempting to focus on something. It's someone I haven't seen since early grade school, but I know him right away. It's Shorty B., the brother of Roger B., I think, who used to ride me to work at I.G. Those behind him are getting impatient because he's stopped, but he doesn't care. He's a tough guy, or I always thought he was, since he saved me from getting beat up a couple of times in grade school, facing down two and three kids at once.

"Little Bobby Baxter," he said, slowly, "I never thought I'd see you in a place like this." He kept looking at me for a moment as if he might be thinking, then moved past.

None of my friends made a joke out of this, which was unusual. I believe the reason they said nothing was the lack of sarcasm in his voice. What had been there instead was disappointment and sorrow and they'd been taken aback.

Of course, I am only able to say this in retrospect. At the time, the reaction in my head was who in the hell does he think he is, I'm old enough to drink anywhere I want, blah, blah, and other ignorance. Obviously, though, I've thought about it since, several or more times over the years, and have concluded that in his mind he was still my protector, an older brother. Maybe he thought, standing there, that he should have let those kids beat the shit out of me back in grade school, maybe I'd have gotten some sense knocked into me to replace what was beat out. What got to me years later was that he'd accepted being there himself.

If you think I stopped drinking because of this, then you've got another think coming, as my father used to say.

Over forty-five years passed before I saw Shorty's face again, when I turned a newspaper page and there he was looking out of a photograph accompanying an obituary notice. It was like being punched in the chest real hard.

*   *   *

The next time I saw Uncle Earl, aka Pee Wee, was the last time, about twelve years after that Christmas Eve, and he was a lone, small figure in a scene that could otherwise have been, on canvas, a Hopper painting.

I'm standing in a field that hundreds of years before had been part of the Bloody Run watershed. The field is growing up in thorny brush, some patches thick and over six feet. It's on an industrial edge of Niagara Falls, cavernous National Carbon factory buildings to the west, the smoke stack of Pittsburgh Metallurgical to the northwest, the one-story General Abrasive office building to the north, flanked by its factory buildings, and Vanadium to the northeast.

Everything is backdropped by a dark, overcast sky. It's early fall, chilly, gusty winds moving across the field. It must be a Saturday, because there are only a few cars in the parking lot, an area of broken blacktop at the far edge of the field, along College Avenue, across from General Abrasive. At this end of the avenue, "college" seems a cruel joke of a name, though I don't think of this at the time. I'm facing General Abrasive, with Hyde Park Boulevard at the field edge off to my right. Behind me and to the left about a thousand feet, hidden by tall grass and brush, is the cellar, the same size as Thoreau's cabin, where I had gone swimming years before.

While I'm standing there, Pee Wee comes out of the front door of General Abrasive and walks across the street into the parking lot. His hairline has receded, but he still combs it straight back. His face and high forehead are bronzed from summer. He's wearing a suit and tie, an unbuttoned topcoat. He walks to the center of the parking lot and stops, looking slowly around. There's no car nearby. He doesn't see me in the field. The wind catches one side of his topcoat and it flares out.

*   *   *

What I was doing in the field, I don't remember. I must have been running the dogs, rabbit hounds, beagles named Hank and Lash. I had no other reason to be there. Hank had been named after Hank Snow, but when I got him I renamed him Hank after Hank Williams. He had a long bay on the trail, mournful, a yodel. Lash was named after Lash LaRue. She was as quick as a whip, had a high-pitched yammer of a voice, and so the two of them made some good sounds running a rabbit together. I never called out to Pee Wee, who probably wouldn't have recognized me anyway, and don't remember him getting into his car or anything else about him that day, other than what I have told you. In my mind, he's still standing in that parking lot.

*   *   *

Uncle Bill was a binge drinker and a mean drunk, too, I understand. Hank Williams, I read or heard somewhere, had a similar pattern to his drinking, though I never heard he was a mean drunk, breaking dishes one after the other like Uncle Bill, who once grabbed a broom and swept the family Pekingese down the cellar stairs. The dog was unhurt, but a fast learner. After its flight down the cellar stairs it never came yapping around his ankles again. In a poem by James Tate entitled "Flight," there's a line or two about a man in the next door apartment teaching his dog to fly. You don't see this, but there are sounds you imagine, or the narrator of the poem does. It's a poem about imagination, among other things.

So if you've never been in a room with a drunk who is breaking dishes, you've got to imagine the repeated explosions of dishware shattering, the lighter sounds of fragments bouncing across the floor, into the sink. Uncle Bill's dish breaking was systematic, accompanied by steady and vicious cursing. He'd jerk open the kitchen cabinet door and go through the dishes, plates, saucers, cups, and bowls, one by one flinging them onto the floor and into the walls. This is why, in our family, we have no china heirlooms, no sets of dishes to pass on.

During these episodes, Uncle Bill's niece, Savilla, ten years old, hid by locking herself in the closet of the upstairs bathroom. This was the niece who put together little wooden models of the ships on which her Uncle had served: the USS Northampton, the USS Yorktown, USS Henderson, USS Paul Jones, USS Salt Lake City, USS Johnson, USS Stribling, USS Shenandoah, and the USS Ingraham, hand-sanded and glued, all detailed, all carefully painted battleship gray. Uncle Bill had seen action at the Battle of Midway, and in the Java Sea, Philippines, Bali Strait, and Aleutian Islands. On leave, the action continued in his mission to destroy the dishes at his sister's house, his rejection of civilian life and all things domestic, propaganda, every bit of it. At sea in both Navy and later Merchant Marine, he stayed sober. On shore, home on leave, he stayed drunk.

Hank Williams died, stretched out in the backseat of a car parked on the street. When I heard this, I was drunk myself. Hank Williams, dead. It was hard to put those words together. No more honky-tonk. What makes this pathetic is that he'd been dead five or six years before I heard about it. I walked home from the bars alone, down 18th Street in Niagara Falls, New York, looking for an open coffee shop. They were all closed and the bars, too. The houses were dark, empty cars lined up along the curb under the dim streetlights. I was the only one on the sidewalk. This is where, when I think of Hank Williams dying, he actually died, in a parked car somewhere in the vicinity of 18th Street and Michigan Avenue, Niagara Falls, New York.

*   *   *

The place is packed and noisy, late in the evening. As closing time approaches, drinkers grow more agitated. Will they be able to drink enough before last call? Who will get to go home with the girls? Four of us were crowded into a booth, drinking pitchers of beer, all young men who otherwise should have joined the Army to break the trajectory of our lives, in that same saloon where I'd been recognized, when an excited young woman approached us in a hurry. She was a regular, as foul mouthed on occasion as any of us, with very black, bobbed hair and skin as pale and smooth as milk over porcelain. Though names continue to be important, I won't reveal hers, but her initials were P.S.

"Watch my purse, you guys," she said, sliding it onto the table. "I'll be back in ten minutes. There's this old man giving me twenty bucks for a quick lay out back."

This was candid, even for P.S., who might have had more to drink that night than usual, but not so much that she didn't catch the looks on our faces.

She tilted her head back. "*With* a rubber, of course!" she announced.

Then we all broke out laughing and she left in a huff. She was back in under ten minutes to retrieve her purse. She didn't buy us a round, but it had felt good to be trusted.

Her initials could have stood for "Post Script" and I'm sure there is more to her story, but I don't know it, and would say the same thing if I did. If she is still alive, she is old enough to be a grandmother and deserves to tape whatever snapshots she wants into those scrapbooks she puts together with her grandchildren.

P.S. Do you think she took someone home with her that night?

*   *   *

It happened nearly fifty years ago, in Louisiana or Missouri or even Georgia, somewhere in the south, where I was hitchhiking and got a ride from a man, perhaps approaching middle age, though he could have been younger. I don't remember what kind of car he was driving, what he looked like, how long a ride he gave me, what we drove past. But I remember his name. After he'd asked mine, he said, "I'm going to tell you my name and you're never going to forget it. It's Henry Parsons. Little bald-headed fella in the comic strips? And two preachers."

*   *   *

Uncle Bill's last name was McCoy. Over the years that side of the family made guarded references to the Hatfields, but a direct connection seems unlikely. The killing down there was already underway by the time Pa was eight years old, and he was born and raised in a region of Pennsylvania that was about four hundred miles from the feuding area. I imagine the slow straggling wave of the McCoy clan that came to America migrating toward Appalachia, meandering and stopping, through New York State, into Pennsylvania and Ohio, down the Ohio River to the Big Sandy, the Tug River, and then Pond Creek and Blackberry Fork. The part of the clan from which Pa, my mother and her brother Billy, and then my sister and I, finally emerged just stopped and settled down before they got there. But Uncle Bill fought in gyms around Niagara Falls, boxing under the name Kid McCoy, before he went in the Navy. He probably fought in the bars, too, where his previously beaten opponents would find him drunk and take turns punching him down into the spilled beer and broken glass. It wasn't difficult to find him drunk. Once his face got shoved down onto the bar, shattering his beer glass. There was no cut man available, though he needed one. He was five foot, six and one half inches tall and packed a punch when sober. He was the real McCoy, but no one ever said he could have been a contender.

*   *   *

Speaking of grudges, both petty and long lasting: a biographer of William S. Burroughs wrote about remarks made at a D.H. Lawrence conference, where Burroughs, Leslie Fiedler, and Alan Ginsberg were together on a panel. We have to imagine the audience. Fiedler had held forth at length, until finally Ginsberg interrupted, saying that "Bill" wanted to say something. William S. then offered that he admired and was influenced by Lawrence's *The Plumed Serpent*. Fiedler reacted with the sarcastic comment that he'd thought William S. had been more influenced by Edgar Rice Burroughs. William S. didn't respond. The thought came to him, however, which years later he revealed to biographer Ted Morgan, that a review had said Fiedler's last novel, *Back to China*, was a "mire of baloney."

I mention this only because Fiedler once made a comment so clever about a novel manuscript of mine that for years I considered it to be a compliment. He was slowly pushing the manuscript across the desk toward me with two fingers at the time. I don't know why he said what he did, but knowing so much about love and death, he may have wanted to give me a little death right there, disguised as love. I've recently decided he hadn't even read the manuscript. He might have already concluded at this time in his life that Stephen King had earned an immortality that would outlast his.

So the next time someone compares your writing to that of Edgar Rice Burroughs, say "Thank you very much," and mean it. You should be so lucky. Edgar was a lover of money and what he saw as the good life, a one-time Gatling Gun instructor, a man who lamented the loss of the natural environment and built a suburb of his own to help destroy it. He actually lived there for a while.

At fifteen, he worked on a cattle ranch near the Snake and Raft Rivers, land marked by the ruts of the Oregon Trail. Five years later he enlisted in the Army and became a member of the Seventh Cavalry, the "Bloody Seventh," the unit with history at The Battle of the Little Bighorn and at Wounded Knee. He was assigned to pursue Indians believed to be in the territory, the Apache Kid, Massai, and others, but never saw anything. This was just a few years before the twentieth century began. Like Hitler, Edgar believed in eugenics. Unlike him, he was conflicted by his racist beliefs. Maybe that's too kind. Read *The War Chief*, cowboy. But he was also the father of Tarzan, who sprang as an infant from his imagination and grew to maturity developing all of civilization's instincts. Tarzan taught himself to read without hearing a single human word spoken, he knew how to passionately kiss the first woman he met, without instruction, example, or practice and, though he killed for food and in self defense, he also sometimes killed only for the pleasure it brought him. He lives in the minds of millions around the world. He'll be a hundred years old before too long. When's the last time you created a character like that?

If someone calls your writing a "mire of baloney," you're on your own.

*   *   *

So Hank Williams, dead, and what songs we got are the songs we got though someone will say hey, give the King a mention, say mystery train, okay, but then somebody'd else say hound dog, but that's the real nothing at all, not Bo Diddley whose little girl on the hill tussled and rustled with Buffalo Bill as Bo put the rock in rock and roll and also put the Bo in there with that one song and some people here also remember D.J. Hound Dog Lorenz, the Hound's around, his night-howling, echo-chambering, radiowaving Niagara into squared-up skewed diddly boxes, distorted, crushed up against old clapboard acoustics, sound hole horseshoe, fretted with railroad ties, dark track, high tension wires strung, strummed overhead humming in all directions, over town and arched bridges and out, everybody's stretched guts, waking or sleeping, sleepwalking, drunk, dreaming, all those sounds and songs suspended in air over this twilight city, this tired, old Niagara, honky tonk blues, freight train blues, heard that lonesome whistle, bucket's got a hole in it, long gone lonesome, can't buy no beer, or finally happy, or what passes here, honky tonkin.

*   *   *

Sixteen years after Hank Williams died, Jimi Hendrix powered the Star Spangled Banner into the stratosphere.

17.

Uncle Bill had left home early, anxious to be off to whatever other frontiers he could find. He joined the Navy and spent the War years at sea on various battleships. He made it home on leave for his sister's funeral, an event he noted by sprawling dead drunk on the front lawn, in uniform, after having toured half the bars in the city, dragging along a widow from the neighborhood. The widow hadn't needed a guide, but she and his sister had been friends in the old days. Neither of them showed up for the funeral.

When he retired from the Navy, he became a Merchant Marine until he retired for good, and spent the rest of his life in a loft overlooking the Hudson River.

He spent a lot of time watching ships on the river. He took pictures of people in the streets, people he didn't know and would likely never see again. He had a rowing machine in the sparsely furnished loft. He believed in staying in shape, in personal hygiene. He continued to drink while awake. Each day he carefully lathered up and shaved as if he were getting ready to stand inspection. He brushed his teeth diligently, a glass of vodka and orange juice balanced on the edge of the sink.

*   *   *

What he left behind I now have in a brown paper grocery bag, sitting on the floor beside my chair as I write: 1) a copy of his birth certificate, Niagara Falls, NY (1911), on which the birthplace of his father, Pa, is listed as "Pa." and "Teamster" under "Father's Occupation." 2) an endowment life insurance policy from Prudential for

$5000, taken out in 1934, with quarter-annual premiums of $24.65, payable for sixty-two years, his mother and father named as beneficiaries, never changed. 3) every Navy training course certificate and test passed recording his promotions from Apprentice Seaman to Chief Petty Officer, starting from 1935, to honorable discharge papers, only one 8 ½ x 11 document laminated: his license from the United States Coast Guard certifying him as "chief engineer of steam vessels of any horsepower." 4) a wallet-sized, tri-fold binder label "Continuous Service Certificate" whose inside pages record ship names, dates, combat actions. 5) seven removed sleeve insignias with eagles and stripes, six bars of ribbons, each with different colored sections, some with tiny metal stars—codes for honors, places served, battles. 6) hundreds of loose photographs. 7) his death certificate. 8) his certificate of cremation. 9) his six sentence obituary notice from the Niagara Gazette.

*   *   *

Photographs: there are photographs of ships at sea, foggy, misty, too far off to be recognizable, street scenes, all taken from too great a distance to be focused on individuals, but more on the aggregate, picture of a lone man on a deserted street at dusk, almost half a block distant, nearly a silhouette, walking away.

*   *   *

Self-portraits: out of several hundred photographs there were perhaps a dozen, probably taken with the help of tripod and timer. The earliest of these were just after he retired from the Merchant Marines, bare from the waist up, unsmiling, barrel-chested, heavily muscled arms, looking as if he could still climb into the ring and go a few punishing rounds, giving it out or taking it. In one photo he is bare-ass naked on the rowing machine, side view, big haunch flexed, back erect, into a rowing stroke. There were a couple of pictures of him dressed up, shirt and tie, ready to go somewhere;

several of just his head and shoulders, face not as well-fleshed as earlier, one of these with face unshaven. All but one of these photographs are taken with him standing in front of a closed door or a wall empty of pictures or decorations. He is not smiling in any of them.

Some months or even a year or two before he died, he had an operation to remove a cataract in his right eye. Infection set in and at the conclusion of prolonged treatment, he lost the eye. A series of photographs documents this. Staring straight into the lens, the eye narrows, discolors, turns marbled, disappears. Now one blue eye stares into the lens, the other eyelid sagging over an empty socket. There's one portrait of him dressed up, wearing sunglasses, another with a black patch.

* * *

Some time after this he was taken to emergency because of blood loss caused by liver failure, where he was stabilized by transfusions. When he regained consciousness, the doctor told him, "Drink and die." Being direct was evidently the order of the day for old, one-eyed, lifelong alcoholics. He quit right then, for three months. It was easy, he said. After all, he'd always stayed on the wagon while he was at sea. When the three months ended, he called Savilla, his niece, back here in Niagara and told her that he'd had enough, he was going to drink himself to death. She was grown up now, of course, and had a family of her own, three children. "Oh, don't do that, Bill!" she said. But he did.

Going through his belongings in the loft and making final arrangements was left to Savilla, who saw to it that he was cremated and his ashes scattered into the Hudson River, according to his last wishes. She passed on the grocery bag of photographs and other remnants to me. She kept a journal of her visit there, her thoughts. The walls were splattered and smeared with blood, she told me, high up, marking his path to the phone where he'd called 911. He'd changed his mind about dying, at least that way, it seemed. He died in the hospital, anyway, where multiple transfusions didn't help this time. Here are a few sentences of what Savilla wrote: "I looked at the night skyline across the Hudson River. What a beautiful sight. No wonder Bill wanted to live here. He had a million dollar view from both his living room and bedroom. The twin towers of the World Trade Center were all lit up. I saw a huge ship slowly drift by."

Can we be thankful that Bill McCoy died before he stared with one eye from his loft windows to see that the twin towers had disappeared from view?

I try to imagine what he'd have said about that, and especially about the war that followed. It's certain there'd have been no long analysis. I can hear his short, raw laugh now, starting and ending abruptly as if it were a sound he was just learning to make, and then his voice, hard-edged, snarly, saying "Propaganda! Propaganda! Propaganda!" He'd have said it three times, staring at you with that one good eye wide, to make sure that if you didn't get it the first time, there'd be no mistake. But why take the imagined word of a dead drunk for anything?

He always made words count, that's why. The last photograph he took of himself, a five by seven of his naked body standing almost at attention, arms straight to his sides, the bottom edge stopping just above the pubic area, had six words written on the back. From his head to his lower ribcage he could have been one of those standing behind the barbed wire when the camps were liberated. The flesh of his face had evaporated leaving a thin, sparsely-haired skull, cheeks caved in, mouth sunken, one eye collapsed. An uneven stubble of beard covered his face. He was standing for inspection one last time, but it had nothing to do with being clean shaven. His once robust chest was gone, collar bones prominent, pectoral muscles flattened, nearly disappeared, ribs clearly visible. His upper arms were so skinny that hands could have circled them, fingertips touching.

Below the ribcage of this wasted-away man standing at attention is an enormous bulge of abdomen. It would fill a bushel basket.

It's an obscene, incongruous pregnancy, skin stretched taut over the diseased liver attempting to expand beyond the confines of the body. This is not someone from the camps at all. This is the last photographic testimony of William O. McCoy. On the back of the photograph he had written "Why I went to the hospital."

If a picture is worth a thousand words, as some people are fond of repeating, I have not given this one all it deserves. But Uncle Bill has provided the six extra words he felt were needed.

*　*　*

The Hudson River has been contaminated with PCBs for years. A cleanup project envisions dredging, dewatering the tainted sludge and shipping it to a hazardous waste landfill here in Niagara County. Some residents have organized to prevent Niagara being this final destination. We're already contaminated enough here, the feeling is, home to Love Canal, and etc. If they prevail it will be a triumph. If they fail, it is possible that some small part of Uncle Bill will be coming home.

*　*　*

The little china figurine of a man has been in our family for a long time, probably since the mid or late 1800s, most of those years forgotten in the jumble of drawers or boxes with other bric-a-brac, old toy parts, assorted pieces of doll house furniture, packets of yellowing, never-used handkerchiefs that were once gifts, deteriorating rubber bands, strayed buttons. During a summer of the 1940s it made it into the gravel driveway alongside our house where it assembled with trucks, tanks, and toy soldiers. Afterward, no child could say how the man's head was broken off and lost. He might have been stepped on in some battle, a flung chunk of gravel may have done it, or the man himself may have been tossed into the air as a result of an exploding bomb. Things happen in war.

There is a blurred memory of my mother taking the headless

body away from us and into the house. She didn't appear to be angry. Whether she was disappointed or sad or resigned I can't say, since it was so long ago, but the broken figurine must have held some meaning or she wouldn't have rescued it and put it away.

Two years later, I reached down and picked up an irregular little mud-impacted ball out of the driveway gravel – the man's decapitated head. This event was the occasion of great exclamation in the family, more for the near incredulous recovery than for something of value being located. Nevertheless, my mother cleaned the head and glued it back onto the body where it remains until the present day. That's one of the few happily-ever-after stories I know.

People often use the phrase "none the worse for wear" when describing the aftermath of such a misadventure, a lost and found: And there he was, the little figurine of a man, wearing his brimmed hat and open knee-length coat, none the worse for wear. But, of course, he was the worse for wear.

This young man, black hair falling almost to his shoulders, had lost a segment of his hat brim on the right side, snapped off, gone forever, and a thin wedge about the size of an infant's fingernail clipping at the top of his left shoulder, angling in toward his neck, the collarbone. These missing fragments may seem insignificant defects, though we should keep in mind that the man himself is only three and a quarter inches tall, with his shoes on, but not counting his hat. Actually, his knees are flexed, canted off to his left, so he's slouching a bit, his face tilted toward the ground. His coat hangs open, exposing a vest where his right hand is tucked into a small pocket, and a loosely tied neck scarf that hangs on his chest. His pants and hat are blue, his white coat blue trimmed, face as pale as his coat, his cheeks a rosy red. The head of a monkey is visible over his right shoulder. This is why as a child I believed this man was an organ grinder. But where was the music box with its crank handle? I don't recall being that inquisitive. Maybe the man was out for a walk on his day off and took the monkey along for company.

Decades later, long after my mother had died, the figurine arose again from a box of clutter, where it once again had been sequestered. Then it was obvious that the monkey clinging to the man's shoulder was draped over his back, its hind feet and tail extending nearly to the hem of his coat, and that the man's left hand, his arm pressed closely down his side, was holding a quart bottle by its neck. The bottle is blue. The monkey is brown, the very light shade of caramel. Though it could be the natural shape of the monkey's face, from a certain angle it appears to be faintly smiling.

*   *   *

Now the figurine sits on a high shelf here in a room with many windows, east and west. If he could see, the man could watch the red stain of suns rising and setting and the changing of the seasons, tree buds leafing out in the spring, sunshine and rain, withered leaves dropping, wind-driven snow whirling, tiny flakes settling. His face is still tilted down slightly, his eyes toward a lower ledge on an east sill, toward the golden shoulder blade of the deer.

Next to the man is a book, taller than he is, *Ten Nights in a Bar-Room and What I Saw There*, by Timothy Shay Arthur, published in 1854. This might be classified as a Sentimental Novel, a melodrama, involving an excessive appeal to the sentiments. Adapted into a successful play, its ill-fated heroine, a young child named Mary, stands in the door of a saloon, singing "Father, dear father, come home with me now." Almost a century later, *The Lost Weekend*, by Charles Jackson, was published. I don't have a copy of that book next to my little blue-hatted man with his monkey.

*   *   *

If you have seen a white-tailed deer running through the woods, you have seen the spirit of the woods come alive, on the move. It's not that rare a sight, of course. Thousands have seen this, even here in Western New York, many over the sights of a gun barrel, though it's much preferred that the deer be standing still. Yet others have seen the deer over the car hood as it launches itself onto the highway, displaced, dispossessed, into the glare of the high beams, a third-degree question that cuts two ways just before impact. What the hell are *you* doing here?

The first deer I ever got up close to was that dead one, back in my Straight Arrow days, on that trail down in the Niagara Gorge. Was it late summer? Long grasses draped over a wide notch in the cliff edge a hundred feet above. This is where the deer had miscalculated, where one errant step had caused its plunge into the gorge. But a deer doesn't miscalculate, does it? Did you ever see one loft itself over five foot of barbed wire or adjust almost in mid-air before diving through a rusted hole in an old woven-wire fence? Do you think for a second that the deer didn't know exactly where it would come to earth?

So it had to have been in a panic, my dead deer, chased by a dog, or several of them, and it was night, the wind blowing and dogs barking and millions of stars in the sky above the gorge, lights shining from the Canadian shore and, yes, maybe it tried to leap that notch and didn't make it.

The following spring or early summer I went back there and retrieved a shoulder blade of the deer, one of the few scattered bones that remained, and took it with me up out of the gorge. Later that year I came upon three more dead deer, crumpled together in nearly the same spot, below the high notched cliff, and this time there was a dead dog with them, a boxer, stiffened, sprawled partially over one of the carcasses.

Ten or so years pass, not as fast as you can snap your fingers, but it seems like it. If you're of a certain age, you know what I mean. I'm sitting in a bar, crowded into a booth with five friends. We're drinking beer, perhaps on our third pitcher. The evening is young, as they say, and we are, too, and we're just getting started. My Uncle Bill is still alive somewhere in the world. We're at that talkative stage when it's possible confidences will be betrayed or personal things will be revealed, and the next morning some of us will be trying to remember how much and exactly what was said, hoping that no one remembers.

The talk turns to hunting deer in Niagara County compared to the Southern Tier. Someone is reminding someone else how he'd emptied his gun shooting low at a running deer the previous season, slugs chewing up the ground. "Trying for the vital hoof shot, huh?" We're all laughing a little.

I break in to tell about the dead deer I'd found in the gorge years before. I intend to tell the whole story, the trio of other dead deer, the dog, the million stars over the gorge, the grass-blurred notch, the shoulder blade I had, painted gold. But someone else interrupts to ask where along the gorge trail I'd found the deer. So many hundred feet upriver, south of the tunnel cave, I say.

"Oh, yeah," someone else says, "right below where the old State Troopers' barracks used to be. Sometimes that's what they did with deer that got killed on the roads. The old heave ho."

"Right," I say. I take a long drink of beer.

You'd think I'd remember what else we talked about that night. I do not.

I had spent years with a gold-painted relic of road kill. And now I've spent many more. It testifies to my embracing the vision of gorge wilderness so completely that the reality on top didn't exist. The natural world and machines had intersected and I'd been unable to recognize it. Is the car-killed deer less sacred than a deer shot in the woods or dying from a leap into the star-filled dark? We have an impulse to put something unpleasant out of sight. Throw the dead deer into the gorge and forget about it. No one will see or smell it there. Toss the dead dog over, too. Out of sight, out of mind, as they say, the gorge and river as garbage disposal. Well, the natural elements at work in the gorge swallowed up and took care of those bodies, spread their bones down among the rocks. Other bodies we've put over the edge, sometimes in great volume, haven't been so easily digested. The whole gorge river should be puking its guts out. We've got to keep taking note of these things, don't we?

I'm keeping the gold shoulder blade. It reminds me of how young I once was, and how often I've overlooked the obvious in favor of dreams. When an infrequent guest looks around the room where it's kept and carelessly picks it up from the window sill to ask, "What's this?" I say "A conversation piece. I've had it for a very long time."

                    *   *   *

Suburbs have claimed huge tracts of land across the Niagara Frontier where the Indian Wars once surged through the woods and along the waterways. Some farms remain. There are public parks, of course, and a few woodlots still standing. But what dominates mile after mile are highways, roads, boulevards, avenues, streets, lanes, and row upon row of houses, garages, and driveways, and lawns planted with shrubs and ornamental trees bordered in flowerbeds.

This is most apparent from up high, from the window of a plane sweeping in for a landing over a mosaic of rooftops, rooftops, rooftops, a sprawling Monopoly board growing out of control, and the houses all packed with lawnmowers, leaf blowers, snow blowers, computers, air conditioners, dehumidifiers, gas or electric stoves, microwaves, refrigerators, freezers, shelves stocked with canned goods, and a can opener, too, electric, at least one in every house.

When, in the front yard of one of these houses, a woman turns up a half peach pit from her flowerbed, it engenders a moment's curiosity, then it's tossed into the basket of grass roots, small stones, and other materials she's collecting for the trash pickup. She's kneeling over the mulched soil as if in prayer, wearing those light cotton gardening gloves with the little rubber dots over the palms and fingers. She's unaware, as are her neighbors, that their houses sit where a peach orchard grew seventy-six years earlier, in a twelve-acre square carved out of the woods, and that the pits last a long time under some conditions.

She is aware, however, of the deer that fan out through the neighborhood each twilight, ghosts moving along the hedges, nibbling the branch ends from her newly planted flowering crabapple trees, eating the nursery flowers, and rearing up on their hind legs like aliens, hooved front feet dangling or stabbing the air as they devour the clusters of red berries from the mountain ash that the man at the nursery had told her would attract cedar waxwings.

At first it had been exciting to see these beautiful creatures through her glass patio doors and the front windows, extreme-screen televisions with exclusive shows of nature moving gracefully over the snowy lawn, entertainment for the whole family. But the destruction they caused became quickly apparent. Now, she doesn't want to kill them herself, but someone should do something. Some of her neighbors, those without plantings, loved the deer, and fed them corn and apples. She's seen as many as seventeen deer congregate on these properties.

It's against the law to feed the deer. This is based on the concern that feeding encourages the deer to group together, facilitating the transmission of Chronic Wasting Disease. There have been no cases of CWD here in Niagara, but so what? There were no WMD, either, but that also seemed only to have mattered to old-fashioned people who believed reason should count for something.

At any rate, one woman refused to stop feeding the deer, stating, I believe, that we took their land away and it was the least she could do. She's been in court repeatedly and may have even served some jail time. Do you think she's repentant? She is not. But people say feeding helps keep the deer herd healthy and breeding, their numbers increasing. This causes numerous accidents involving deer running into the paths of cars, which more than justifies the bait-and-shoot practices currently underway in several area towns and suburbs.

This action was taken after many heated town meetings where other solutions were discussed, such as trapping and relocating the deer, birth control pills or birth control administered by hypodermic darts, etc. Only the idea of lecturing the deer on abstinence fell short of receiving serious consideration.

Let's look at numbers in Amherst, one of the locations under siege by deer, and which also possesses an interesting name, which we'll get to later. Low estimates put Amherst's deer herd at eight hundred. Births in just one season could easily jump this to twelve hundred. In spite of over one thousand deer being shot by police or other officials over several years, there were still five hundred and eleven car-deer accidents in a subsequent year, 2004. We'd guess most of these deer died. One driver death occurred in the early months of the following year.

None of the fifteen hundred or so dead deer that we know of were thrown into the Niagara Gorge. Those shot in the bait-and-shoot were butchered, "processed" the newspaper called it, and the venison donated to the Food Bank of Western New York. One thousand deer at one hundred pounds each comes to fifty tons of venison. That's a lot of steaks and stew meat and burger, and anyone who knows anything accepts the fact that somewhere between the dead deer being hauled out of the woods and the Food Bank a few steaks probably strayed away.

But however you look at it, a lot of people here are eating a lot of venison these days, which reminds me of the poet Gary Snyder. He once said, and he may have been discussing one of his poems at the time, that when enough people have eaten enough deer that the deer would take over. This, he said, smiling in away that suggested some of us understood something that others didn't, with a fixed smile that seemed to linger long after the joke was over, would be known as a takeover from the inside, a phrase commonly known in the corporate world.

The bait-and-shoot has made the sounds of gunfire echo through the woods more than any time since the Indian Wars. We are told the sharpshooters wait in tree stands, so that when they aim at deer, their rifles are pointed toward the ground. This is an important safety consideration since they are, after all, discharging firearms in heavily populated areas. Nevertheless, one incident, that is to say one rifle bullet, has gone through the second-story window of an Amherst home, lodging in a opposite wall. This was reported as a ricochet "after striking a deer." A newspaper article reported the police chief as saying the officers weren't being unsafe and that those involved in the bait-and-shoot had been trained with rifles and were members of the department's emergency response team.

But training and emergency response team memberships aside, the bullet did go through the window. Perhaps the bullet ricocheted off the shoulder blade of the deer.

* * *

Lord Jeffrey Amherst was Commander-in-Chief, the British general, as if being a Lord weren't enough, in charge of the war-won territories on the Niagara Frontier, not to mention North America. This was a long time ago, before America had become America. Amherst thought the Colonials were rabble and the Indians were worse.

He had no appreciation of the tribes and their complex relationships, loyalties, hostilities, grievances, or interests. He couldn't have cared less. So he cheated the Indians out of land, which certainly wasn't a first, just a local example. He refused to give small gifts of food to hungry Indians. He treated them all the same, allies, enemies, those who might have been friends. He was in favor of distributing blankets from a smallpox ward to the Indians. He was watching the store in 1763 when the Devil's Hole Massacre took place. He tried to put a spin on that when he reported back to his superiors in England, but was relieved of his command and called back across the ocean.

This sterling record led to his being honored by having a town on the Niagara Frontier named after him. In that town, Amherst, the Lord Amherst Motor Hotel is located, its name advertising lodging for those who drive. Deer are throwing themselves in front of cars in this town. The authorities are shooting the deer, many of which are nearly tame, to prevent them from doing this. Deer were, and remain, very special animals, we'd call them sacred, to the tribes of the Six Nations, who believed them capable of resurrection. The words "ironic" and "ironical" came to mind as I wrote these last few sentences, but I decided they were silly words, empty of power to summarize any of this. You choose a word, if you can think of one, that's appropriate.

*   *   *

In January of 2006, the *Amherst Bee* noted that a resident had called authorities to report two deer standing in the back yard near the sliding glass door. There was concern that the deer would try to come inside.

*   *   *

Gerry Rising, in his Nature Watch column in *The Buffalo News*, noted that high numbers of deer are destroying our legacy, altering the character of fields and woodlands, consuming native wildflowers and other plants, bushes and tender saplings, so voraciously that forest regeneration is impossible. Alien species of plants unpalatable to deer are invading. Hunters killed about 230,000 deer in New York State in 2010. In the same year an estimated 70,000 deer ended up as roadkill in the state. Not nearly enough, obviously, Rising and others might say, especially not in the right places. Where have the wolves and cougars gone, now that we really need them?

18.

Eleven heads and twenty-two arms, one pair for each head, were hacked from their bodies and then attached to wooden poles. I imagine the arms being severed from the bodies at the shoulders, and tied dangling from the poles just below the impaled heads with thongs of rawhide lashed around the exposed knobs on the ends of the humeri, the long arm bones. This act of terrorism was carried out by Western Indians against British soldiers here on the Niagara Frontier in 1760. This was about a century before the great slaughter of the plains Buffalo, which should in no way be construed as a delayed act of retribution, and two years before the Devil's Hole Massacre, the massacre that wasn't a massacre.

Those eleven British soldiers were dead before their heads and arms were cut off, I'd guess. There was no video footage of them begging for their lives, chert arrow points fronting those straight arrows in drawn bows positioned at their throats. Technologies yet to be invented would make this refinement possible centuries later. Otherwise, a videotape wrapped in buckskin might have been left outside the gate of Fort Niagara during the dark of night.

But this was a reality show with real objects and body parts in the real world, an array of poles along the trail, each with a head and a pair of arms, blood streaked, pale British skin paler yet, fingers slightly curled, the heads jammed onto the pointed wooden stakes that probably went up through the ragged necks into the nasal cavities behind the faces to make them stay on. Were eyes opened or closed? Some of each? What color? There's no report of such detail.

As far as we can tell, the Indians can't be credited with inventing beheading, though they may have initiated it independently. It's doubtful they'd heard of Anne Boleyn's beheading, or the demise of Mary, Queen of Scots, or Sir Walter Raleigh. The Reign of Terror, during which tens of thousands were beheaded by guillotine, hadn't yet taken place. Still, all of this considered together, along with the beheadings currently taking place in the Mideast, suggests there may be a universal urge to behead.

My Grandmother Baxter would have certainly beheaded that porcupine if she'd had a sword or an axe. Without either of these, she resorted to a club, a makeshift at that, a tree branch she'd picked up from the forest floor. Does the lack of technology make us more brutal or less?

Grandmother B. shouldn't be characterized, however, by this one incident in a long life. For all I know she may have gotten to a point, poor thing, where she just had to kill something. But she was also, for a time at least, an artist, a painter of pictures. She may have ended up, with my Grandfather, as what's commonly known as "well-to-do," but they'd started out poor, believing in hard work, scrimping, frugality. During the early years of their marriage, when the bed sheets wore so thin in the middle portion that you could almost see through them, they were salvaged, not torn up for cleaning rags. My Grandmother carefully cut them lengthwise, down the center, repositioned the thicker, unworn edges alongside one another and sewed the sheets back together. The thin portions were now on the outside edges and they slept on the seam, or perhaps to the sides of it. Whether she did the sewing by hand or used a sewing machine, I don't know. I only heard the story once.

Cutting someone's head off has the appeal of finality about it. It's an injury so severe that the person's never coming back. Human beings have recovered from horrific and massive injuries, but never that. One of the early arguments for the use of the guillotine was that it would relieve those about to be executed of the fear of being buried alive.

In Europe, we're told, "hanging by the neck until dead" was considered a low class way to die. Beheading was the more honorable way to go. In Italy this method of execution was, in the beginning, reserved for gentlemen and ecclesiastics. As always, the upper classes get all the breaks. In China and Japan, however, it was a disgrace to die as a result of beheading.

During WWII the Japanese beheaded a captured American pilot, Donald Armstrong, on an island beach. At least this was the location imagined by poet James Dickey when he wrote about his friend's dying in a poem called "The Performance." To give his friend's death a dignity that his execution denied him, Dickey imagined Donald Armstrong, an amateur gymnast, at last doing a perfect handstand just before he was to be killed. His executioner is so moved by this act of courage and the flawless performance that he breaks down in tears. He beheads him anyway, of course.

Prior to the invention of the guillotine, the executioner swung a broadaxe down onto the neck of the condemned. One of the arguments against the use of the guillotine was that almost anyone could operate the new device and a lot of civil servants skilled in the use of the broadaxe would be put out of work. Like everyone else, many of them had families to support. But the counter-argument was that the less skilled of these failed to sever the head with one stroke and so the condemned suffered while the axe fell for the second, third, or even more times. And it was messy, too. The use of the guillotine, then, would be a giant step for mankind, a great technological and humanitarian advance, the embrace of an apparatus that almost guaranteed the instant separation of the head from the body. Its advocates were successful, and the guillotine was enthusiastically put to work on men, women, and even children, about 2,500 of them during The Terror between 1793 and 1794. That was a whole lot of suffering alleviated.

Beheading that number of people in a relatively short time required multiple guillotines, naturally. Still, in one location so many were executed one after the other that the ground couldn't absorb all the blood. Dogs gathered to lap it up. This may have amused the crowd that had assembled for the entertainment, though it's unlikely this was recorded for history.

About fifty years later a meat delivery truck pulled up and

parked in front of the grocery store in Dorset, Ontario, Canada. It was August and there were blocks of ice in the truck, cut from the Lake of Bays the previous winter. A thin mixture of watery blood leaked from beneath the rear truck doors onto the dusty street surface. I must have been young, and shy, too, because most of my memories of this are of the street and of the delivery man and my father from the knees down. I had stolen enough glances upward to see the truck, and the man's little smile when he spoke and then my father's big smile. A dog had appeared and begun to lap at the blood.

"Bloodthirsty hound," the man had observed, accusingly.

This being clever had made my father smile. It was a common phrase that even I had recognized, being illustrated with real blood and a real hound – even more appropriate because it had actually been a real hound, with short hair and long, floppy ears, which I hadn't realized at the time. Maybe it was a scene and comment that was often repeated by the delivery man in front of little grocery stores in little towns across that region of Ontario, but it had been new for us. This was about six miles by dirt road to where my Grandmother had bludgeoned the porcupine to death in the woods, perhaps within a year of that same summer.

Do you wonder what sort of pictures my Grandmother painted? They were landscapes. Do you know the poem "Looking at Pictures to be Put Away," by Gary Snyder?

I have a years-old picture of my wife, Loraine, standing in front of our fireplace, facing the camera. Over the mantle is a circular, convex mirror about eighteen inches in diameter. At the top center of the wooden frame is the carved figure of an eagle, wings spread. All of the frame, including the eagle, has been painted gold. Loraine's long, black hair falls to her shoulders. She is French-Canadian, a descendant of the Huguenot. There is a bird, a drab raven, perched alertly on top of her head. It's not a real raven, but a blackbird, maybe. I never found out for certain, which I regret.

This photograph, has, however, gone missing. A sustained search for nearly a week, through folders, stacks of papers, picture

albums, shoe boxes, and dozens of larger boxes of papers, page
by page, has failed to find it. Maybe I put it in a special place so it
wouldn't be lost, then forgot. The resealed boxes have been labeled
"not here" with a black magic marker. But it is here, somewhere,
though not finding it may have turned out for the best. It remains
the perfect, flawless photo in the imagination, with the wonderful
symmetry of the eagle-mirror and all, where it will be preserved for
as long as the imagination lasts.

There's no mistaking the robin in one of my Grandmother's
oil paintings. My father used to make fun of that robin, that it was
too fat. Looking at it all these years later, it's not so bad, that robin.
They have a habit of puffing themselves up, looking more plump
than they actually are.

The only other painting I have by my Grandmother is also an
oil, two feet by one and a half, also with trees in it, scraggly pines
and deciduous, with water and stone, the remains of an old stone
bridge, truncated you might say, which will permit us to go back
to beheading and final thoughts about that. Who says that ruined
bridges don't lead anywhere?

Before that, though, there's a little more to tell about a tree,
two dogs, and me. I don't know what kind of tree. This would have
disappointed my Grandmother, who loved trees and birds and the
natural world. She could probably have named the tree, but I am
only guessing here.

The tree I'm talking about is gone now, so there's no way of
knowing. It was a long time ago. I had not yet grown a beard, so I
couldn't have been older that late teens, early twenties. It was a big,
old tree, hardwood, ash, red oak, something. It towered high above
the other trees in the woods, maybe eighty feet tall, with forty feet
of straight huge trunk before massive limbs branched out. This was
a tree in an enchanted forest, with a circumference of twenty or so
feet at its base. It had probably been a finger-sized sapling in the
seventeen hundreds, at the time of the Devil's Hole Massacre and of
those eleven beheaded soldiers, their arms with hands, pale fingers
slightly curled, nails dirty, lashed dangling from the poles.

I was inside this tree with a pair of rabbit hounds, all of us looking out of a hole through which we'd crawled to get inside. This hole might have been chopped at, enlarged, a half century earlier. Dim axe marks were still visible on the dead wood around the edge in some spots. The cavity inside the tree had started by then and the axe wielder might have been after a raccoon that had taken refuge there. A thick curl of inner bark had advanced toward the hole in a years-long attempt to heal the wound, but had failed.

Actually, I'd been the only one who crawled in. The dogs had easily leapt inside, at my urging, since the bottom edge of the hole was about a foot and a half from the ground. I held their collars lightly as I knelt. The hole was off-round, slightly taller than it was wide, but had presented an opening about two feet across. Above the hole was a barkless, dead-wood scar shaped like a blunted sorcerer's hat, a forest tree spirit, ghost face, stained eyes darkly visible. My face was near the center of the hole, Lash's face to my right, the top of her already graying muzzle near my cheek, and Hank's face to my left, the top part of his head near the right ear touching my jaw. His mouth was slightly open, tongue hanging out a little. My nose had caught the light, and is slanted downward at the same angle as Hank's muzzle. The entire core of the tree has rotted away high above our heads. I could stand up if I wanted. Sun rays come in another opening thirty feet or more above us, which frames a tiny patch of blue sky.

It's a hot day in August, midmorning. We'd started out early while it was still cool, the grass soaked with dew. The dogs had spent a couple of hours chasing rabbits or searching for them. Now, the sun nearly overhead, we are all ready to quit for the day.

Do you know what rabbit hounds smell like after such a morning? Probably not how you think. They smell as if they are part of the fields and woods. Their paws and the tufts of hair between the pads and their front legs and chests, and the short, smooth hair of their heads, and hanging ears, and muzzles have all been bathed and rebathed with dew and they are awash with the scents of crushed green grass, and sweet clover and wild carrot and dandelions and dried leaves from the woods. I sniff at their heads and they sniff me back. It's certain they smell better than I do.

I remember all of this as clearly as if it happened just a few days ago. Sometimes a mere fragment of a thing, the smell of a newly mowed lawn, brings the morning back. It's like a dream, those memories, the sounds of the dog's voices on a trail, the rustling of their tracking through fallen leaves, my own voice as from a distance calling them, calling them, the sunlight falling. But I know it's not a dream. We were in that tree. I have an old black and white photograph that proves it.

*   *   *

*   *   *

A high wind has gone through the night before. In the morning, I went out to check on damage and discovered a large limb had snapped off from one of the giant pines in the front yard. The limb was about fifteen feet long, and nearly six inches in diameter where it had broken from the tree about twenty feet up. Among its thick needles was a sloppy nest of dried grasses and twigs. Inside the nest was a single baby bird, a naked, pudgy blob of flesh with no feathers at all, not even pin feathers, but alive, it's wobbly head waving around, beak gaping open to be fed. You just can't walk away from something like that, can you? What was I supposed to do – call for the cat?

Birds this young usually die, even if people try to save them. But the kids said, "Oh, look! A baby bird! How cute!" and we said we'd try. Somebody found an earthworm, which disappeared down its throat like a magic trick. We didn't realize that fifty worms could disappear the same way and that the blob would be shrieking for more – and that this was every day, all day long. How do mother birds do it? And they usually have more than one.

We brought the whole nest, with the bird, into the house and put it into a deep cardboard box. Let's shorten this story. Here's a question for you: how long do you think it takes for three teenagers to start whining about trudging out to the manure pile by the barn every morning before school to fork it over and collect, let's say, enough worms to fill a cereal bowl, even if they're taking turns? Didn't take you long to answer? You really can't blame them. You may have been a teenager once yourself – and how many worms are there in a manure pile? What? You only found three? *And here comes the school bus!*

A note on earthworm preparation: if you've watched a mother bird, say a robin, pulling a worm from the ground, you realize the worm's enduring some severe stretching, some trauma. It may be pecked several or more times once extracted from its hole, gathered up in the beak, pinched, dropped, picked up again. This puts the worm in a state of shock and probably injures it, also. It doesn't feel much like going anywhere after this treatment.

Earthworms gathered by humans, say from under a board or similar environment, are vigorously alive. You feed several to a baby bird and when it opens its beak to get another, one of those it already swallowed makes an escape attempt. We experienced this first hand. We just kept poking the worm back down until it stayed.

It's only in retrospect this observation can be made. We probably would have been reluctant to soften up the worms by beating them, for example, with a little stick, even if we could have gotten enough of them.

Loraine, desperate, called our veterinarian. Dr. Badger, already elderly, who took care of our large animals, horses, cattle, hogs, did not laugh. He was a somewhat taciturn man, anyway, so maybe he laughed later, but I doubt it. "Dog food," he said. "It's got everything the bird needs, protein, minerals, roughage." We were not to get the red-dyed kibble stuff, but the dry, brown chunks about the size of marbles. We already fed this variety to our dogs. This food was to be soaked in water first. Loraine started feeding the bird these swollen chunks, which were eagerly accepted, by extending them impaled on a toothpick. Maybe it looked to be a long narrow beak to the bird. I made jokes about it starting to bark like a dog. This was easy enough for me to do. I had to go to work, after all, and Loraine had to feed the bird almost continually.

I had wanted to name the bird something dramatic, maybe after the gale force winds that had buffeted the East Coast, the tail end of which had swept through the Frontier and broken the tree branch. This was a storm, one of many, whose name I can no longer remember, certainly no Katrina. I would have settled for "Tornado," or "Hurricane." The bird, however, was christened "Birdy-bird," and this pronounced and repeated in rapid, high falsetto tones. Try it yourself. It's almost like human chirping, isn't it? Birdy-bird began to answer with shrill, prolonged, single notes.

Birdy-bird flourished on the dog food. It gobbled chunk after chunk, chirping for more until its crop was so jammed that when it opened its wide beak to chirp the last chunk was visible and the voice stifled into silence.

Fast forward: Birdy-bird's feathers grew out. It spread its wings in the box, walked around, spent no time at all in the old nest. Its wide beak narrowed. It fluttered repeatedly against the closed flaps of the cardboard box. It wanted out. So we took Birdy-bird outside into the yard and placed him(?) on a low branch. Just as we got back to the porch the bird launched itself into flight, gliding to a clumsy landing on the first step. It didn't like it out there with all the tree branches and leaves moving in breezes and *other* creatures, birds like it? making funny noises. It wanted back in the house where things were stable and the noises it heard were those of people talking and saying "Birdy-bird!" and its own voice.

We kept it up for days. At least he was learning how to fly, high, low, to glide, to land on the ground, on the perch of a branch, a twig – then we put him out on the back porch, a rough, damp concrete in the shade with overhanging lilac and forsythia branches. We closed the door and watched through the window as he walked around a little, looking up at the door. Finally, he spotted a sow bug making its way across the concrete, eyed it up, took a peck at it, missed. It took eleven tries before he nailed it. It is only a coincidence that this is the same number of British soldiers that were beheaded not too far from here in 1760.

Gradually, Birdy-bird grew comfortable with spending more time outside. He eventually got to staying all day in the large trees of the yard and even in the woods behind the house. He still wanted to come in at dusk, though, and spend the night in an old cage we'd resurrected. Loraine would go outside and call "Birdy-bird!" and he'd fly in from wherever he was.

When we had visitors that summer, Loraine would sometimes say, "Oh, yes, all the wild creatures are our friends here," or start to tell Birdy-bird's story – and get raised eyebrows in response. Then she'd say, "Watch this," and step into the yard and call out "Birdy-bird!" and down he'd come from a tall yard tree or the woods in a great gliding swoop to perch lightly on her outstretched hand, her shoulder, or head. The looks on their faces were worth all the feeding, she told me later.

As the weeks passed, Birdy-bird ate less dog food. Some days he wasn't interested at all. The insects he was now capturing were probably a much more tasty diet. Then there came a twilight when he didn't respond to calling by flying down. He answered, but stayed high in a tree. There were owls out there, Great Horned, but he was going to take his chances. In the morning he flew down to Loraine's shoulder to say hello.

That fall, great flocks of blackbirds gathered and came swirling by, heading south, settling temporarily into the pine grove and woods behind the house with a cacophony of voices and fluttering of wings. Sometimes they'd roost there overnight, leaving as dawn broke. One morning, Birdy-bird was gone, too.

We may have felt silly out there that morning trilling "Birdy-bird! Birdy-bird!" into an empty woods and sky, but I only have a vague memory of that. I remember we both experienced some relief, and some sadness, too, because we realized we'd never see the bird again.

But we did. After a long winter he came back in the spring and called out a shrill note from a tall tree and glided down to perch on Loraine's shoulder when she answered with his name. He stayed around most of the summer. He returned the next year and the year after, as well. The third year he'd no longer come down to Loraine's shoulder, but would answer for as many times as she'd call his name. The fourth year there was no sign of him.

That seemed about right. Three years plus might be about the normal life span for such a bird in the wild, with hawks and owls, prowling house cats and other predators and dangers, including cars and fools with guns who kill for the sake of it. That was one of the years, too, we read in the newspaper that flocks of wintering birds had become such a nuisance in some southern locales that the authorities flew over in planes at night and sprayed a detergent mixture over the wooded areas where they'd roosted. This destroys the natural oils in the feathers and the birds then die of "exposure," pneumonia.

We were privileged to have our lives intersected by this wild creature that ended up teaching us more of its language than the other way around. We may have broken the law since we were not licensed wildlife rehabilitators. Is there a statute of limitations on such things? There are probably millions of these common birds, so

us interfering in one such bird's life was probably of little conse-
quence. It's clear that Birdy-bird imprinted on humans, especially
Loraine, but the condition appeared not to have been so hardwired
as is usually assumed to be the case. We came to believe Birdy-bird
had been a female, which explained her return each year. She was
coming back to nest and raise young where she had grown up. Out
of habit we continued to say "he" when referring to her. It is comforting to think that Birdy-bird successfully mated and that down
through the years her descendants have come by here in spring
and fall migrations, unaware, of course, that for one of its great
grandparents this was a very special place. Still, there are undoubtedly naturalists and others, perhaps ornithologists, who are purist
enough to say we shouldn't have interfered, but screw them.

Anyway, this is how I came to have a photograph of a woman
with long black hair, with a bird perching on her head in the serene
confidence that it belongs there.

*   *   *

*   *   *

Mexico: October 2006: Severed human heads are being publicly
displayed in central Mexico as drug lords eliminate their enemies and
use the heads to intimidate law enforcement officials and others. Authorities say the practice is common, with seventeen heads counted for

the year as of 22 October 2006. Many such heads are left with blood-stained notes, such as, "See. Hear. Shut up. If you want to stay alive."

In one instance, gunmen threw open the doors of a nightclub and rolled five heads onto the dance floor. In another, two heads were positioned in front of a car dealership in the town of Zitacuaro. This town is known as a wintering ground for monarch butterflies. The ancestors of the butterflies that winter there may have been fluttering and gliding along the Niagara Gorge near Devil's Hole in 1760.

19.

My mother is partially in the small black and white snapshot, though she tried to avoid it. A portion of her skinny arm shows and a sliver of housedress that she'd made herself so faded that the pattern has all but disappeared. She is holding a swaddled infant up and away from her for the camera. It's healthy looking with an unsmiling face, appearing so much like every other infant that I can't tell if it's me or my sister. The background is the paint-free, narrow clapboard of our house on the industrial outskirts of Niagara Falls. There's a poverty in the picture that makes me think of the photographs accompanying James Agee's *Let Us Now Praise Famous Men*, not that there's a photo-quality comparison. Photographs published in that book were taken by the accomplished Walker Evans.

Our poverty was nowhere near that unrelenting, that profound, as that captured by Evans. We were blessed. We had indoor plumbing and electricity and drinkable water that came out of taps. We had a coal furnace and my father had a job that bought enough food and the tons of coal that came down the chute into the cellar bin at the beginning of winter. There was a woodstove and kerosene heater in the house for cold days before hard winter set in and when it was on the way out, to conserve coal. There was enough money for beer. It's irrational for me to identify with the poverty depicted in *Let Us Now Praise...* but an emotional association surfaces nevertheless. Once poverty takes hold, in reality or in the eyes of others, it's tough to get loose. Rich is one thing, but poor lives in the bone. I understand something of my mother's fierce pride in that infant she held up for the camera, whoever it was, and shyness, humility, resignation and the special joy that was hers. Some of that is off camera, obviously.

The brilliance of Agee and the power of his documentation is clear. He cared about those people, the sharecroppers whose lives he recorded and they grew fond of him. His presentation of their circumstances often lifted the harsh details and artifacts of their lives into the light of a dignity approaching nobility. But his secret lusts, secret from his writing subjects at least, and his rummaging through their worn articles of clothing in their absence, even sniffing them like a dog, and then describing this in his writing, was a skulking betrayal of trust. Agee was sharply aware of this and more than once used the word "obscene" to describe his invasive exposure of the families' lives he wrote about. The real name of one of those families in the book was Burroughs, for what that's worth, and in spite of its dedication page, some surviving members of those people who were the subject of the book still remember they were never presented a copy when it was published, as revealed in a recent film documentary.

*   *   *

About the end of WWII my mother crocheted a little white dress for my sister, Brenda, who was about four years old. Since the photograph of her wearing the dress is undated, this attempt to date it is guesswork. She is sitting sideways on a boulder that might weigh over four hundred pounds. This huge stone is one of a pair of similar size that my father persuaded a nearby farmer, who'd unearthed them while plowing, to position on opposite sides of our gravel driveway where it entered the street. These boulders had undoubtedly been rolled along for hundreds of miles by advancing glaciers and then deposited, when the ice melted, where twelve thousand or so years later, a farmer would uncover them. The farmer dragged them to our driveway location using a chain and his horse. All of this seems to have take place in another time and country, doesn't it?

My sister's hair has been braided into pigtails, which have been positioned and tied behind her head with ribbons. My father's nickname for her was "Pigtail Annie." She sits on one of those boulders, her face open with that unguarded innocence often seen on the faces of young children. The future spreads in front of her as expansive and full of possibility as the wide blue sky that day. To the extent she's aware of it at all, she has an absolute trust and faith, as she sits for the camera in her new dress, that the future will be full of sunshine and gentle rain showers in which rainbows will reveal themselves, everything more incredibly beautiful than any of us can imagine.

*   *   *

*   *   *

"In the Rouen asylum there was an idiot known as 'Mirabeau,' who *for a cup of coffee* would copulate with a dead woman on the dissecting table. I'm sorry you couldn't have introduced this little episode into your book: it would have pleased the ladies. It's true that 'Mirabeau' was a coward, and untrustworthy of such an honor, for one day he flunked it badly when faced with a woman who had been guillotined."
– Flaubert

*   *   *

There you go, Gustave.

*   *   *

For most people who grow up in poverty and then, by a lightning strike of good fortune, say winning a lottery, suddenly find themselves filthy rich, there is no smooth transition into all that money. So maybe the first thing they do is to buy a new Cadillac, a Lincoln, or one or two of each, and a big motorboat, a house, a starter castle in an outer suburb or gated community, hire a housekeeper, and a groundskeeper, start referring to him as "my man," get a pinkie ring, rings on all your fingers, on your toes. They take vacations, cruises, go to Vegas, join the country club, donate big money to the church. And then they find themselves being interviewed on some television talk show as if the money made them suddenly have something worth saying, but they are the same as they always were, except now millions of people are hanging expectantly on their words to hear things like "We were poor, but we didn't know it." What? So you were not only poor, but also stupid?

The interviewer, the audience, they all get what you're saying. You didn't have a lot of money, but you had a roof over, enough to eat, loyal friends and such a loving family that you didn't even miss the material riches. After all, everyone in the neighborhood was in the same boat, weren't they? How could any of them tell that some people elsewhere, far away, were much better off? So the whole neighborhood was poor and stupid.

In your dreams, and late at night, you're as poor as you ever were, forever stuffing rags under the door and around the loose windows to keep the cold air and drifting snow out, sitting close around the kerosene heater playing cards, wearing two shirts and sticking newspaper pages in between them for insulation or, too proud for that, throwing your shoulders back and shivering, pretending it's not that cold yet, who needs a coat or jacket? You remember picking up half-smoked cigarette butts from the street, and that quick joy when you spotted one of them first and pounced on it. There was even a name for these in the neighborhood: Hollywood butts. And even now, with all your money, you use and reuse brown paper bags, carefully smoothing and folding them to store in the cabinet under the sink. Some are as thin and fuzzy as old flannel shirts, as ancient feeling between the fingertips as parchment. You look for a long time at the ragged sole-flapping sneakers before you drop them into the garbage. The laces are still good. You've got half a junk drawer full of them. You wince every time you throw something out. I could use that sometime, you think. With all the good restaurants you've been in, some winter days you want to sit down at home to a plate of steaming navy beans on a slice of bread, a little pepper. The taste of these beans and the smell of kerosene or a wisp of smoke from a woodstove can make you so homesick you can feel your heart breaking.

*   *   *

So there's my Grandfather and Grandmother Baxter, the whole family gathered around, their two sons and their wives and the five grandchildren. This is unusual only because both sons and their families are visiting at the same time. Grandfather is sitting alone at the small breakfast table, eating a soft-boiled egg, which is perched in a china egg cup, its narrow end lopped off. He is dipping a tiny silver spoon, which has been designed for this, into the egg. The chrome device that accomplished the precise shearing of the shell tip lies on a linen napkin on a countertop. He makes a joke, something on the order of "Why did the chicken cross the road?" for the benefit of the grandchildren. Everyone is laughing a little, when he makes what we all understand is the real joke, because he is inordinately fond of puns. "And that's no yolk, son!" he says, holding the little spoon aloft.

Now we are all laughing harder, dutifully, since we've all heard variations of this before, repeatedly, sometimes linked to the varnished yoke for a pair of oxen which hangs on the living room wall above the mahogany secretary. "And that's no yoke, son!"

Then he cuts off the laughter by declaring "We have a lot of fun for poor people!" He has a brittle, fixed smile on his face as he looks at all of us, as if challenging someone to say something, maybe one of the grandchildren, "Are we really poor, Grandpa?" or one of his sons, "Just how much money do you have, Dad?" but no one says anything, not even "You call this fun? What in hell's wrong with you?"

There was no way of telling whether he intended this oft-made declaration as ironic, knowing full well that he was wealthy or if, at ground level, he still thought of himself as poor. It's probable that the irony resulting from hanging the worn oxen yoke above the mahogany secretary was incidental. Such a crude restraint for joining beasts of burden at the neck eventually produced the money necessary for fine furniture and other luxuries. But there was, of course, no direct link between the dumb, castrated animals that once shared the yoke on display in my Grandfather's home and that particular secretary – which in any case, was designed and produced by craftsmen with notions of their own about luxury items. The mahogany was Honduras, from the exotic rainforest tree that has become rare today, inlaid with curly maple, that species of tree that grows in the northeastern region of North America from whose sap maple syrup is distilled. American Indians were the first to make this syrup, and the sugar, which was the major sweetener in this country until about 1875. Straight Arrow would have had much to say about this had the card series continued.

This kind of thinking, however, seeing the natural world connected by various webs, stories, threads, names, tensions, actions, histories, and so on, leads one along the path of going quietly insane. It is best not to follow this path too far into the deep woods where the light begins to fail. The rock maples will begin to crowd in from all sides and telling the difference between a rabbit and a hare in the midday twilight will be even more impossible than what might have been previously believed.

*   *   *

What most clearly illustrates for me the faltering journey from poverty to riches is Johnnycake, corn bread, a slab of which is slathered in maple syrup and eaten as dessert. The corn meal is stone ground, home baked, and hot from the pan, perhaps buttered, and then liberally doused with maple syrup, a gallon of which has been brought back from Northern Canada and served on dinner plates whose patterns are trimmed with gold. This treat was served at the end of a meal at Grandfather Baxter's, once a year, Thanksgiving or Christmas. The corn bread was coarse, aromatic, hearty, with a thin crust on top, not the homogenized pale yellow of a packaged mix. It was probably close to the original cornbread eaten by the early settlers, another gift from the Indians, who had developed several highly specialized varieties of this grain, including sweet corn and popcorn, by the time the Europeans had come splashing ashore asking, "What's for supper?" This is something for you to think about if, at some future date, you find yourself clutching an extra-large popcorn as you settle into the seat of a darkened theater to watch *Dancing With Wolves II.* Nearly a quart of amber maple syrup has been decanted into a cruet of crystal with a tapered stopper and we are all urged by my Grandfather to pour it until it covers the plate.

* * *

Where the name Johnnycake came from: researchers called etymologists, a specialized kind of historian, note two possibilities for
"Johnnycake," which they call a corruption. This means it started
out as some other word or phrase and then lost its purity as it was
changed, either on purpose or by error or the mixing in of some
foreign element. I don't know how these etymologists actually do
the work to trace words back, but I like to imagine them pouring
over old texts, day after day, fingers moving slowly over the lines
of print and even handwritten pages of letters, diaries, journals, and,
in this case, old cookbooks and recipe collections until, under the
yellow cones of light cast by their desk lamps, they come upon a
description with a name that sounds like "Johnnycake."

I imagine their joy of discovery when "Shawnee Cake" was
found, and also "Journey Cake," which had been used as far back
as 1775. Less than two hundred years later, my Grandfather Baxter was calling it Johnnycake. It's easy to visualize Shawnee Cake,
the name for the cornbread cooked at open fires by the Shawnee,
becoming Johnnycake. All it would take is a few dozen misheard
mutterings through beards, being spun through the accents of the
French and British, and being shouted by semi-literates as instructions to troops about rations, etc. And Journey Cake, too, has a
rightness about it. You could stuff your pockets or bedroll with
chunks of this sustaining cornbread when embarking on a journey,
a long march, a trek through the forest. The cornbread itself took a
journey from those first cooking fires of the Shawnee to the Angli-
cized Johnnycake, and now even that name is disappearing as the
cornmeal sits nameless, except for a company logo, in boxes on su-
permarket shelves, though we deplore this particular journey's end.

* * *

You probably know people, and I sincerely hope you are not
one of them, who after putting sugar in their coffee, continue to stir

long after the sugar has dissolved. When six or seven stirs will do it, they keep on stirring, spoon clinking, clinking, clinking, clink, clink, clinking about one hundred and sixty-three times. Clearly, this is a petty grievance, make no mistake about that. There are at least several million other offenses to complain about before mentioning this, but I'll get to those later. Remember that people are being killed every day for less, and who says these things have to be considered in order of importance, anyway? These compulsive stirrers have limited knowledge about common elements in the world: hot coffee, sugar, number of stirs required, etc. Do they imagine that after the thirty-seventh clinking stir, let's say, that there's still undissolved sugar in the coffee? Do they believe if they keep up this incessant clinking for an hour that somewhere a bride and groom will kiss again and a genie will arise from the swirling coffee to grant them three wishes? Say what you will in their defense, these clinkers are simply unacquainted with the principle of diminishing return.

My Grandfather Baxter was one of these. Johnnycake disappeared from his plate until only crumbled pieces remained in a shallow pool of maple syrup. These he went after with the fork until finally the granules that had escaped were small enough to slip between the tines. Then he switched to a spoon and the scraping and clinking began, interspersed with the spoon going to his mouth every little while where it was enthusiastically licked clean. Clink and scrape, clink, scrape, clink, scrape, scrape – a lengthy paragraph would have to be comprised of these words to even begin approximating this process or perhaps an entire page. Imagine that, if you will. Meanwhile, no one could leave the table until the last person, who was my Grandfather, was finished.

So the scraping and clinking continued. One of his rules seemed to be that a finger could not be used to trap a particle of cornbread against the edge of the spoon. The spoon alone, then chased tiny fragments of cornbread, no larger than a comma in newsprint, around and around the plate until, one by one, the exhausted fragments gave up and allowed themselves to be captured. When none of these were left, the spoon began working on the syrup, which by now was nothing more than a stain, a smear, a discoloration of the plate. But thirty or so clinks and scrapes would produce a half drop of syrup, so the process went on. For this, the plate could be slightly tilted, though gravity no longer had an influence on the nearly invisible film of syrup that remained. Finally, the plate was so clean it appeared polished. In most households it could have been returned to the cupboard and no one would have known the difference. "May I please be excused?" one of the grandchildren would ask and, when the answer was in the affirmative, the rest echoed the question and they all fled the dining room in horror to the kitchen, where they stood quietly, arms at their sides, while the adults talked briefly after the meal. Okay, so I exaggerate, but only a little.

This was a man who'd experienced the Great Depression and so food was not to be wasted, no matter the effort required to eat every last trace of it on the plate. If you had to expend ninety calories to get three, so what? Once poor you were never absolutely certain just because you'd been fortunate enough to have one meal, that you'd ever get another.

Now, the grandchildren, for entertainment, got to help wash the dinner dishes, or at least to watch, since they couldn't be trusted not to drop one. It's obvious as the plates emerge from the steaming rinse water that most of the gold trim had been worn away. The ritual of clinking and scraping went on every day in that house, not just after Johnnycake. There was the juice from roast pork, the remnants of applesauce, the grease and gravy from Yorkshire pudding and other food to be cleaned up, used, every bit.

*   *   *

20.

During the Depression, Pa, my Grandfather McCoy, worked at lumbering in Pennsylvania. He operated a steam crane called a loader, which ran on rails at the bottom slope of mountains where it lifted huge logs to railcars after the trees were felled and trimmed and rolled down the mountainside within reach. He must have sent some money home to the family in Niagara from time to time even if he did drink up the rest. On the rural, industrial northern edge of the city of Niagara Falls, about a mile from Bloody Run, his wife, Ida, and two daughters and two aged grandmothers lived in an old farmhouse. The son, who would become my Uncle Bill, was already gone or ready to leave. They kept chickens, one milk cow, and a garden.

The hobos of that era were riding the rails, legs dangling from open boxcar doors, and trudging over the dusty roads of America. They made marks on the picket fence of the McCoy homestead, which indicated that a good family lived there. The marks and symbols were a language shared by these homeless men that told of available food, if there were a mean dog on the property, and so on. Historians of this period have documented the marks and can also tell you what a bindle was then, and a bindle stiff. These men chopped and hauled wood and did other chores in exchange for bread, soup, baked potatoes, whatever the family could spare. Some nights they were allowed to sleep in the barn. In those days the flow of water over Niagara Falls was nearly at full volume and so most nights, unless it was very windy, they would have heard its muted roaring in the distance as they fell to sleep.

Ida, my Grandmother McCoy, who died when I was very young,

was a little twig of a woman, I'm told, who slept during those years with a pair of sewing scissors on her nightstand. She did not intend to harm anyone with them, but she knew that not all of the men passing through were honest and honorable—and in the event that bad intentions showed themselves some night, it was her plan to turn the scissors in the moonlight so they would catch the light. The glint of reflected moonlight would make them think she had a gun.

* * *

When the McCoy household disintegrated, what was left of the furnishings were divided among the children's families, cousins, and so on. Of the three items I remember, my parents ended up with one, which has been passed on to me. There was a black bearskin rug, open-mouthed head attached. This was spread out in our back-yard next to the field one summer afternoon as the old house was emptied and twilight deepened. In the morning it was gone. My father might have dragged it to the side of the road for garbage collection. Someone may have stolen it. I want to believe it resurrected itself during the dewy night and snuffled off into the darkness.

Another item came from the cellar of the old home where Pa had a couple of chairs and a table, where he drank when he was home. This was his den, where he could invite a friend or two down the narrow stairs for a drink and a game of cards. Next to his chair was an ashtray holder, homemade from a single wide board about an inch thick. Someone had jigsawed the silhouette of a standing cat, about two feet high, paws together, back arched, tail straight up. A thin metal ashtray was fixed to the top of the tail. The whole cat and its base had been painted a flat black. Its eyes and whiskers had been brushed on in white. A half inch circle of red paper had been glued just below where the tail joined the body. You may think of this as a visual example of lumberjack humor. When I think of this ashtray-holding cat and its decoration, I remember my Uncle Bill and how his favorite expression, "Ain't that the cat's ass!" may have been established in his young mind. This piece of folk art disappeared, too. Maybe it impatiently flicked the ashtray off its tail and followed the bear into the field.

The one piece of furniture that came into my parents' house was the Victrola, made by the Victor Talking Machine Company, Camden, New Jersey. It is in our old farmhouse today.

* * *

Now I am home alone again as I had been when I started telling these stories. It was a cold day then, and I'd had a Joplin CD turned up. Years passed. I was going backward and forward at the same time. This time it was mid-October, unseasonably warm, no frost predicted in the long range weather forecast. Nearly forty thousand were reported dead from an earthquake in Pakistan, tens of thousands more suffering, thousands injured, in cold rains without adequate shelter or food. This number would double in the days that followed. And here I am in my warm house, noting the existence of an old Victrola.

* * *

So the bear went snuffling off into the dewy field, followed by the cat, together lifting their heads to gaze at the new moon rising, the cat mewing querulously, the bear resisting the impulse to cuff it gently to make it keep quiet, since the bear knew they had to be silent as they trailed east along the railroad tracks heading out of town. They gave the hobo jungle a wide berth, even though they could imagine the warmth from the smoky fires, even though the odor of simmering pork and beans was enough to make them dizzy. The bear could also detect the scent of whiskey. He could have used a drink to rinse away the memory of people walking on him all those years. They were heading for the deep woods in Pennsylvania, to the other side of the mountain, and must have made it, because neither of them were ever heard of again after that night they left the backyard.

In my parents' kitchen, a nicked and marred porcelain-topped kitchen table, equipped with two slide-out leaves and its sensible silverware drawer, sat heavily on the linoleum. The porcelain was the yellowish color of heavy cream with soft green edges, supported by wooden legs. This is where our parents sometimes sat drinking coffee from heavy mugs and talking in quiet voices on a weekend. We were kitchen dwellers. Even now I experience a moment's discomfort when someone says, "Let's take our drinks and sit in the living room."

Often, as our parents sat there, the clunking sounds of their coffee mugs being replaced on the porcelain, my sister and I, and you can guess how young we were by this, were amusing ourselves with slim brushes from a paint set and a jar of water. We were allowed to trace the letters and cast iron designs of the wood stove with water. These wet letters were quickly dried by the heat of the stove. There could have been a lesson in the making there, something about the futility and impermanence of tracing the words and designs of others, but the same thing would have happened, of course, even if all the words had been new, all ours, or mine, brushed in water on the hot iron. So the practical value of all our artistry was that we added some miniscule amounts of humidity to the heated winter house, while we learned about fire and water, two of the earth's basic elements. In the kitchen, our parents stirred sugar into their coffee, six or seven clinks, and so, at some level, we were also learning about hot water, sugar, and the number of stirs required. Those early lessons really take hold.

That first winter we played all the records stored in the Victrola. We played Bing Crosby's "White Christmas." This Decca record had been much used and had a crack in it, so that seventy-eight times a minute the song was interrupted by a sharp noise as the needle jumped the damage. But we all know that's the way Christmases are sometimes.

While you may be familiar with "White Christmas," even if you are not Christian, it's far less likely you are familiar with "Hallelujah, I'm a Bum." It was a song about those hobos, those tramps, though we acknowledge the distinction made by the names, that not too many years before had left their curious marking on the McCoy fence. The remembered words are something like "from the east and west they come, they sleep in the dirt and they wear a shirt that's dirty and full of crumb.... Hallelujah! I'm a Bum!"

I wanted to be a bum when I grew up and go hiking in my dirty shirt, with my bedroll, walking and trudging and sleeping in barns and riding boxcars across the country. That record was a treasure and I cranked the Victrola to play it over and over. Once I looked for a safe place to put it where the fragile record would be in no danger of being knocked off onto the floor, and finally nestled it securely on the soft cushion of my father's easy chair – where my sister promptly sat on it. It snapped into pieces with the sound of peanut brittle breaking and I never heard the song again.

This wasn't, I'm sure, the first stupid thing I'd done, and it was far away from being the last, but it's the first one I remember doing. On the other side of the record, the title forgotten, was a song about a drunk sneaking home late at night, shoes off, trying to creep up the stairs to bed, stammering and laughing and narrating as he goes. His wife calls out "Is that you, John?" and he answers with inebriated mirth, "Yes, it's me! Who was you expecting?"

I imagine a crooked road leading from this record to Jack Kerouac and *On the Road*, *Dharma Bums*, *Desolation Angels*. Do you think he may have cranked up some old Victrola to listen to it? Have you read the short story "The Portable Phonograph," by Walter Tilberg Clark? In addition to being about the forgotten classes in America, "Hallelujah, I'm a Bum" is another Christian song, of course, and Kerouac, interested in eastern religion, was a Beat, friends with William S. Burroughs, who wrote, I repeat, among other books, *The Place of Dead Roads*. Do you think that all of this ties together into a big loose knot of nothing? A lot you know.

Kerouac, like my Uncle Bill McCoy, was in the merchant marines, though unlike him, he was discharged after a short time as mentally unsuitable. He died, like Uncle Bill, a drinker's death, liver bloated, veins in his throat rupturing, vomiting blood. It's not a pretty way to end an episode, is it? Try this then. It's near the end of October 2005. The number of Americans dead in Iraq reached two thousand today. Is that better?

* * *

Update: early September 2007. American troops dead, 3,742. Iraqi police and army, 7,408. Iraqi civilians, estimated range from a low of 50,000 to a high of 715,823.

* * *

My Grandfather Baxter, in the last years of his life, sat in his living room chair after dinner, drinking whiskey on the rocks, which he stirred with a finger when he poured another shot into the glass. Grandmother Baxter, the one-time porcupine slayer and painter of pictures, had been dead several or more years at this time. He was Church of England, an Anglican. To amuse himself he would, on occasion, without getting up from his chair, throw his arms wide and intone, "Man hath but a short time to live! He riseth *up* like a hoppergrass and is cut *down* like a jackass! *Blessed* be the name of the Lord!" He was having a lot of fun for poor people.

You can try this at home. I've italicized the words he emphasized so that you can get that rhythm going. Have a couple of drinks first and think of Jack Kerouac and my Uncle Bill McCoy.

* * *

The Hatfield and McCoy feud of the late eighteen hundreds may have been, in part, stimulated by genetic predisposition. In April 2007, an Associated Press article reported the McCoys had an inherited disease which caused, among other symptoms, racing hearts, severe headaches, and too much adrenaline, which led to short tempers. They also had a tendency to grow tumors in the adrenal gland, the eyes, brain, and other locations. Of course, a Hatfield stealing your pigs could also piss you off enough that you'd start the killing without the prodding of any of the aforementioned.

Genetic researchers have known about this disease for many years, but kept it a secret. It's difficult to say why. Perhaps they had in mind the formation of a special military squad of McCoys, prone to quick rages and an urge to kill. Please take note of how I resisted saying "at the drop of a hatfield." But now they are searching for descendants of the McCoys to warn them about the risks of their legacy.

This is almost in time. We raised hogs, here, on the Niagara Frontier, pigs, about 1978, a hundred years after the original dust-up that left a dozen people dead, but none of ours got stolen. My grandfather, Pa McCoy, was a kind and gentle man, though a drinker, it's true, who was once straight-jacketed with the DT's in Niagara Falls Memorial Hospital, summer time, windows open, and he could be heard yelling on Memorial Parkway, a block away. There's a memorial for you. But he never killed anyone that I know of, never even got angry, was nearly always smiling. He did have a tumor the size of a California orange cut out of his back, from underneath a shoulder blade. Family lore has it the size of a grapefruit, but that might be an exaggeration so I reduced it here for the sake of verisimilitude. At the same time, we should keep in mind that grapefruits may have been smaller in those days.

Pa was a fiddle player, and a caller, too, in his younger years. He also played the harmonica, and the wooden spoons, though his abilities with the latter were undoubtedly diminished, as they say, by a subsequent digit deficiency. He couldn't read a note. One of his fiddles is still in the family, though it's gone to finishing school and become a violin. My Aunt Honey, one of his two daughters, played the piano, expressed a fierce love of family her entire life, was subject to brutal migraines, was quick to anger, and died in a nursing home, of other causes, with a sizeable tumor growing in her throat. His other daughter, Florence McCoy, who was my mother, died suddenly of a cerebral hemorrhage three years before my father died. This was years before autopsies were much considered and so, now, with the recent information about the McCoy clan affliction, the possibility of brain tumor presents itself: cause of death, cerebral hemorrhage, caused by tumor. My mother was a happy person, who would often break out singing for fun, played the piano really well, and the fiddle and violin, I've been told, and didn't display fits of anger or any other of the McCoy behavioral problems. The whole family was "musical," people said, forgetting about my Uncle Bill.

Me, I play the radio. Some things just die out or skip a generation or two. My sister, though, could plink out several piano numbers at the age of seven or eight and, once, when asked to play, sat at the piano in Sunday School and proudly tinkled out "How Dry I Am," while singing the words. My mother was mortified. My father, who'd taught her the song, thought it was hilarious.

*   *   *

The McCoy family took a lot of snapshots in the old days, but almost never turned them over to write down a date, to note the name of an individual, or to list the names of everyone in the group photos. Who would ever forget them? Anyone in the photo could easily name all the others in the group that day, and wouldn't the summer of 1934 be unending, the sound of waves onto the beach, the picnic blankets spread, the house freshly painted, morning glories and hollyhocks blooming in the background, wild raspberries forever ripe in the warm sunshine?

Of course it would be, at least in the snapshot, and so Otto Mc-Coy sitting in the driver's seat of that roadster, both hands on the wheel, big smile on his face, will last forever, poised to drive off somewhere, the envy of everyone. It was that image that established the year of another snapshot, since the license plate of the car was dated 1914, and its rear canvas top with its oval window showed as a blur in the background of the second photo.

In this black and white photo, Pa McCoy is visible only from the knees up. He's sitting on something not shown, dressed in a rough, unbuttoned overcoat with wide lapels, under which is a but-toned vest. A heavy dark shirt is buttoned all the way to the throat. His rumpled pants are finely striped. A dress hat is tilted slightly to the back of his head. His deeply lined and furrowed face is unsmil-ing here, reflecting years of hard work and hard drinking. He ap-pears to be in his late fifties to mid-sixties. Actually, he is forty-two.

His right hand balances on his crossed knee, and is holding a pistol which is pointed toward the edge of the photograph. It's a revolver, his finger on the trigger. This is his hand with the mid-dle finger missing, having been surgically removed, including the knuckle. The hand doesn't look any less capable of anything, ex-cept that gesture requiring the middle finger, but the pistol makes up for that. So that's my old Grandpa Pa, he got he car, he got he gun, he has a few drinks every now and then, he's got most of his own teeth and most of his fingers. If it gets any better than that on the Niagara Frontier, he wants to know about it.

*   *   *

21.

Ethel Baxter is a name that hasn't been spoken aloud many times in recent decades. She slipped quietly beneath the earth, as most of us will eventually, as have most of those who've lived before us, into an unending anonymity that grows more profound over the passing years. This is merely fact, not a lament. She'd had the benefit of a long life, the satisfaction and consolation, if that were the case, of giving birth to two sons and seeing grandchildren born and beginning to rise into their own lives. Ethel was Grandmother Baxter's first name.

Her maiden name was Bullock, her father was Albert Bullock, and his father was Charles Bullock, whose wife was Ann Caston, from Wales, England. This was Ethel's grandmother. These Bullocks were not related, except by serendipitous oddity, to the oxen yoke later on display in Grandfather and Grandmother Baxter's home. A bullock is a steer, an ox, a castrated bull. The obsolete definition of a bullock, however, is a bull, so that back in Ann Caston's time, that meaning may have been the vital one. Over the years, the word lost its testicles. And that, son, is no yoke.

Ann and Charles were my great, great grandparents, but all these names mean nothing to you, nor should they. The names are in the light of day only because I wrote them. They would have otherwise remained as unknown as the names of the eleven British soldiers beheaded on the Niagara Frontier in 1760. Somewhere, their names may also be recorded.

We don't have the details of events leading to their deaths. They may have been killed in battle and then decapitated. They may have been captured first and then beheaded. If that's what happened, then some would call their deaths a massacre. We can't keep up with all of these, some of which involve the deaths of such large numbers of people that massacre no longer suffices to describe them. We say genocide, then, and holocaust.

A list could be made of all such slaughters large and small, from the earliest days of recorded history to the present, but that would result in a long book that would never end, listing numbers of how many killed and dates and "events" with which many of us would be unfamiliar. According to the Tutela Legal list, for example, in 1981, seven hundred and sixty-seven died in The Massacre at El Mozota, men, women, children, the very young and the very old. There was an effort here to record names. Three hundred and fifty-eight of these deaths were infants too young to know they had names, and children under thirteen years old. Does anyone know the names of the tens of thousands of Iraqis killed? How long will they be remembered? When the inhabitants of entire villages in Rwanda are hacked to death who's left to know their names? Sometimes it's tough to keep insisting that names are important.

*   *   *

It's curious that the Grandmother Baxter oil paintings, the one I'm starting to think of as The Fat Robin, and the other of the collapsed stone bridge, are both unsigned. I've pulled the rusty finishing nails that held the cardboard behind the stone bridge, thinking her name, or at least a date might have been written there, but there was nothing. It seems Grandmother Baxter was foretelling and contributing to her anonymity while living.

*   *   *

Annie, a widow, lived by herself in an old farmhouse a half a mile back off the main road, which was dirt, up in the north woods. She was in her eighties, older than Grandmother Baxter, who went up to visit regularly when she spent summers in the woods by the lake. Grandmother Baxter's middle name was Ann, perhaps after her grandmother, Ann Caston. The widow and my grandmother would have been a pair of Annies if Grandmother Baxter had ever permitted this informality.

But once she did allow herself to be driven by my father in his old Ford, accompanied by Uncle Don and me, into the back country to visit Annie. We discovered the farm had been stripped bare of timber since the year before. Of the fifty acres of tall pines that had surrounded the homestead and barn, only one pine remained, which Annie had refused to let the loggers cut. It towered well over a hundred feet, I forget the exact height, but she'd had her son, who was a bush pilot, buzz the top in his plane and get a reading.

We wandered around the place, leaving the two women alone to visit. A spring trickling down the mountainside had been diverted though a galvanized pipe into a large wooden tub, its outside damp and moss-covered, so that the work horses could drink fresh water. People could take a drink there, too, using the rusty tin can hanging from a fence post nail. I took a picture of the pine tree with my father standing in front of it.

On the way home, Grandmother Baxter and I in the back seat, she told the story of how Annie had fallen ill during the previous winter. The snow had been so deep that a vehicle couldn't get to her farmhouse. Neighbors hitched up the work horses, put Annie on a stone-boat and dragged her out to the road. I imagined her wrapped up in quilts, the steam rising from the horses, white breaths flaring out of their nostrils. A stone-boat was a number of logs lashed together like a raft. When new fields were being cleared for farming, boulders and stones were piled on it and pulled away by the horses.

After a few minutes of silence, just the car bumping along over the dirt road, my Uncle Don, who was now driving, said, "Poor old Annie!" I believe he emphasized the "poor," maybe by drawing it out. My father and Uncle Don started to laugh. "*Poor* old Annie! he repeated, and they laughed harder. They may have had a couple of beers earlier. Actually, I'm pretty sure they had.

"Now, boys... " Grandmother Baxter said.

"Dragged her out on a stone-boat!" my father said.

"Now," Grandmother Baxter said, "It's not nice to..."

"Wolves a snappin at her heels!" Uncle Don said.

Now they were really laughing and Grandmother Baxter pressed her lips together into a thin line and didn't say another word the rest of the way home.

The dust from the road spumed up behind us and the poor old Annie story came floating back from the front seat a few more times, even though it was difficult for the brothers to get all the words out because they kept laughing. We were having a lot of fun for poor people. I'd wanted to laugh, too, but I didn't because of Grandmother Baxter. I kept it pushed down inside, which is a good thing to do, because you can save it for a day when things aren't going so well and you can let it out then.

When the photograph of that remaining pine was developed, it showed the whole tree, top to bottom, but I'd had to back off so far to get it all in the picture that my father, who'd been wearing a tee-shirt that summer morning, was only visible as a white dot. That's the way it is sometimes, isn't it?

If I were an artist I could fix that with my own perspective on it and there'd be a half dozen or more other paintings that would come from my memories of that day. You can probably think of some of them. You can probably see my father clearly, patiently standing in the bright sunlight against the trunk of that pine tree, watching me walking away, backward, looking through the lens of the little 120 camera, walking backward again, slowly, looking again, walking, farther and farther away.

*   *   *

Max lives in Niagara Falls, NY, and paints in oils. He's a real-istic painter and he's very good. In his backyard is an old shed with a double door, the top half of which swings on hinges independent of the bottom half. This is called a Dutch door. On the top half he paints a horse's head and shoulders as if that part of the door is open and a horse is in the shed looking out. His neighbors call the SPCA and report him for keeping a horse in the city.

I want to tell you that the horse's name was Eagle, but that's not true—and that Max had painted straw and a pile of manure on the floor of the shed that was so realistic visitors held their noses and walked around it when they went inside, but that wouldn't be true, either. He was that good, though.

So Max is on the front porch where he has an easel set up, painting and drinking. He's enjoying the summer afternoon. Sue is in the kitchen washing dishes. She can't see him from there. After a while Max takes a break and lights a cigarette. The next thing you know, the turpentine he has spilled on his leather shoe has caught on fire. By the time he feels his foot getting hot, the flames are going pretty good. Kicking his foot around just makes them burn brighter. It's way too late for him to grab a blank canvas and paint a fire extinguisher. He yells out to his wife, but because he's so inebriated or because some artists aren't particularly good with words, there's a disconnect and the important thing he wishes to communicate is short-circuited.

"Shoe," he yells, "I'm drunk!"

Sue continues washing dishes. Big deal, she thinks. What's new?

"Shoe!" he yells again. "I'm *drunk!*"

Maybe by the third or fourth time he shouted this she heard some edge of meaning in his voice. When she found him dancing around on the porch with his foot on fire she came to the rescue by throwing a pot of dishwater on the flames. It was then she noticed he'd been working on a painting of hundreds of well-dressed people, a scene inside a crowded theater. Unnoticed by any of the crowd, a tiny flame, no bigger than one of the points on a man's breast pocket handkerchief, is licking at the bottom edge of the stage curtain. A single wisp of smoke curls upward. I'd guess there was no serious injury to Max's foot, but being an artist is still dangerous work. He could have, as we all know, been burned to a crisp.

* * *

I once wrote a short story called "Jack Gets a Thesaurus," in which a man's foot, or at least the cuff of his pants, catches on fire. This takes place in a saloon and doesn't end so happily. It's too long a story to include here, but the first sentence is, "It's cruel and murderous and children of all ages love it."

22.

I will tell you a story, but it's complicated, and some of it happened a long time ago, almost a once-upon-a-time story, and some of it not so long ago at all, though it may seem so. You will love the story, but I cannot tell it now. There was a bad fire here lately and I was burned to a crisp. You may think I'm making perfect sense under the circumstances, or at least some sense but, still, I'll tell you the story later.

* * *

This is not that story. There are only a few pages left, and you may be wondering where all of this has been going, how it's going to end. There were the buffalo, and deer, and that golden shoulder blade. There was Johnny Cake and maple syrup, Georgia O'Keeffe positioning her bones, a bear that used to be a rug and a housecat that used to hold an ashtray becoming uneasy friends and wandering off together, and Richard Brautigan and my Grandfather Pa crawling on their hands and knees down some long, dusty road. There were the Burroughs' brothers singing their broken blues, Bloody Run, stories about drinkers, and way back there, Straight Arrow, the best friend you ever had, and the flutter of monarch butterflies down through the years and Kid McCoy, Uncle Earl and Christmas, the Columbia and *The Book of Shit*, cowboys and Indians, foxes, pigeons, including the vanished passenger pigeon, reflecting pools and a cave painting, poems and porcupines, and an assortment of other stories told for the sake of telling, because of the voice that came out of the dark.

It would be comforting, I suppose, if all of this could be woven into a warm blanket, say a four-point Hudson Bay. But why would you expect that? If you are the sort of person who makes solemn remarks about "closure," I know just the kind of movie ending you don't like, and I can see you now, emerging from the darkened theater as the credits scroll inside, squinting in the sunlight, looking around, and saying, "But what happens next?"

That is the big question, isn't it? If it can't be answered anywhere else, doesn't it seem fair to expect that at least a movie or a book, in their limited contexts, could do it? Some do. Maybe you can remember how significant these have been in your life. My apologies that the best I've offered here is a minor confluence of stories, even if they do go from buffalo to colonoscopies to unicorns. Actually, the words "colonoscopies" and "unicorns" were mentioned to acknowledge their realities, but in depth discussions of these are absent.

More regrettably absent were narratives about the War of 1812 that raged across the Niagara Frontier, when the British burned their way across the landscape, a missed opportunity to extend the idea of being destroyed by flames and rising from the embers with a story, all of the foundations of our lives filled with love and humor, courage and killing, hatefulness, cruelty and violence, joy and suffering, and nobility and shamefulness. How can you tell a lifetime of stories without talking about all of these? Well, you knew this was a meandering from the start.

Please consider cutting some transparent plastic sheets, the kind used to store photographs in albums, to the size of these book pages. You can write your own stories and thoughts about these neglected topics on these sheets with the proper marking pen, one side only, and insert them between pages where dates or subject matter make their inclusions appropriate. You will create a contemporary "palimpsest" of sorts, which is a word I've wanted to use ever since I first learned it many years ago. This will also make the book more yours than mine, especially if you include some personal history, and maybe a few connective sentences to stitch them in place.

For my part, I hope that at least one of these stories does a fade at the end like a sad, old love song, with repeated notes that get softer and softer, until finally they disappear. Yet there's an echo in your mind, an expectation that one more note is about to sound. It stays that way forever.

THE DENOUEMENT

Raccoon hunting has become gentrified. Hunters take hounds "worth thousands" into the woods at night, I have read, and these hounds chase a raccoon until it climbs a tree. Judges then award points for a variety of things and the raccoon is left up the tree as the hunt moves on. Back in the day when I took part, it was a blood sport. We hunted for the meat and the hides – and it was widely called "coon hunting," and locally, "coon huntin'," not "raccoon hunting." Even the name is now gentrified.

Five of us hunted together a lot, and I will tell you their real names, though I could be lying: Otis Browder, Willie Dunbar, Bob Harper, and Willie C. Matthews. These were all grown men and I was a boy or, at best, a young man, seventeen, eighteen, nineteen. These men, as I understood it, were all from Alabama originally, and how they ended up in Niagara County is an old story involving work in the factories during and after the War. But I had the feeling that some of them had known one another in Alabama, had even grown up together. Some of these men were black, African American, and those of you who believe you have an instinct for names may have already decided which were black and which were not. Maybe you're right.

These names were magic to me – and even today if I say them aloud those dark woods of years ago come back, the voices of hounds on a trail, moons and stars through leaves, shouting and laughter. When three or four hounds are working a trail and it starts to heat up – the deep, drawn out bay of one hound overlaying the treble shriek of another, the bellowing mixing and echoing in the woods – then sometimes one or two of the men get to hollering back, shouts of encouragement to the dogs, excitement, joy, noises you seldom hear coming out of a human mouth.

Maybe the thought of grown men running through the woods at night whooping and hollering isn't your idea of good times. I wouldn't tell you to your face that you'll never know what you've missed. But you won't. You've got to be chasing after the hounds and thrash into a thicket of brambles in the dark or run full tilt into a strand of barbed wire to find that out. Then you'd be doing some hollering of your own.

Dunbar knew this. He wasn't very tall, short, even, often getting tangled in the bramble patches, staggering sideways to get out. Some nights he'd wear two or three pairs of pants, old dress pants, usually, where the holes and rips wouldn't match up and so there'd be no bare leg poking out anywhere. This gave him some protection against thorns and barbed wire.

One night he didn't put on the extra pairs until we got to the woods. The dogs were already barking and baying as we unloaded them. We were all waiting for Dunbar. "Hurry up!" we were yelling. In the glare of everyone's flashlight beams, hopping on one foot, half falling, trying to get a booted foot through a pant leg, he was in perfectly good humor, laughing at how pissed we were. "Boys," he said, "I got more pants than any man my size!" This made everyone more furious. He was already having a good time.

So how did a punk like me get to go with them? Well, I enjoyed it, which they knew, I accepted it as the privilege that, without saying, they let me know it was. I also kept my mouth shut, and I had a dog in the hunt, as they say, a pretty good one, if I do lie so myself. But the real reason, I believe, is that I was young and skinny and when a coon was up a tree hiding somewhere beyond the reach of three-cell flashlight beams, they sent me up the tree.

My job was to climb up and find the coon, get it to change location – or in extreme cases, get it to jump out. It would be reluctant to do this, with the chop-barking dogs and men and flashlights below. From the coon's new position, even perhaps having bailed out and scrambled up a shorter tree and out on a limb, its eyes would shine yellow in the flashlight and one of the men on the ground would put a .22 slug right between them. That'd be one in the sack, and the imaginary judges would award points, and we'd all move on. Points would have been awarded for a coon retrieved the instant it hit the ground, hounds kicked away, while the body was slid neatly into the burlap before teeth tore the hide and reduced its value.

One night we got nine. Other nights we got three, or four, or one, or none. Some bloody struggles took place in those woods. I won't tell you about them.

How does roast coon taste? Good. Sort of like bear.

How do unshelled peanuts from Alabama taste? Also good. Every year Bob Harper would get a hundred pound sack of peanuts either shipped up or he'd go down home for a visit and bring one back. When we went coon hunting he'd jam the big pockets of his army fatigue jacket with peanuts and during the night, without a word spoken, he'd slip me handfuls of them. He'd put peanuts in his mouth, shells and all, and chew until the nuts inside dissolved. Then he'd swallow, and spit out the pulpy residue of the shells, or at least most of it. I imitated him and did this, too, which I believe amused him, though he never said anything. But he could hear me spitting out the chewed shells, and once, in the fringe of light cast by a flashlight ray, I saw him smiling slightly, I think. We were doing roughage before it was popular.

My back yard dog pen was about thirty feet from Willie Dunbar's dog pen. On weekends up to a dozen men congregated there, each with hundreds of stories, none ever repeated, all of them about down home, the south, some of them true, I suspect, though which ones it was impossible to tell. After a while it seemed to me that the ones who lied the most also protested the most that they weren't lying, punctuating their stories with oaths that they were telling the truth.

Once, a guy whose name I never got, pulled up in a car and flung the door open, already talking. It was a cold winter day, ground frozen, no snow, and he remained half-seated in the car, one foot out on the ground, the other on the gas pedal, gunning it constantly as he talked animatedly, waving one arm, one story into the next. He kept repeating "And if I'm telling a lie, may the Lord strike me dead before I mash down on this asscellerator!" He had everyone laughing. He was afraid the car would stall if he let it idle, and he wouldn't be able to get it started again. The Lord didn't have a chance to get him before he mashed down. He was mashing down one time after another. You could tell he was from the south, because otherwise he'd have said, "before I step on this gas pedal."

There was also a thin man, approaching elderly, who showed up regularly, who had a high-pitched voice, a ready laugh, and an enthusiasm for story-telling. He'd coon hunted a lot in his youth, spent a lot of time in the woods. He was afflicted with a terrible stutter, but nobody made fun of him and everyone waited patiently while he stuttered his way through a story. His nickname was "Preacher." He told a story about a friend whose dog, out coon hunting, got bitten by a rattlesnake, high on a front leg. The dog was limp, leg "swolled up the size of a man's leg" by the time they carried him home. The friend had poured a pint of kerosene down the dog's throat, but "he died anyway."

Once during those years I bought a dog from Otis Browder for one hundred dollars. It was a good looking hound, a bluetick about a year and a half old, just getting started. Otis had that kind of smile that wreathed up his whole face, mischievous, in on some joke you wished you knew about. Just looking at him made you want to start smiling, too, ready to laugh at whatever was coming. About three weeks after I'd bought that dog, Otis showed up, smiling. He had a guy who wanted to buy it. But the dog was mine. It was near Christmas and Otis was out of work. If he could sell that dog again, he'd have money to give his kids Christmas presents.

Well, I thought, I was about ready to give up coon hunting, anyway. My life had started to go in different directions. I let him take the dog. Now he owed me a hundred. I didn't see him again for seventeen years.

I was living in the country by then, in a place with a long crushed-stone driveway. When a pickup came crunching in and stopped, engine running, I walked out to see who it was. Otis sat there, smiling, an open six-pack on the seat beside him, a can in his hand.

"Want a beer?" he asked.

"No thanks," I said. I couldn't help but smile myself.

He told me he'd been retired for a few years. He looked older. He was leaving, going back down home to Alabama, ready to be there, do a little fishing, maybe some hunting. I asked when he was leaving and he said, "Day after tomorrow." Then he pulled out a wad of money and peeled off tens, one by one, counting them out and handed them to me through the open window. "There's that hundred dollars I owed you," he said. "Thanks," I said. "You take care of yourself, now." He'd never stopped smiling.

I'd guess we talked a little more, but if we did, I don't remember what about. I didn't ask him about Dunbar, or Harper or Willie C., which we all pronounced "Willisee," and he didn't mention them as I recall. He could have, I suppose, but I don't think so. That was the last time I saw or heard from Otis.

When I remember him, I think of his smile, the day he pulled into my driveway and paid me, and what seems now to be the last night we spent in the woods together, him, Willisee, and me. It was cold, the end of the season, coons getting scarce, an all-around bad night where the only coon the dogs had run, treed up a huge old oak. The flashlights couldn't locate it. The tree was twenty feet up before there was a limb, so climbing was out.

*   *   *

Otis and Willisee decide we need to get that coon. It's only a few hours until dawn and we'll wait. The coon should be visible then. They tie the hounds to low brush away from one another. They bark treed every so often, but finally get shouted into silence and curl up in the leaves. We build a little fire.

Soon we're all stretched out on the ground ourselves, on our sides, around the fire like uneven spokes, faces turned to the flames. We don't speak for about twenty minutes. This isn't unusual for me, because I keep my mouth shut around them. These two I believe grew up together, somewhere in Alabama and they have a history I don't know anything about.

Then Willisee scissors a pack of cigarettes from a shirt pocket with two fingers and extracts one from a hole in the bottom of the pack. He lights it from a burning twig he picks up from the edge of the fire.

Otis has watched the whole procedure and gets a smile going. "Willisee," he says, "why is it you black guys all open your cigarettes from the bottom?" Willisee doesn't say anything. He's big enough to swing Otis by his ankles and knock his brains out against the oak tree.

Otis is really interested now, starting to laugh a little. "You just trying to be different from a white man?" Now the smile has taken over his face. "You already different enough!" he says, and begins to laugh. He got himself going now, him really laughing, steadily, not loud, not as a taunt, but down-deep amused for sure. He making his own fun.

Willisee, he don't say nothing. Him just hang his head down low, smoking a cigarette he took from a hole in the bottom of the pack.

* * *

There are two ways this story might have ended: 1) Dawn broke. We could see the coon, shot it, got it, and went home. 2) Dawn broke. We still couldn't see the coon and went home. Truth be told, and if I'm lying may the Lord strike me dead before I finish writing these words, I don't remember if we got that coon or if we didn't.

* * *

Otis and Willisee live near one another in some Alabama backwash. They go fishing for catfish together, sitting in the sun on the riverbank, two old men who came through. Willisee still opens his cigarettes from the bottom. Otis doesn't say anything about it. I made that scene up, of course. There's no chance this ever happened. But I'm a sucker for a happy ending, as delusional as the next person about some things.

*   *   *

On Opening Cigarette Packs from The Bottom: In the routine of your daily life people you scarcely know, or don't know at all, bum cigarettes – at work, down at the Supermart, guys hanging out in front of the liquor store. "Got a cigarette?" they ask, stepping forward expectantly, eyes on the shape of the pack showing in your shirt pocket. If you have opened the pack from the bottom, that permits you to mumble, "No, man, I'm cutting down. Ain't even opened this pack yet," while you push at the pocket a little, sliding the pack up far enough to expose its top, verifying what you said. At this point, the supplicant retreats. He doesn't want to get in the way of your self-help efforts. If he's wild-eyed loony enough to insist – "Well, open it now and gimme one!" you've been in trouble from the start. The next move is up to you.

*   *   *

If denouements existed in real life, they'd go unceasingly on, one after the other until the end and even afterward, one last, tired drum roll. In stories, just one is recommended, but even if tradition is ignored, and another is tacked on, and then another, and so on, it's eventually over. The story exhausts itself, and so it is here – with this one last series of remarks about raccoons.

The blood sport of hunting them has not stopped. Wherever there are coons in America, it goes on, and where there are few, or none, men set out with hounds to kill other animals, jackrabbits, coyotes. They even mix greyhounds into the pack so the prey can be caught on the ground and the dogs can "pile on," as it's described. It doesn't appear these guys hunt for much except the kill. I wonder what the men I hunted with years ago would have thought about that.

I haven't killed any coons since those years. Now they live in the barn here, beating down trails in the long grass with their comings and goings between the barn and the creeks, following the same path each day. One year three mother coons raised young ones in the barn, second floor, burrowed in between hay bales. The little ones chittered loudly in their burrows, sounding angry, then frightened, but in reality probably just hungry, calling out for mothers to return so they could nurse. At dusk we sat in the yard here when the young ones had grown older and watched them trailing after the mothers as they ventured out of the barn, single file, tiny duplicates of the adults, hurrying along so they wouldn't be left behind. There were so many in the barn one year I'd holler "Here I come!" when I walked in, and upstairs the thumping of running feet against the wooden floor sounded like children playing, scrambling to hide. By the time I'd get up the stairs, the barn would be silent, nothing moving, not a coon visible anywhere.

They've ruined a lot of hay here over the years, digging burrows between the bales, and by defecating and urinating on it, usually on the highest stacked bales where they doze during the day, an ideal vantage point to see what's going on if they're disturbed. There's no awareness on their part that the hay is valuable to me, but it's payback anyway. You think there's a judge somewhere awarding me points? I have moved from hunter-gatherer to herdsman, raising beef cattle, and I am curious about the landscape into which I might be wandering next and whether or not I will recognize it when I get there.

*   *   *

Author's Notes

There are some debts, of course, that can never be repaid. Often these are debts of gratitude. If you have lived to a certain age, you know what I am talking about, because you have accrued such debts yourself. So it is with me, and with *Niagara Digressions*, the book you are now holding.

Its publication marks a culmination of many years of writing, during which time I have been blessed with extraordinary help, much of it indispensable. Although it's often been said by other writers in reference to their publications, I need to repeat it for this one: without the help I received, this book would have never been published. This is not some spasm of pre-publication modesty or humility or generosity or any of that. It is the simple truth. In keeping with the entry to *Niagara Digressions*, I'll make the acknowledgements of the help I received in a little story, so that you can appreciate them in a long context.

When I was twelve years old, I wrote a 52 line, imperfect end-rhyming poem about nature, the changing of the seasons, in block letters both large and small, titled "Up North," that covered both sides of the lined, 8 1/2 by 11 inch white tablet paper. I remember sitting at the porcelain kitchen table working on it for hours and finally asking my mother for help. She gently suggested "hunter's dog" to rhyme with "hollow log," a suggestion I accepted, and her penciled-in words are still at the end of that line where I'd asked her to put them. My father was so impressed with the poem that he folded the page three times, into a rectangle of about three by four inches, so he could put it into his pocket and take it to work the next day to show the guys. There was a porcupine in that poem of long ago and there are porcupines in this book. Isn't that something?

Jump forward about five years: I am now writing shorter poems, still end-rhyming, about hunting, and submitting them to the *The*

New Yorker, my marketing perceptions almost impeccably flawed. There was an opossum in one of those poems. What is it with me and small, gray animals?

In Trott Vocational High School I'd been hungry to learn about writing and some teachers inadvertently helped. One teacher read aloud to the class – a poem by Kipling involving the repetition of the words "boots-boots-boots-boots" that made me resolve to never write such lines. Another described one of the Queens of England, I believe it was, as a "pulchritudinous strumpet" with such delight that I could tell he loved words, even saying them, and I went right home and looked those words up and have never forgotten them. (I've had very few opportunities to use the phrase over the years, so I pass it on in hopes that good fortune will smile upon you more broadly.)

I continued to write, trying short stories. Then, some years after high school, I found myself in the living room of a friend, who lived near Cleveland and 18th Street, Niagara Falls, New York, to whose house I had just walked seven blocks. On the plywood coffee table between us was a copy of *The Beagle Hound Journal and Basset Hound News*, where he had tossed it after casually flipping through its few pages. It was a very fine issue, with a slick, red-trimmed cover, which depicted, rendered in black ink, a rabbit in mid-leap. Inside was a story called "Crazy Man's Hunt," about hunting rabbits in the Niagara Gorge, written by me. My friend hadn't seemed too impressed by this, even though he, too, was a hunter, and this was my contributor's copy. It takes a lot to impress some people

That same day, as I remember it, though this memory may be faulty, I picked up a *Time* magazine from the coffee table. In it was a review of a novel, *Rabbit, Run*. I'd written a short story titled "Run, Rabbit, Run." This guy had all but stolen my title. How'd he find out about it? But I had a real rabbit in mine, not some character nicknamed Rabbit. I knew immediately that I had a long way to go. I mumbled this to my friend. I was 22. John Updike was 28. Later, I got that novel from the library and read it. It became clear that "a long way" was understatement of monumental proportion. I kept writing, anyway.

Then, and this was years later yet, but still so long ago the occasion for it has faded, a small group got together and threw a surprise party for me: my sister, Brenda Piza, Loraine, and friends Larry Coleman, and Wayne and Mary Jane Lehning. We probably had the requisite cake and ice cream, but the focal point of the evening was the electric typewriter they had chipped in to purchase as a gift, a Smith Corona with an extra long platen. I remember sitting on the floor and unwrapping it. Retire the old Underwood upright, they told me, and get to work. What's a gift like that worth? I'm not referring to the value of the typewriter, which wasn't paltry for any of them at the time, even split five ways, but their demonstrated belief in me as a writer. It's true that I thanked them that day, but I do it again now, for the turning point that it was, in retrospect. Now I had to get serious.

Loraine made that typewriter sing. Everything I wrote, essays, poetry (not rhyming any more), short stories, research papers for school, and the revisions of all of those – she typed. Free from poking out what I had written in longhand with two fingers, I wrote more. Years passed, during which new technologies began to appear and ribbons for the Smith Corona started to get hard to find locally, and we turned, after much discussion and with some trepidation, to a Sanyo word processor, a computer, with a printer. This was still the early days of single-sided, five inch floppy discs, one of which sort of ran things because the computer had no memory, and a printer that made us smile when it ran – because it sounded like someone typing – and we walked right out of the room and it went on, industriously, the text rolling out on a long scroll of pages that could later be separated along lines of perforations. I felt like Jack Kerouac, by proxy twice removed.

It had started with us plugging in the necessary cords and making connections, then opening the first of several three-ring notebooks jammed with operating instructions. This was back when the technicians had zero interest in the concept of user friendly. We bent our heads over the first page. Step number one was: "Boot up."

We looked at one another and started to laugh. Boot up? That's what we did out in the barn before grabbing pitchforks to clean the manure and sodden straw out of calf stalls. I went off to work. Loraine worked on those notebooks and figured it out. Then the essays and poetry started to flow – and then a novel manuscript, and then a revision of that manuscript, and soon another novel was in progress. Several short stories were mixed in there. The first novel was revised again, and again – for a total of seven times, finally. It never got any better. It might have gotten worse. The theme was superficial. The dialog I wrote was so wooden it could have been used as kindling. And some of it was.

During this time Loraine was also my critical reader and she was very good at it. She had an unerring ear for dialog, both good and bad, and for the subtleties of relationships, for motivations, who would say what, and why. She made the distinction between the reality of spoken language and the illusion created by writers who mirror that reality, but do not attempt to record it. An unbalanced sentence or awkwardly expressed thought didn't escape her attention, either. Along with her close reading observations came unintended lessons in humility – I can't tell you how many times I said to her, hours, days, or even weeks later, after our discussions, after my stubborn resistance evaporated, that she'd been right, absolutely right, all along.

By the time the little typewriting printer quit for good, I had four novel manuscripts in various stages. We got another printer, four or five generations along, that required a special cord be made to connect it. Some time afterward Loraine called an 800 number to ask for help. The man in New York City, I believe it was, asked for make and model numbers, put her on hold. When he returned, he said the units were incompatible, that it just wouldn't work. She told him that she had it working just fine, and only wanted to know how to make it set proper margins. Then she started laughing into the phone – and they spent thirty minutes talking, Loraine telling him step by step how to make it work, him taking notes. At the end of the conversation, she got the answer about margins. She'd traveled a long way from the little village of "Boot up."

Years later the whole system self-destructed, all of the saved manuscripts retrievable only as word salad, incomprehensible gibberish. Loraine and our friend Liz Sieb went up into what we'd come to call "the computer room," the narrow little bedroom in the northwest corner of this old farmhouse, where they'd spend hours, day after day, searching out those lost manuscripts, and a few scraps of something new I'd started – that would eventually become *Niagara Digressions*. Now that room is empty of people, cluttered and unused, and has been for years, but their voices and laughter still echo there.

The new effort was to be a book of nonfiction in which Loraine would appear. I wanted her to read it when it was well along, in big sections, if not the whole thing at once. Christine Osypian, a friend who was already familiar with my handwritten first drafts from her work as webmaster of the Niagara Heritage Partnership site, offered to turn my additional scribbling for the book into printed copy. That was help I welcomed. She knew how to follow those arrows leading to sentences or parts of sentences that had been written out of order, the instructions, such as "Go to A back page," and "insert here, next page," or "New para pg 143." She could pull tiny paragraphs that had been crowded sideways into page margins back into the narrative, could read eight-letter words when only two of the letters were legible, knew when I'd made mistakes because I was tired, and would grant me unspoken allowances, such as she did, for example, when she learned that cut and paste for me involved scissors and Scotch tape. I have always felt that first transformation of handwritten, rough copy into printed pages was a magical part of the writing process, and I believe Christine did, also, though she never said anything about it.

After the following multiple revisions of that first draft, word changes, sentences smoothed out, material added or deleted, and so on--it was ready for the readers. Eric Gansworth has been part of that group of two for decades plus. He is reliable, perceptive, insightful, direct. No detail is beneath his notice, no long range perception something he'd neglect to thoroughly consider. If a word choice is 97% evocative on the connotative level, he wants the other three. He is alert for the sentence or transition that permits even a slight potential for misreading. He is especially good in the recognition of the symbolic implications of images and larger scenes and events. There is no manuscript of mine over the years that has not been improved, sharpened, as a result of his questions and comments.

He's so good at this, in part, because he is an accomplished writer. As such, he's worked to achieve standards he can then extend to others – and he has also fully embraced the responsibility of marketing as an integral component of writing. He studies publishers; he reads widely. It was at his strong urging that I submitted *Niagara Digressions* to Starcherone in the first place. He knew that the press was interested in the unconventional, and he believed that Ted Pelton, the editor and publisher there, receptive to the innovative, might give the manuscript a chance. He was right on both counts.

Ted Pelton did not accept the book for publication. But he didn't reject it outright, either. He saw immediately what I was doing – and gave very high praise to parts of it, including portions that made use of old-fashioned story telling. He was equally direct about what I didn't accomplish. He envisioned a more focused book, more gathered, more muscular, more tightly aimed, and asked me to consider revision to those ends. He never mentioned which sections, but he wanted about twenty-five percent of it gone. I agreed right away. And swallowed hard later. How to cut that much from a text whose intrigue derived from repeatedly jumping into the dark in the first place?

But a more appropriate question: how fortunate was I to find an editor so appreciative of the book I'd written (it was in there), perceptive enough to understand what needed to be done, and confident enough to give me a chance to shape the book he could see? I got to work. When I shared the news with Liz Sieb, she offered to see it through with me. (Christine and her family had moved to Florida, but were keeping tabs, sending encouragement.) I started tearing out big chunks of the book, tossing them aside, little pieces, fragments, condensing passages, considering whether or not connections were being lost, writing new paragraphs, pages, wincing. I was supposed to be taking out. I haunted Liz, watching the computer screen over her shoulder to see how things fit. Liz was very patient. Her mantra of "No problem, no problem" was reassuring.

Of course, there is no suspense here. You know that Starcherone, Ted Pelton, was pleased with the revision and accepted *Niagara Digressions* for publication. He then asked if I might assemble a group of photographs for the book, sensing these would extend the kaleidoscope of images already present, creating a complementary dimension. He was right again – and this was a natural for Harry T. Brashear, photographer, significant other of Liz, and proprietor of 10th Planet in Newfane, NY. Years before, out of his own interest, he had already photographed the deer pelvis and vertebrae on the fence post when I'd told him the story. Now he took the family snapshots and other photographs and put them into the proper digital format so they could be used in the book, coaxing the older ones from the haze of the past into sharper focus.

In the final stages of manuscript preparation, Niagara Falls historian Paul Gromosiak read it over to verify dates and other factual information. Betsy Potter, artist and long-time bird watcher, had read it previously to make sure I had not, as a layperson, made some stupid mistake in the bird stories or in musing about their behavior. Over the years, the entire process of writing the book had, in easily one hundred instances, been helped along by Diana Bonura, who found time to type letters where I sought information, chase down a library book, photocopy those pages I just "had to have," prepare text I'd use at a reading, search files for documentation I'd lost. When just two days remained to deliver the final and completed manuscript, my daughter, Suzanne Parry, visited from Oregon. She did not arrive via wagon train over the Oregon Trail, which would have been appropriate. She flew in on United, many thousands of feet over it, though a cartographer might have pointed out its fading traces far below. At this time the manuscript was locked away in a

Document where, because of my technological deficiencies, I was unable to get at it. I still had changes, paragraphs to add. Though her visit hadn't been planned with this in mind, her timing was excellent. She was able to open the Document, to splice in those last substantial revisions and get it sent off. Because she is the daughter of Loraine, it was more than fitting that she had a hand in that final step.

The preceding paragraphs have followed a relatively direct route – but have not mentioned others, teachers both formal and informal, who helped along the way. I've already risked putting those mentioned into a category of question: "What? Is this guy so delusional he thinks he's written a companion piece to the seven volume *Remembrance of Things Past* and everyone who touched it or him along the way must be noted? These people weren't helping. They were enablers. They should have stayed out of it." Maybe that's so. But I reveal them nevertheless – and trust they will survive such criticisms.

Gerard Dombrowski, former publisher of *Abyss*, has supported my writing from early on – publishing my early work in *Abyss* – and has taken it upon himself over the years to provide me with a library of fine volumes I would have otherwise never acquired. Once, suspecting I had fallen on hard times, he drove from Dunkirk to Buffalo, NY, to buy me breakfast (bacon and eggs) in a Main Street diner, and to chat me up about the littles. The coeditors of the locally-based Slipstream Press, Bob Borgatti, Livio Farallo, and Dan Sicoli have been supportive over many years, publishing my poetry, an essay, a short story, a chapbook, *What I Want*, and *Looking For Niagara*, a book length collection of poetry. Larry Coleman had gone on to publish *The Little Mag*, in which he published work of mine as well as others from across the country. At the State University of New York at Buffalo, the late Professor Ann Haskell guided me into imagining the silhouettes, the shapes, of essays and permitting the writing to flow into them. Professor Irving Feldman once spoke at length about a single sentence I had written. It was of moderate length, grammatically correct. It did an adequate job of what it was supposed to do in context. I'd taken notes while he was speaking, writing down everything he said. When he finished, he asked me if I'd understood. I said that I had not, but that I'd written it all down and was sure that at some time in the future it would all come clear to me. Years later I came across that page of notes while looking for something else – and I did understand. The short of it: the sentence was perfectly ordinary and that was its problem. Generally, Feldman's position was that if a passage in a piece of writing approached excellence, then all the writing surrounding it should be lifted to that level. When I suggested that might be impossible to achieve, Feldman agreed that it might be, but that didn't mean the writer shouldn't try.

Others have cleared the path for me – Ralph Black at the State University of New York at Brockport quickly swept aside what could have been bureaucratic impediments to permit my use of interview material from the Writers Forum interview series in this book. Nearly twenty years in the classroom at Niagara County Community College kept me dancing – students there seldom heard me say anything about writing they'd leave unchallenged. Omar Blackwell's technique was to make a seemingly innocent comment about a piece of writing and to then smile quietly while others clamored to voice their opinions. George Carveth, former student become friend, could be relied upon then and now, to provide tough, argumentative critique. Mike Cochran's reality-based commentaries go straight to the heart of the matter, followed by fundamental questions. Michelle Vanstrom's interest in the way the ordinary can rise into metaphor often leads to keen, reflective analysis.

Colleagues and others read, commented on, and critiqued my writing during those years and beyond: Bill Bradberry, Paul Dominick and his wife Jan, Don Ferrick, who took pages of notes, observations, comments, and questions and never let me get away with anything, the late Bill Justice, Kathy Kifer, John C. Merino, Bill Michelmore, Gene Miller, Sue Phillips, the late Eleanor Robinson, Don Sleight, Art Taylor, Norm Tederous, a wonder at comparative literature, Dave Tobin, D.R. Wagner, and Brandon Warden, also a note-taker, and Grant Wolcott.

Another friend, the late Dan Keily, spent hours at my kitchen table where we discussed one another's manuscripts. One of the last times we got together, to discuss a novel manuscript of mine that involved groups of people in opposition, Dan started the discussion by asking, "For whom do we root?" That turned out to be a very fine question. I still smile inwardly to think of it, the content and the phrasing. I don't believe I was able to provide a satisfactory answer. It's still a good question that I ask myself from time to time, especially for nonfiction, and I believe I have come down on the side of telling the story as truthfully as possible, or lying about it so skillfully that no one can tell the difference, and letting the readers decide for whom to root.

To each person mentioned in these notes: Thank you. Those two words may seem feeble and common when measured against what has been given to me. But those to whom they are addressed should know they are offered with deep gratitude, in recognition of the gifts which were given.

At this point I might be asked, repeatedly, as I have been in the past about other pieces of writing – in fact, have already been asked several times about *Niagara Digressions*: "How long did it take you to write it?" I'm caught off guard, as always. I hesitate. I want to say it took me three years, but then I half-remember there are signposts in the book that suggest it was closer to five years. Should I subtract the periods of days, weeks, or sometimes a month or more when I did no writing at all? I was thinking about it during those inactive times, jotting notes, reading, researching. Aren't all of those part of the writing process? And then the only meaningful answer becomes clear, though it might not satisfy those who ask the question. The truth: it took me about seventy years to write *Niagara Digressions*, and I had a lot of help along the way, a lot of help.

PERMISSIONS

Quote from "Jack Gets a Thesaurus," by E.R. Baxter III, was first published in *Slipstream* 21, Niagara Falls, NY.

Chapter 9 was previously published in *Hold.Com Underbeat Journal*, issue # 2, July 2003. Fingerprintpress, Depford, NJ.

A large part of Chapter 15 first appeared in *New Madrid Journal of Contemporary Literature*, Vol. 2:2: Summer 2007, entitled "Thought of the Week." Reprinted by permission of the Department of English and Philosophy and Murray State University, Murray, KY.

Excerpts from *Reflections on the Death of a Porcupine and Other Essays*, by D.H. Lawrence, the Cambridge Edition of the Works of D.H. Lawrence, edited by Michael Herbert, Cambridge University Press, Cambridge, Great Britain, copyright 1988. Acknowledgement to William Heinemann Ltd in the UK and Viking Press (USA) copyrighted 1915, 1925, 1926, 1928, 1934, 1968, in respective territories. Reproduced by permission of Pollinger Limited and the Estate of Frieda Lawrence Ravagli.

Excerpts from "The Barn," by E.R. Baxter III, previously published in *The Hartford Courant*, 25 December 1985, Hartford Connecticut, 25 December 1985, under the title "The Barn: Thick with Mysteries of Years – and Christmases – Past." Used with permission.

Excerpts from Straight Arrow cards (included as collectible premiums in boxes of Nabisco Shredded Wheat), *Book One* and *Book Three*, copyrighted 1949 and 1951, respectively, by the National Biscuit Company. Used by permission of Post Foods, LLC.

William Stafford, excerpts from "Traveling Through the Dark," and

PHOTOGRAPH CREDITS

p.76 - (author as little kid, with Lloyd Harpham): Florence (Mc-Coy) Baxter

p.106 - (mother fox with young ones): Loraine L. Baxter.

Insert between pp.112-113 - (painting by d.a. levy): Harry T. Brashear.
 - (d.a. levy with D.R. Wagner & Grady Jones at kitchen table): E.R. Baxter III.

p.119 - (author reading at Wintergarden): Loraine L. Baxter.

p.145 - (vertebrae on fencepost): Harry T. Brashear.

p.237 - (author with dogs in tree): Robert E. Levering.

p.242 - (Loraine with bird): E.R. Baxter III.

p.247 - (girl on rock): Florence (McCoy) Baxter.

p.255 - (steam-powered log loader on rail, Otto B. "Pa" McCoy, center, circa 1898-1908): photographer unknown.

p.266 - ("Pa" McCoy with pistol): photographer unknown.

p.285 - (three men with dogs): E.R. Baxter III.

p. 303 - (author photo with tea mug): Loraine L. Baxter

E.R. Baxter III, Niagara County Community College Professor Emeritus of English, has been a fellow of a New York State Creative Service Award for fiction and a recipient of a Just Buffalo Award for Fiction. Previous publications include *Looking for Niagara* (Poetry, 120p., Slipstream Press), and the chapbooks *And Other Poems*; *A Good War*; *Hunger*; and *What I Want*. Baxter is also a founding member of Niagara Heritage Partnership (www.niagaraheritage.org).

Also available from Starcherone Books:

Kenneth Bernard, *The Man in the Stretcher: previously uncollected stories*
Donald Breckenridge, *You Are Here*
Blake Butler and Lily Hoang, eds., *30 Under 30: An Anthology of Innovative Fiction by Younger Authors*
Joshua Cohen, *A Heaven of Others*
Peter Conners, ed., *PP/FF: An Anthology*
Jeffrey DeShell, *Peter: An (A)Historical Romance*
Nicolette deCsipkay, *Black Umbrella Stories*, illustrated by Francesca deCsipkay
Sarah Falkner, *Animal Sanctuary*
Raymond Federman, *My Body in Nine Parts*, with photographs by Steve Murez
Raymond Federman, *Shhh: The Story of a Childhood*
Raymond Federman, *The Voice in the Closet*
Raymond Federman and George Chambers, *The Twilight of the Bums*, with cartoon accompaniment by T. Motley
Sara Greenslit, *The Blue of Her Body*
Johannes Göransson, *Dear Ra: A Story in Flinches*
Joshua Harmon, *Quinnehtukqut*
Harold Jaffe, *Beyond the Techno-Cave: A Guerrilla Writer's Guide to Post-Millennial Culture*
Stacey Levine, *The Girl with Brown Fur: stories & tales*
Janet Mitchell, *The Creepy Girl and other stories*
Alissa Nutting, *Unclean Jobs for Women and Girls*
Aimee Parkison, *Woman with Dark Horses: Stories*
Ted Pelton, *Endorsed by Jack Chapeau 2 an even greater extent*
Thaddeus Rutkowski, *Haywire*
Leslie Scalapino, *Floats Horse-Floats or Horse-Flows*
Nina Shope, *Hangings: Three Novellas*

Starcherone Books, Inc., is a 501(c)(3) non-profit whose mission is to stimulate public interest in works of innovative fiction. In addition to encouraging the growth of amateur and professional authors and their audiences, Starcherone seeks to educate the public in self-publishing and encourage the growth of other small presses. Visit us online at www.starcherone.com and the Starcherone Superfan Group on Facebook.

Starcherone Books is an independently operated imprint of Dzanc Books, distributed through Consortium Distribution and Small Press Distribution. We are a signatory to the Book Industry Treatise on Responsible Paper Use and use postconsumer recycled fiber paper in our books.

Starcherone Books, PO Box 303, Buffalo, NY 14201.